BraveHeart Women
How to be *Inspiration in Action*

Volume 1

BraveHeart Women
How to be *Inspiration in Action*

Volume 1

Edited by Cynthia Krejcsi
Editor in Chief, BraveHeart Women Publishing

BraveHeart Women Publishing

BraveHeart Women Publishing
Los Angeles, CA
© 2010-11

Published by BraveHeart Women Publishing
www.BraveHeartWomen.com

ISBN-13 9780979112607

Cover Design by eVision Media
Clip Art courtesy of www.jackhaas.net

This book is dedicated to every BraveHeart Woman
who is rising to share her voice in the spirit of collaboration . . .

And to Cynthia Krejcsi, BraveHeart Women Publishing's Editor in Chief,
on behalf of every author in this book, thank you for pouring your heart into
the creation of a masterpiece . . . .

Ellie Drake
www.BraveHeartWomen.com

Table of Contents

Foreword

The BraveHeart Women Global Community is for women who want to inspire or be inspired. It is a place where women bring their own sense of inspiration and their own mission in order to collaborate for a common purpose. In the BraveHeart Women Community, we empower each other, and in so doing each woman discovers and realizes her own deepest potential.

When women express their voices together, the voice of collaboration becomes more powerful. When enough women inspire one another to shift into a more conscious state in which they create personal, professional, and global change, they will initiate a shift in the consciousness of humanity.

This book is a dynamic tool that will enable women to get their message out into the world. It is a vehicle by which women can collaborate to educate, inspire, and encourage each other to rise to the next level of humanity and to thrive as they do so.

Within the chapters of this book, BraveHeart Women visionaries and communicators are expressing their voices from a fully individualistic place yet also in a collaborative manner, enabling them to show up fully for themselves and also to show up together. By expressing her own voice, each author is empowered "within" by reaching deep inside herself to tell her own authentic story and identify the lessons she has learned. She also empowers "between" as she shares her story and her specialized knowledge in lessons that serve as a template of success for each of us. Each woman who has contributed to this book becomes a beacon of light to show us the way and to inspire us to join in this great collaboration.

My experience of getting to know each of the authors you are about to connect with and learn from has been both enlightening and fulfilling, and it is an honor to be part of each woman's personal and professional journey and also part of our global collaboration. Let me introduce the BraveHeart Women who will be sharing their wisdom with you in this book:

- **Mariel Hemingway** lived her childhood seeing members of her creative family become self-destructive. This set her on a quest to be creative without being self-destructive in her own life. She'll share with you how she found balance by discovering that she was her own best teacher and inspire you to find your own teacher within.

- **Radha Conrad** describes how she experienced several major insights once she started to keep a diary documenting her constant shoulder pain, which she traced to a deep discontent with her life. She will show you how you too can become empowered by gaining clarity in your own life.

- **Anne Johnson** empowers women entrepreneurs in today's global market by showing them how to change their mindset about selling products and services and by teaching them to overcome their most common fear of selling.

- **Janie Pighin** shares her own personal story about being a caregiver and raising two handicapped children in an empowered way. Her experiences inspired her to teach others how to go from a Victim to a Warrior Caregiver mindset, and she'll show you how you can do it too.

- **Kim Kiyosaki** had a great job and lived on the island of Oahu, Hawaii, yet she woke up one morning feeling, *There must be more to life than this.* Soon she was learning how to run her own businesses rather than just learning a job. Kim has taught millions of women around the world how to tap into the Rich Woman inside of them. She will show you what might be getting in your way and how you can ignite the Rich Woman inside of you.

- **Audie Perove** struggled with low self-esteem and loneliness after losing her father when she was eight years old. It took her years to come out of her shell, but working through her own pain instilled in her a passion to empower children. She'll show you how to nurture children so they will develop healthy self-esteem and have the self-confidence to reach out for and accomplish their dreams.

- **Dr. Kim Silvers** tells you how a life-altering spiritual experience helped her learn that to be a true healer a doctor must have an open heart. As a dermatologist, she chooses to teach women, including her current patients, why doing cosmetic work alone will not make them feel beautiful. The key is to shift the way you see yourself from the inside.

- **Gloria Loring** had several serendipitous experiences that made her start to think about the role coincidences played in her life. She'll share with you how you can allow coincidences to guide you in manifesting the life you want.

- As a seven-year-old child **Dr. Pamela Zimmer** had a vision of a heaven on earth where people were beautiful on the inside as well as on the outside. This instilled a passion in her to help women raise their consciousness to the next level. She will show you how you can reach the next level by identifying and changing your limiting beliefs.

- **Dr. Sugar Singleton** is a medical doctor with a love for true healing, as opposed to the traditional methods of only treating disease. She assists women in releasing their unproductive cellular memories, thereby removing the energy blocks that are keeping them from being successful and that might also lead to disease in the body. Dr. Sugar explains how releasing your cellular memories can enable you to experience true self-esteem, fulfillment, and prosperity.

- **Tari Bussard** lost her best friend in a car accident when she was 18 years old. This set her on a journey to discover why she herself had been spared. She'll show you how paying attention to your intuition can lead you to seek and find your life purpose.

- **Nancy Markham** spent the '60s at home raising a young family, but over the years something inside her started to simmer. The feeling that she was getting ready for something finally bubbled up to the surface when she was in her 50s, and she began to open herself up to new experiences. She will show you that it's never too late to let your intuition lead you on the journey to realize your spirit.

- As a ten-year-old with a paper route, **MaryEllen Tribby** learned many valuable lessons that contributed to her later success as a CEO, online marketer, and entrepreneur. She'll show you some of the lessons your children can learn by taking initiative and responsibility—such as developing relationships with customers, starting the day with a sense of pride and accomplishment, and setting and exceeding a financial goal—and how these can lay the foundation for success as an adult.

- On the surface **Tara Marino** appeared to be a happy young wife and mother who had everything she could ever want. Yet one night she had a meltdown. This was actually the beginning of her discovery that there were three aspects of herself that needed to be in balance in order for her to feel fulfilled. She will show you how to get in touch with those three aspects of yourself and how to keep them in balance.

- **Penny Wanger** met **Nanci Moore** when she was starting her own business and visualizing a business partner. Nanci was also starting a business but had been struggling with reconciling her heart with her business intellect. Together they explored ways that business could be carried out when led by Soul. They will share their new business model with you and show you how this new way of doing business can assist you to live your best life.

- **Sheila Kelley** discovered something that changed her life while she was filming a movie about strippers. While a man watching the movement finds it erotic, a woman's experience is freeing. And so she developed S Factor to empower women with their sexuality, their body, and their female nature. She'll show you how to free yourself by embracing your natural body and heightened natural feminine movement.

- Sisters **Arlene Schmidek** and **Cathy Dool** were successful business owners when their father's illness necessitated that they take over the family business, which was operating at a loss. They turned it around and then went back to their own business. They learned some difficult lessons when they took their eye off of the business and then the economy took a downturn. Now they share what they learned in order to help you create and maintain a sustainable business of your own.

- **Lynette Chartier's** journey began when her baby died from a heart defect. For years, she pushed down her emotions and kept moving forward, ignoring debilitating health challenges, stress headaches, and other warning signs. After her mother's death she realized that she didn't want to die with her music still inside of her, and so she decided to put an end to the things that were holding her back. The golden nuggets of wisdom she shares here will guide you on your own spiritual journey.

- A debilitating car accident injured **Kathy Kolbe's** brain so badly that she couldn't speak in full sentences. Because of the drugs she had to take, she didn't even know what she wanted for dinner much less any emotional preferences. Unable to utilize the cognitive or affective aspects of her mind, she relied on the more instinctual part of her brain that had to do with her natural drive—the conative domain—to retrain her mind. She will show you how you can experience more joy, peace of mind, and a sense of accomplishment by trusting the conative part of your mind.

- After working for a company for 23 years, **Rebecca Hofeldt** took some time off for relaxation and self-discovery. As she tried new things, a true awakening was triggered deep within her. Discovering a hidden talent for writing poetry transformed her life. She believes that there is a poet within everyone, and by sharing her own journey poetically she hopes to inspire you to tap into the poet living inside of you.

- When **Dr. Angela Sorensen** experienced a family health issue, she realized she'd have to maintain her energy reserves so that she could deal effectively with the unknowns ahead. She shares the process she created to keep herself mentally strong and physically fit so that you too can have optimal vitality and approach life with excitement, positive energy, and a sense of adventure.

- When **Rolonda Watts** was growing up, she didn't see anyone on TV who looked like her, but that didn't stop her from visualizing herself as an actress. When the dream didn't materialize as soon as she hoped, she followed the path of journalism until she had the opportunity to act. Along the way she also developed a few other talents, as well as an openness to possibilities. She shows you how taking small steps toward your dream will build momentum and provide the motivation to achieve your goal.

- **Cynthia Krejcsi** has been learning to follow where Spirit leads her. When she ignored the voice inside and stifled her true self in order to "fit in," she squelched the powerful woman inside of her. But when she followed the urgings, she began to grow, embrace change, shift her perspective, and move into her power. She'll show you how you can claim your power too.

- **Rijuta Tooker** longed for a life of peace and calm, yet even when living in the idyllic setting of a yoga retreat in the Bahamas she still felt an emptiness in her heart. A job at the U.N. and the opportunity to study with a spiritual teacher in New York enabled her to live a life focused on peace and loving oneness. She'll share simple principles and practices that will enable you to align yourself with your highest values and become a force for peaceful change.

- **Kammy Haynes** grew up hearing mixed messages from her father and mother that made her confused about competing or collaborating, winning but not celebrating, being strong and smart yet appearing weak and demure. These mixed messages haunted her until she realized that she didn't have to choose one approach over the other. Her lessons will enable you to work through the mixed messages in your own life and to approach situations with a new and more positive perspective.

- **Shelley Redford Young** set out to find the easiest and healthiest way to achieve her optimum health, weight, and appearance. She discovered that the answer lies in keeping our bodies in a more perfect pH balance by choosing foods and drinks that are more alkaline, like the human body. She'll educate you about which foods are acidic vs. alkaline so that you can make conscious, health-minded choices to stay in balance and enjoy maximum energy and vitality.

- The death of **Lisa Buckalew's** 17-year-old son set her into a tailspin of grief, despair, and anger. It was only when she gave up, when she surrendered, that she began to wake up. Creating art enabled her to express some of her deepest feelings, and so the process of healing began. She will explain how the power of surrender can make it possible for you to connect with yourself in ways you have never imagined.

- For years **Bonnie Hooper** suffered excruciating pain that finally led to back surgery, but then a different type of pain surfaced. Depression set in when the physical limitations required during her months of recovery forced her to depend on others to get around and also led to substantial weight gain. Her story will inspire you to overcome your own limitations by following up on opportunities to grow and change.

These are the dynamic BraveHeart Women who have collaborated in this book. They share their individual stories and life lessons. In doing so, they join their voices together in collaboration, inspiring women to rise to their next level of personal, professional, and global success and thereby shifting the consciousness of humanity.

And so I welcome you to BraveHeart Women Publishing: The Voice of Collaboration!

Dr. Ellie Drake

Founder of the BraveHeart Woman Global Community: for Women Who Choose To Be Inspiration in Action; and BraveHeart Women Publishing: The Voice of Collaboration

$\mathcal{F}$inding Your Authentic Self

by Mariel Hemingway

I guess I'd describe my life as being one gradual aha moment. I'm not a person who learns things overnight, so there isn't one specific insight or experience that changed the course of my life or suddenly brought me awareness. My whole life has been a learning process.

I come from an incredibly creative family with a wonderful heritage. My grandfather was a renowned author. But there was a tremendous amount of mental illness, physical illness, and a lot of dysfunction in my home, not so different from anyone else's. And I think the reason that I share with people is because I know that I'm not unique. Just because I'm a celebrity doesn't mean that I'm exempt from the ups and downs of life. Everybody has difficult life experiences to deal with. But there were several suicides in my family: My grandfather committed suicide; his father committed suicide; my grandmother's father committed suicide; my uncle, my great-uncle, and my sister committed suicide. And then my mother had cancer, and I was her primary caregiver from the ages of 11 to 16. My father had heart disease, and I knew that there was diabetes in my family. So basically, I lived my childhood in fear. I feared getting ill, having a disease. It was about survival. I wanted to survive what I'd been brought into.

This isn't to say that there weren't great things about my family, but there were many things that worried me. I have a sister who's still alive, and she's mentally unstable, so I was worried that one day I would wake up and I would be crazy. And I used to suffer from depression. I always had a fear that something was going to come over me, but the beautiful gift is that my fear actually propelled me into this world of health and wellness and working out to be fit.

What it did initially was make me an extremist. I did everything to the extreme. I tried every diet. I've been macro-biotic, high protein, low protein, no fat, all fat. I've done food combining. I did Fit for Life®. I did the Beverley Hills Diet. I drank coffee solidly for one year. I ate air-popped popcorn and nothing else for a really long time. I did some weird things.

But I did all of this because of my desire to find balance and a sense of self. I was in a business that was all about the way you looked, so inside I had this fear. I had very, very low self-esteem. I had the fear of getting sick and going crazy. But I also had a deep desire to be loved, like all of us do.

It wasn't until I reached about the age of 40 that I realized I was actually my best teacher, my best healer, my best nutritionist, my best guide. And I'm still learning. Not only have I done every diet, but I've probably followed every guru, I've tried every system, I've done woo-woo things, and I've done great things. And all of it has given me a wealth of information and knowledge about who I am. But I finally woke up one day and thought, *I don't have to give all my power away in order to be healthy and happy and love myself. I need to find that within me.*

It took me a long time to do it. That's why I share about where I come from in this field of health and wellness. I have a cookbook out, called *Mariel's Kitchen,* and a company called Mariel's Kitchen, and I make cookies that are gluten free and sugar free. These foods were designed for my ex-husband, who had cancer—similar to my mother. But we went about dealing with his cancer totally holistically, and he was cured by lifestyle, food, exercise, creating silence in his life—real alternative measures.

I'm so inspired to share my journey with people because I know that the answers lie within myself. Right now I'm writing my next book with my partner, Bobby Williams. And it's about connection. It's about connecting in nature, and it shows us that nature is our greatest guide. One of the things that saved me as a kid was that I always got outside. I lived in Idaho, and being outside was really my teacher. It was the place where I felt most at home and the most comfortable with myself. I was so lacking in self-esteem and so fearful of getting sick and of all these different things in my life that it wasn't until I was out in nature, climbing or in the woods, that I felt grounded and at home.

My passion is to share the idea that food and home and health and adventure and connection to nature are ways to find your authentic self. That's what my entire life is focused on, and it's what my current book is about. Helping myself always comes first with me—not in a selfish way but in a selfless way. The more I discover about me, the more I empower myself to listen to my own intuition and to my own inner guide, the more powerful I become in the world. And then I want to share what I've learned, because my own self-love gets translated into a generous giving of that love to others.

When you have enough for yourself, you actually can give to others. It's an old idea that if you can't love yourself, you can't love anybody else. There's a voice inside most of us, not just in women but in men as well, that is sort of self-deprecating. Not everybody has it, but I certainly grew up with this degrading, nasty voice in the back of my head that was always making me wrong. Nothing was good enough. It was the *don'ts, nots,* and *should haves*—all these different things were destroying my sense of well-being. However, when I slowed my life down enough, got back in connection with nature, I really discovered that there's no one-size-fits-all in the way that you eat and the way that you move and the way that you are in life. Then I realized that I really had something important to tell people, to inspire them to find their own teacher within. For me that comes through being in nature, but it's also just being mindful of everything you do. It's about being present. Yoga taught me about being present in the body.

My desire in life is to keep sharing how I know from experience, because I think that's the only place from which people can truly teach. I call it experiential knowledge because you have to experience something to really understand it. Then it becomes cellular. So I go out into the world and I'm able to share what I've learned. What drives me now is no longer about survival. Before, I lived life feeling like I was sliding every single day. Now I feel connected. I love myself. That was a really hard thing for me to learn how to say. I thought that was weird and kind of egotistical. But it's not. True self-love makes you feel joyful to be in your life.

Many of my earlier issues had to do with my lifestyle choices. I was drinking too much caffeine. I had too much stress in my life. I wasn't honest about some of the things in myself that needed attention, about my past or my history or my relationship. But once I got very clear and very honest with myself about my life, all that depression started to melt away. It was just not a part of me anymore. And I started to lose the story—the story that my parents gave me, the story that my genetics gave me, the story that the environment gave me, the story that the business I was in gave me. I started to shed a belief in the story. I started to absorb that I was my best person.

I discovered that I was the best person to give myself love. I was the best person to feed. Lifestyle is about everything you do. It's about being present in every moment. It's about the thoughts that you have when you wake up in the morning. It's about how mindfully you do things. It's about making ceremony of making tea in the morning. It's about what choices you make to have breakfast. Do you take 5-20 minutes of silence a day, just for you? Lifestyle is about all the things that I realized gave me a sense of joy and freedom and acceptance of myself that I never had before.

By shifting your paradigm, you shift your world into a world that works for you. And the minute you do that, when you have the faith and the courage to do it, everything starts to fall into place. You feel financially supported. You feel loved. You feel accepted. You feel better about the way you look. All kinds of things happen when you're following your true path. And your true path is guided by you alone. I can give you tools. I can help. You can help another person. You can be a parent to a child. But the truth is that the real guidance comes by really getting in tune with who you are. And that's about being very honest, learning how to breathe, and really connecting to the food that you eat. It's about being conscious and making conscious choices about everything that you do.

Finding Your Authentic Self

And then you experience a knowing. And the knowing only comes from your knowing. It only comes from you. I knew it intellectually. I knew the information. I knew where I wanted to be. But it wasn't until I got there that I truly experienced knowing. I knew that I wanted to be my own guide, but it didn't really come together until I had the courage to say, *I am my own guide,* when I started asking the questions, *Who am I? How do I show up in the world?* You really have to be honest about it to be able to say, *It's not my job. It's not my parents. It's not my religion. It's not all these outside things that make up me. Those are stories that I've told myself. That's the programming that I come from. The truth of me has nothing to do with what anybody else outside of me has said or set up or how I was brought up, not any of it. It all comes from within.*

I've always been Mariel Hemingway and not Mariel Jones. While I was married for 24 years, I tried to be Mariel Chrisman. Finally I decided that was not me. And then I began to have this understanding, this knowing, and I said to myself: *I guess I don't have to be Ernest Hemingway's granddaughter or Margot Hemingway's sister or the girl who was in* Manhattan *and had an Academy Award nomination. That's not what defines me. It's not who made me up. I can make myself up new every day.*

That's what's beautiful about coming to the age I'm at now, knowing that I am getting younger by the way that I think and knowing that there are 86,400 moments in every day to have a new thought about myself, to be different, to be reborn every time I decide that I want to be better and more me every second. That's what I want to share with people. You have the same 86,400 moments in each day to do something different, to make better choices, to make loving choices, to be kind to yourself. And if you screw up, who cares? The point is, you're always there. You're always given enough information, given the guidance. Nature's always there to guide you. It's always present. Learning how to breathe costs no money.

We've been given all of the tools within us to be the best we can be. We just don't believe it. We've been told a story that at age 65 we're supposed to retire and that around age 75-85 we're dying. It's a lie. It's just a story we've been told; and we believe it, so then it becomes true. It's very hard to buck a system that says that's how they want it. You have to have courage to say, "No!"

I've raised two kids. They're 20 and 22 now. I had a great time raising them, but that doesn't mean my life is over. It doesn't mean I'm not making good films right now, that I'm not a part of doing what I love to do. It's just about making conscious choices and being really aware of where you are and being honest about that.

Probably the most difficult thing about being your own guide is to be really clear that when things come at you—when a partner, a friend, or your child says something to you that makes you have to look at yourself; or when someone says something hurtful to you and you wonder why—these are opportunities to look into your own mirror.

It's difficult to learn to tune in to these experiences, but once you do it, the more you do it, the easier it becomes. It's difficult to have something come into your face and realize that it's true: *I do act like that. I behave like a baby sometimes. I shriek and I want my own way and I want to be right.* But when you start to realize it, the next time it comes up, you laugh: *Yeah, yeah. I really do like to be right. That's my thing.* You start to recognize it. And the first step of letting something go is recognition and awareness. It just starts to dissipate the more you let it: *There's that voice saying I need to be right again.* It's no big deal. It's not to make you wrong. It served its purpose for many years. But you get to a certain time in your spiritual growth when you don't need certain things any more. What doesn't serve you should fall away, but you have to allow it to by acknowledging it when it comes up. Unfortunately, people too often listen to the bad voices and say, *That's so bad! I'm so bad!* And they berate themselves for their mistakes instead of saying, *Yeah, well, there it is.*

It's also important to understand that this bad voice is not you. Your authentic self is a loving self, it loves you, it IS you. It's the child in you, the happy you, the accepting you. It's the one without the problems. It's the limitless you, the cheeriest you, the playful you. The other stuff comes from the programming. It's what society tells us we're supposed to be like, but that's not who we really are. Always remember that the loving, kind, conscious, and aware voice inside of you, although sometimes hard to find, is who you really are.

You're your own YOU. You are already wonderful now. You already have the perfect body. You have everything you need. Everything about you is already where it's supposed to be. Sometimes you have extra weight on you. Sometimes you have habits. That's not who you are. That's just something that's attached to you. And that's because of the story, because of the environment, because of choices. Your perfect, delightful, beautiful, successful, and inspired you is already here. You don't have to go out and find her.

Once you acknowledge this, you realize that your best you is already here. She wants to be there for you. She wants to be the best being. She wants to show up and make you feel good about yourself. Coming to that awareness is the first step. If that's true, then all these other voices and habits—cigarette smoking, eating too much sugar, doing this or doing that, not taking enough time for yourself—they're all just story.

We get wrapped up in the story, believing that it's real. It's got chains on us and it's holding us in prison. But it doesn't really. A powerful transformation happens when you realize that you're already free and you say to yourself, *I can already do what I need to do in my life because I'm already here and powerful. I'm already free.* That will ignite your own ability to manifest the life that you already are meant to have. It's just about acknowledging it.

You have to remember to do it every day, though. It's not like a practice that you just do once. It's not a magic potion. Habits are so ingrained in us, and society wants us to keep those habits; but if you keep with the thought that you're already there, you already have this tremendous power. We're so much more powerful than we realize.

Many of us don't want to step into our power because we're afraid of it. It was very hard for me to do. People would say, "You're successful." But

I hadn't stepped into my power. I played victim, and I victimized myself in my own marriage. It had nothing to do with my husband. He didn't do anything wrong, but I made myself out to be less than I was because I was scared of my own power. Women in particular are so afraid of not being loved or liked or accepted that we dumb ourselves down so that everybody else can shine a little bit brighter, because we think that's what we're supposed to do. We think that's kindness. We think that's a good thing. The truth is, when you don't step into your power and own your power and your light and your incredible, extraordinary beingness, then you're doing a disservice to everybody in your life, because they're not getting the best of you. It's just another one of those stories that we're scared of our power because we think being in power is egotistical. It's not.

Stepping into your power means you've got a point of view. It means that you are who you are and you feel good about that. It has nothing to do with ego or bragging. It's really just about being. And you don't have to be a bitch either. It's not about being in the business world and being a bitch. It means, *I feel really good about me, and I own me—my unique, individual me. I'm not owning somebody else's vision for me or a religious belief's vision for me. I'm owning the unique me that I've discovered I am.*

The way to get in touch with your power is to acknowledge first that it's already there, and then take steps. For example, being your own nutritionist means being honest with yourself about your habits. *I drink too much coffee,* you can say to yourself. *Okay, this is a step I need to take. I need to pull back on the coffee. Maybe I need to cut it out completely.* I know that I'm an addictive personality. When I gave up coffee, I had to give it up cold turkey, because I can't do things halfway. When I used to eat bread, I ate a whole loaf. I was just that person. And if you know that's who you are, and you're honest about it, you admit, *There are certain things that sabotage my well-being. Eating too much sugar does it, so I need to give that up. And because I'm addicted to it, I need to go whole hog. I need to just say, "No more."* You need to repeat this for at least 21 days, because that's how long it will take to break the emotional addiction to it. We can feel oh so sorry for ourselves and think it's so hard to do; or we can play "poor me," trying so hard but never succeeding. Ultimately, you either do something or you don't. When you do it, you feel amazing. Isn't it more important to feel amazing, younger, and more vital than to drink too much coffee?

Step up to the plate and do something that makes you better. If you know you have a problem with something, change it. It's not about "kind of" doing it. You can't "kind of" be pregnant. You're either going to do something for yourself or you're not. That's where the male energy comes in. I learned this from my partner, and I learned it through adventure with him. He takes me rock climbing, and I know that I'm either going to fall off this rock, or I'm going to take the next step. It becomes black and white when it comes to making good choices for yourself. You don't take grey choices into your life.

Some people who aren't addicted to it can wean themselves off of coffee, or they can just pull back and have one cup a day. It's likely if you're that person, you're not overdoing it anyway. So it's about being super honest. And then when you know that you've got an issue with something, find out what people do when they have addictions to this or when they do too much of that. What are some of the solutions?

In the case of someone who's constantly running and doing and feeling as though she doesn't have time for herself, my solution would be to tell yourself, *I'm more important than all the things that I pretend run me. So I'm going to get up 15 minutes early and I'm going to take 10 minutes to sit in silence. Or I'm going to take 10 minutes and make myself breakfast rather than run out to Starbucks® and get a muffin and a choco-latte mucka mucka drink. I'm going to make time for me, so I have to get up a little bit earlier.* When you give yourself time, time expands, and you find that you have more of it in your life.

Excuses are for people who don't really want to change. If you really want to make a difference in your life and you really want to own your power, make changes where you can see that they're needed. Everything always seems harder when you think about it, but actually doing it is never quite as bad as the thinking about it. We spend so much time dreading the work it will take to change. When you're dreading or thinking about it, you're in the future or you're thinking about the past, when it was so difficult before. That's not being present. When you're present, you take action in the present. You know that something's good for you, so you just do it in that moment. There's no thought about how it will be or how you're going to feel or how you used to feel.

You can play games with yourself, but that's just old patterning. There's a voice inside, a tape playing in your head, that does want to sabotage you. That's the old mind wanting to hold on to the old story because you're used to it. I remember coming to the realization that maybe I was addicted to not feeling good. Maybe I liked this whole drama of always searching for something. When I got honest about the fact that I was totally addicted to being messed up, then that started to go away. That's really not who I am. I just thought that story worked best because my entire family was that way. So you unpeel the onion. You start to realize why you do that. It doesn't make your mom or dad bad. It's just something they learned and passed on to you. Just don't listen to the story.

Think about the amazing global impact we will have when all women connect with their inner teacher to find their authentic self, when they start to take care of themselves, love themselves, and step into their power! When you are authentic, you lose the story you've been given by your parents, your teachers, and society. You take responsibility for your life and for the choices you make. You stop being a victim. You start to make conscious choices about your health and well-being by choosing healthy, natural foods, staying fit, and connecting with nature. You are considerate of the environment and begin to do things to protect it, and you realize that we are connected to nature as well as to each other.

Find your authentic self. Go ahead and step into your power! And love being your own unique, individual you!

About the Author

Mariel Hemingway is an Academy Award-nominated actress, model, yoga instructor, mother of two daughters, and a leading spokesperson for holistic and balanced living. Making her acting debut at the age of 13, she has appeared in over 30 films and made numerous TV appearances. Mariel is the producer of a yoga video entitled *Rodney Yee/Mariel Hemingway: 15 Minute Results Yoga,* as well as the author of three books that lay out the foundations of healthy living: In *Finding My Balance* she uses yoga practices as jumping off points that lead into her reflections about her own life. In *Mariel Hemingway's Healthy Living from the Inside Out,* she shares tips and techniques that she's learned over 20 years, including types of yoga and meditation that changed her life, ways to strip "noisy" foods from your diet, exercise as a way to connect with yourself, grounding yourself by allowing time for silence every day, and ideas for making your home a nurturing and creative space. *Mariel's Kitchen* is a guide to cooking nutritious and delicious meals in the midst of a busy schedule. Arranged seasonally, the recipes demonstrate how easy it can be to use locally grown, seasonal produce in your meals. In 2009 Mariel also launched a new lifestyle company called Mariel's Kitchen.

You can listen to Mariel and her partner, Bobby Williams, every Wednesday on their Hay House Radio program, *Earth Healers: Live Your True Nature.* Mariel is also an active participant in the BraveHeart Women Global Community and can frequently be seen on "A BraveHeart View" on *BraveHeart Women TV.*

To find out more about Mariel and her work, visit her website at www. marielhemingway.com.

Your Gifts Drag You Where You're Supposed to Be

by Rolonda Watts

When I was growing up, there wasn't anybody who looked like me on TV. There weren't any black anchorwomen. There wasn't any *Cosby Show.* If you saw somebody black on TV, everybody would say, "Look! Somebody black's on TV!" I think when I had this dream of being on television, it was being able to envision a place for me even though there wasn't a lot of opportunity at that time. I knew TV was a place where I could excel and be a leader. And even though there wasn't anybody to point to and say, *I want to do what she's doing,* I still always had a vision of me being there.

I had so many really good teachers who helped me prepare to get where I wanted to go, and I applied for and completed a lot of internships. I also went to journalism school.

The other day I was at Spelman College, and I was telling a story about something that happened to me when I was a senior there. I was supposed to have read this book for an African American literature class—Ralph Ellison's *Invisible Man.* I was involved in several projects at the time—I was the editor of the school newspaper and I was the lead in a play—and I was just so busy I couldn't get it done. But I wasn't too worried because I figured that I could just go out and get the CliffsNotes® to this classic.

I went to the bookstore, and the saleslady just looked at me. I'll never forget that look. She peered over her nose and said haughtily, "There are no CliffsNotes® to such classics." So I had to go home and start reading the book for the next morning's class.

I made it through the first chapter, the battle royal, and then I fell asleep. And the next thing I knew, the alarm clock was ringing; and I had to rush to class and give a book report on this book that I had not read. I still wasn't too worried, since I had the gift of gab. I went to class, and I talked it up about Ralph Ellison and what a great writer he was. I discussed his impeccable use of the English language, and I told the class that the best chapter that exemplified everything I was talking about was the first one, the battle royal. I continued to go on and on about the metaphors and the symbolism.

When I finally finished yakking, all the other students told me that I had done a great job. When the teacher asked the class, "How do you think she did?" people were saying things like, "She was fierce! She really knocked it out of the box!"

When class was over, the teacher said, "Everybody leave except Miss Watts."

I waited until everyone else had cleared out, expecting to get many accolades for my report. She asked me, "How do you think you did?"

I said, "You just heard the other students. I did great!"

She replied, "How do YOU think you did?"

And I said, "I think I did pretty good."

Next, she asked, "Did you read the book?"

And I said, "You just heard me give the book report."

And then she came back with, "Miss Watts, I know you read the first chapter. But did you read Ralph Ellison's *Invisible Man*?"

And I said, "Not really."

I'll never forget this. She slammed down her book as she looked at me across this sea of desks, and she bellowed, "How dare you cheat Ralph Ellison!" She went on to explain that Ralph Ellison was a black man in America who had to be invisible just so that one day I could be seen. And he had to be quiet so that one day he could write words that I would recite. And then she just pointed out that here I was at a historically black college with this wonderful opportunity to make a difference in this nation, to go places, to be seen, where everybody else had to be invisible. And that was when I realized that I had also just missed a perfect opportunity to educate my own classmates about Ralph Ellison.

And I think that really had an effect on me. Clearly it did. I'm very emotional about it. And to this day, I have Ralph Ellison's *Invisible Man* in my office so I never forget what I'm here for. I think that one situation put me .2 from being a summa cum laude graduate. But it made a point too, if you will. And I think that really inspired me. The point hit home for sure. I think that might have had a lot to do with my determination, on many levels, not to try to get overt and also to be religiously adamant about my visibility. Now here I am heard and seen on TV and in films all over the world. It was a definite turning point for me.

My mother was another major influence on me. I think that self-esteem starts at home, and she was always very much into positive thinking. Basically, I'm always happy. I just see it as a choice, and I love being happy. That's my state of being. It always has been. I love to laugh, and I love to have a good time. I think positive.

There are times, yeah, when you wonder, *What's the next step in my life?* You especially think about the future in this business as you become older and you're making choices. Business isn't the way it used to be. Unless you're a hoochie momma with no brains, they really don't want you on TV. We're in changing times.

I think that as industries change and time moves on things are different, and change is being embraced. Sometimes those changes require that one's self-esteem gets a little booster. Then what I do is I just pray. I have a lot of faith. I read a lot of self-help books. I talk to my mother, who is extremely positive and insists on positivity. My mom and dad are very much into that. Misery is not a choice for us. You do something about it.

I think it's normal to go through difficult times, but it is expected that you'll pull yourself out of them. It's constant work. It always requires maintenance. Affirmations that you repeat to yourself really help too. Over and over, I'll say: *I am good enough. I am just enough. I'm brilliant, wonderful, and smart.*

My father is an artist. He's a retired chairman of the Fine Arts Department, but he's a woodcutter. And my mother is an educator. She's a retired associate dean from Wake Forest's great School of Medicine. So my mother's very heady and my father's very artsy, and I think I'm a combination of them both. At times, I'm extremely serious and very driven, and then there are times when I'm just fun and giddy and really enjoy the light-hearted side of life. I think that's a good combination of my mom and dad. Both were very, very serious about education. We come from a family that founded a college. My great, great grandfather started Bennett College in Greensboro, North Carolina, in the basement of his church. My parents are over-achievers. They have two master's degrees, and my mom has a doctorate. She started college at the age of 16. Wake Forest has established an endowment in her name. My parents are really good at what they do. They're also very generous people who are very active in the community. I'm very proud of my family. My parents are just dynamite people.

My parents expected a great deal from me. It wasn't about whether you were going to college—it was what college are you going to? My father is Roland, and I'm Rolonda. I'm the apple of his eye, and I never feel as if I'm anything but great in his eyes. And my mom is the same way, just a little tougher. They both just have great expectations. So while I didn't see any role models on TV, I certainly did have them in my life.

Many people aren't as lucky as I was in having exemplary role models at home. But even if you have no role models in your life, you can still dream. One of the most important tools in life is visualizing. You have that dream, you see yourself doing something, and you just love what you see. It's something we do as children; yet I think that as we get older, we lose so much of those dreams and the ability to visualize them so clearly.

When I was a kid, I would lie on my back in a big green pasture and look at the clouds and dream about what their shapes looked like. And I dreamed about being an actress on the stage. I didn't necessarily need to see it on TV, because I saw it in my head. And I carried it around every single minute of the day. I didn't have to wait for a certain time to see it. I became everything that I am because I dreamed it at some point in my life.

I think dreaming is extremely important, along with visualizing or seeing yourself where you want to be. I always wanted to be an actor. But when I got out of school, if you weren't singing and dancing on Broadway, there was no place for you. So I took on another career. Thank God I fell in love with journalism and took that path. But it was when I finished my talk show years later, when I was almost 40 years old, that I had an opportunity to act. I didn't have a contract, but I moved to California. And that's when I started acting. And now this year—at 51 years old—I am a leading lady in 3, and possibly 4, films. In *25 Hill* I appear with Corbin Bernsen, who is well-known for his acting roles in *L.A. Law* and *Psych*.

I honestly believe that your brain is like a ballistic missile. And if you set your brain on a goal, it's going there whether you like it or not. I have this saying, *Your gifts drag you where you're supposed to be.* Maybe that dream about being an actress way back when I was a little girl never went away. So it's still manifesting itself. And it doesn't happen in our time. It happens in the Universe's time. That's because everything else around you has to be ready too. I may become a big movie star. Who knows? But I'm going to be open to it.

I'm getting really jazzed by the fact that I landed a lead role. That's going to inspire me to dream another dream now, because I know it worked. So the thing is just keeping faith and keeping your dreams very clear and not giving up on them. I think of the Langston Hughes poem: "Hold fast to dreams, for if dreams die, life is a broken-winged bird that cannot fly." That is a real mantra of mine.

I think that my family, my history, my culture, the great writers of the Harlem Renaissance—all of those people who were artists and survived and left great pieces behind—they all have influenced me, and I can be part of that community. As my auntie Maya Angelou always says, "Your crown and all the jewels in it have already been bought and paid for. Your job is just to wear the crown well. You have a legacy to follow as well."

Your Gifts Drag You Where You're Supposed to Be

Recently I've also completed my first novel, *Destiny Lingers*. It's a story that's been in my head forever. I jokingly say that when my friends and I would go to the beach, they'd bring a book to read and I'd bring a book to write. I would just write this story I couldn't get out of my head. I kept writing and writing every time we went there. Finally it got to be about 100 pages. My friends said, "Whoa! You're writing a book here. Why don't you just write it?" And I replied, "It's a novel. Why don't I just keep going?" I was so into it. It was a project that went on for over ten years. It was something I kept writing. Finally, I took some courses in memoir writing and creative nonfiction at UCLA; and I used this plaything, this little book I was writing, as the piece I would work on. People were just blown away by it, so then I started working with a writer's circle of women who were published writers. And they said, "Ro, this isn't chick lit. This is really good literature. Keep going."

I was inspired, and I surrounded myself with positive people. Out of everything I've done, writing that novel was the hardest. I took a year off, and I really got serious about it. Right now it's being shopped to the publishers. And now I start part two. I start the screenplay. It has taken on a life of its own, and I really expect it to be tremendous. I see that as going into the second act of my life now. I really see myself as a writer—and a screenplay writer as well.

I believe that everything that we have comes together and coagulates in different forms at different times. And right now, one common thread I see through every thread that I do is storytelling. One day it might be reporting on *Nancy Grace* like I did the other day. It might be doing the voice-overs for the *Judge Joe Brown* show or *Curious George,* it might be narrating my own book, or it might be writing a screenplay.

Trying something new really thrills me. And I don't even think about failing. So what if you fail? What's worse is if you don't try. So many people are too timid to even try. That's crazy. I obviously don't have a problem making a fool of myself. And I get bored easily, so I'm always looking to try new things. It keeps life very interesting. I'm not one of those people who do the same thing again and again and again. However, sometimes I do dip back into my former careers and the skills I developed earlier in my life.

In my news career, long before my talk show, I was an investigative reporter. When I left that business to do the talk shows and then later left there for Hollywood, little did I know that I would be coming back and doing *Nancy Grace.* The reason I had the opportunity to do this was because of my investigative reporter background. So even when you do one thing and then switch to do something else, you never really leave that background experience behind. I'm an investigative reporter and always will be. Columbia University gave me a journalism degree to prove it. That's something I will always have. If the industry changes or I change, the stories don't change. There's always a story to be investigated. So I know I'll always be needed somewhere.

Do I want to do investigative reporting every single day? I don't know about that. But I'm always there to be a contributing reporter. Or maybe I will decide I want to do that again. I just think that it is interesting how things repeat themselves. I like doing everything. I laugh and say, *By the time I get back home to God, He's going to say, "Girl, you all used up!"* I'm going to use everything God's given me to the fullest. I think that's our way of giving back to God. If God gives you a gift, how you use it is your gift back to Him.

It's so important to use the gifts that you're given. Nelson Mandela says that it doesn't serve any purpose or it doesn't serve anyone for you to keep your light under a cup. It doesn't serve anybody when you don't show your light. That's just a waste. I think that's a wasted life if you don't exude all the beauty that God has put in you. If you don't show that, then having it serves no purpose whatsoever, and that's just unacceptable. Everybody's got a little light.

You take little steps. Not everybody is going to take the bold leap of moving alone to Hollywood to try to become a star. A lot of people can't do that. But there are little things that you can do. Take a community acting class. Take some type of course or hang out with a group of people who enjoy the same things that you do. That leads you to the next step. If you're passionate about something and you just give yourself a little tease of it, you're hooked. So I think that while you may not make a bold move, a little move is good enough. Take a course. Go to the YWCA and see what they're offering. Go to your local church to see what they're doing. Maybe the girls in your neighborhood want to start a writing group. Go to seminars. Join BraveHeart. Join a volunteer group. It doesn't have to be a monstrous move. Just a small move is enough to get your heart to leap.

I'm thinking again about my book that's going to be a big blockbuster, that's going to turn into a movie. Remember, it started off as a piece of notebook paper sitting on a beach. I had this idea for a story. Then it became 365 pages and 90,000 words. It was so hard to do that.

I kept dreaming about what it was going to look like when that book came in the mail, actually published and with a hard cover. I imagined that instead of having to host a talk show every day, I'd be on everybody else's talk show. And I'm envisioning and still envisioning, because this is a long process. I've been waiting months to get an answer from a publisher. I understand this is the way it works, but this is tough work and I still haven't heard anything. My editor says it's that thin slice of hell called "waiting."

But you've still got to keep the faith going. I'm wondering, *Did I do all this work for nothing? What are they saying? Do they hate my book?* But I stand by my work. I know that book is going to make it, and I just have to be patient and wait until it happens.

I have to keep my vision active and alive. I don't even think about failure. If the publishers don't pick it up, I'm going to publish it myself. Either way, that book's getting out, doggone it.

This is where those moments of self-doubt turn into bad self-talk. There are times when I have to catch myself, watch the things I say to myself. If somebody said those things to my friend, I'd slap that person across the face. We are our own worst enemy sometimes. We claim that we're so downtrodden because our parents or our teachers did this to us. No. You did it worse to you than they ever did, because you believed it. It's little things. You lose your keys and say, *I'm so stupid.* You walk past a mirror and say, *I'm so fat.* What do we think we're doing to ourselves? Nobody can do worse to you than you do to yourself.

Why do you think you're stupid? Something happened a long time ago and you believed it, and then you kept proving it to yourself. And every opportunity you get you call yourself stupid. Why? Sometimes you have to just stop.

I think sometimes we do things without self-awareness. Whether we're eating too much or we're not exercising or whatever it is, we're not being aware. You've got to watch. At every party you go to, they're serving alcohol. You've got to be aware of how much you're taking in. If you go out to dinner every week, you've got to really watch what you're eating. Our life is full of abundances around us, and if you just walk through it blindly then you are going to over-indulge. We need to be aware and be in tune with our body and ourselves.

Having some type of spiritual practice helps you stay in tune with yourself. God is my best friend. I'm not really religious, but I'm very, very spiritual. I start my morning, every morning, reading the *Daily Word* and concentrating on the Word. My friends and I call each other back and forth and say, *The word for the day is this . . .* , just so we have a connection with it. For example, today the word is *ascend.* I allow my spirit to soar and be one with God. I just concentrate on my ascending. Whatever I do, I try to think of taking things to the next step, taking things higher. That's my word for the day. I also read a lot of quotes. I love quotes. Right now, I'm reading *The Writer's Quotation Book,* a little companion book that has positive sayings. These are just little things that I do.

I love affirmations. I love being around positive people. My mom always said, "You show me your friends, I'll show you your future." I just try to stay positive. And I often walk around my house in silence. My studio's in my home, and most of the time all you hear is birds tweeting. I love my loud music at certain times, and I love watching TV—the news—but when I'm in that mode of writing and working and concentrating, I just have to stay steadfast and focused because I'm doing so many things at once. When it's quiet, then I can hear my voice and I can hear God's voice.

Writing is also a great way to break free of a lot of issues and to open up parts of yourself that you don't even know. Writing is an incredible way of connecting with yourself, even if it's just free writing. Maybe it's writing three pages every morning. It is so healing. It's the letter that you never send. It's the writing that you never show anyone else. But it unlocks something inside of you that may surprise you—some pearls of wisdom. I think we have tons of little angels trying to bust out, and maybe writing in the silence of your own moment is the way to uncover them and set them free.

Everything we need we already have. I think trusting that is important too. Stay positive. Focus on the positive, not the negative. Hang around with positive people. Happiness is a choice. People tell me, "You're so happy." I say, "It was a choice today—a conscious choice."

I'd encourage everyone who is reading this to go ahead and allow yourself to dream. And visualize that dream coming into being—see yourself doing something you love and then just love what you see. Dreaming about something and visualizing it as if it is already happening is going to make that dream manifest in your life. You might have to hold on to that dream for a while and hold it fast through some of life's ups and downs. But if you are very clear about your dream, stay open to the possibility, surround yourself with positive people, use the gifts that you've been given, and don't give up, then when the time is right, your dream will materialize. It has to!

And always remember that your gifts drag you where you're supposed to be.

About the Author

Rolonda Watts is a journalist, talk-show host, actor, producer, voice-over talent, and writer. As a result of her work in radio, TV, film, and the Internet, Rolonda is known by audiences all over the world. She began her career as an investigative reporter, receiving an Emmy nomination when she was at WNBC-TV in New York. She later became an investigative reporter and anchorwoman for *Eyewitness News* at WABC-TV in New York.

Rolonda began to attract national notice when she was host of Lifetime Television's talk show *Attitudes*. Next, she joined the newsmagazine *Inside Edition* as a senior correspondent, weekend anchor, and producer. But many viewers really got to know Rolonda when she hosted her internationally syndicated talk show, *Rolonda,* which ran for four years. After leaving her talk show, she went to Hollywood and began her acting career.

Rolonda is known for her voice-overs on *Curious George* and *Judge Joe Brown.* She's also the voice of the Boeing ad campaign. And soon you'll be able to see her with Corbin Bernsen in her first lead role in a movie, *25 Hill.* Rolonda is also in two other movies that will be released soon: *Christmas Mail* and *House Arrest.*

In addition to her work in numerous TV shows and movies, Rolonda recently completed her first novel, *Destiny Lingers.* She is also an active participant in the BraveHeart Women Global Community and can frequently be seen on "A BraveHeart View" on *BraveHeart Women TV.*

Rolonda has been the recipient of numerous awards and honors. New York City, East Orange, and Newark, New Jersey, have each established an official "Rolonda Day" in honor of her journalistic, community, and humanitarian works; and the McDonald's Corporation has also honored her as a "Broadcast Legend."

For more information on Rolonda and her work, visit her website at www.rolonda.com. You can also find her on Facebook at www.facebook.com/rolondafanpage as well as on Twitter at www.twitter.com/rolonda.

$\mathcal{E}$xpect a Miracle

Drawn from *Coincidence Is God's Way of Remaining Anonymous*

by Gloria Loring

Miracles do not happen in contradiction to nature, but only in
contradiction to that which is known to us of nature.
-St. Augustine

It was 6 a.m. on a Friday at the NBC Studios in beautiful downtown Burbank. I put my carry-on bag on the chair in my *Days of Our Lives* dressing room and took out my script, makeup bag, and shoes. I was "first up" that day. My scenes were being taped first, because I had to catch a plane to Houston to participate in the Jack Benny Memorial Tennis Classic to benefit the Juvenile Diabetes Foundation (JDF). When my scenes were completed, I rushed to my dressing room, packed my carry-on bag, and lifted it from the chair. Lying on the chair was a printed business card that read, "Expect a Miracle." I wondered out loud, "Where'd this come from? It wasn't here this morning." The card had appeared in response to a journey I had begun two years earlier, a journey that was going to transform my life.

It began when my four-year-old son, Brennan, was diagnosed with diabetes. It seemed incomprehensible to me that all my efforts to take perfect care of him had somehow failed. He had not been sick even one day until he got chicken pox six weeks before the diagnosis of diabetes. I was told that he would have to take insulin injections for the rest of his life, and it was most likely that diabetes would shorten his life by one-third.

A year later the intersection of two events set me on the path toward "Expect a Miracle." One morning Brennan asked me, "Mommy, when will

23

my shots be over?" I couldn't bring myself to say *never,* so I answered, "I don't know, but we're working on it." I decided that I would find a way to raise money for diabetes research and JDF. I had also been cast to play "Liz Chandler" on *Days of Our Lives.* During my first months on *Days* I overheard recipes being traded. An idea formed: I would put together a cookbook to raise money for JDF. *The Days of Our Lives Celebrity Cookbook* was born. Encouraged by the fact that *Days* had ten million daily viewers, I collected recipes, pictures, and autographs and told everyone who would listen about my plan. The project inspired lots of support; within ten months, I had everything ready to go, except money for printing.

I was getting discouraged, yet I recall thinking, *I didn't get this far to give up now. Something has to happen.* It was at that point that "Expect a Miracle" showed up; and within 24 hours, a man I had met years before provided what I needed. He was in Houston at the tennis tournament and as we were talking about Brennan's diabetes, an inner voice whispered, *Tell him about the cookbook!* I did. He offered $10,000 to underwrite the project. Then he introduced me to friends who chipped in another $7,500 that night. Within one month the cookbook printing was fully funded. The cookbook and its sequel, *The Days of Our Lives Celebrity Cookbook Volume Two,* raised one million dollars for diabetes research and JDF.

A Pithy Perspective

In the years following, I told the story of "Expect a Miracle" many times, usually punctuated with, "Isn't that an amazing coincidence?" One time someone responded, "Yes it is. That's because coincidence is God's way of remaining anonymous." I repeated it immediately, knowing I wanted to remember what I'd just heard. Albert Einstein is responsible for this pithy perspective. I send him my gratitude, because his wisdom changed my way of looking at life.

I'd always believed something great and powerful existed. I just didn't know what—or Who—that something was or where He/She/It could be found. "Coincidence is . . ." gave me an idea of where to start looking.

As I began researching the interplay of God and coincidence, I read that Carl Jung coined the phrase *the Connecting Principle* to describe the source from which coincidence flows.

What is this divine source/Connecting Principle that brings us coincidences? It is that essential creative nature within us and around us that both leads and accompanies us through our journeys. How do I know God/the Connecting Principle exists? Through coincidence. Through what I call evidence-based living. It's my adaptation of the concept of evidence-based medicine, which means to put theory aside and look at what actually happens. My cookbook experience provided evidence that I was not alone, that something greater than my individual self was listening and responding.

Coincidences appear because of what we feel, think, and do. They are attracted by the choices we make, consciously and unconsciously, and the depth and strength of the thoughts and feelings we have. The creative process that led me to "Expect a Miracle" was accompanied by intense feelings of love and urgency because of Brennan's daily struggle. Those feelings found focus in publishing the cookbook to help cure his diabetes.

I didn't see it until later, but there was a step-by-step process that led to the success of the cookbooks. The process that attracted the support of coincidence moved through four stages, or what I call the Four I's— *Inspiration, Intention, Inventory,* and *Investment.*

Inspiration

The moment of inspiration may feel like a nudge from a place deep within. You might notice it as a "gut feeling" or a sense of warmth around your heart. It generates enthusiasm. The idea attracts you and you have attracted it. You feel energized when you think of it, speak of it. This energy is an important key to attracting coincidences. Science and religious traditions agree that there is an underlying principle of energetic connectivity. Three perceptions shared by scientists and saints help us understand the source of coincidence:

1. **We come from and exist within the same source.** Physicists tell us that the universe is made of a single unifying substance—energy. Mystics also tell us that there is an "exquisite unity" to all of life. Recently, a group of scientists and theologians redefined God as the principle of simplicity and unity that underlies all the complexity at the surface of things.

2. **Each portion of the universe contains the wholeness from which it was created.** A spark of electricity contains the same qualities as an electrical current. A drop of water from the ocean contains all the "ocean-ness" of its source. The world's major religions tell us that God's spiritual and creative energy is within us.

3. **There is an endless process of energy being transmuted from one state to another.** Creation is an ongoing process, and each of us is a member of the creative team contributing toward the creation of coincidences.

Inspiration is the first step in the creative process of bringing inner possibilities to our outer reality. Inspiration has the potential to connect you to everything and everyone you need if you take the next steps.

Intention

Now let's imagine your inspiration as a goal and phrase it as an *intention*. Intention is the planting of a seed. Mine was, "I will create a cookbook to raise money for diabetes research." When you form an intention, you encourage your connectedness to the source of all possibilities. As you verbalize your intention, you are giving notice to God and coincidence that you believe your dream can come true.

If your inspiration is asking you to let go of some element of your life, you might not know exactly what you're moving toward, but you can begin to picture the qualities your vague goal might embody. Perhaps you feel you must leave your job but aren't sure what job you want or what is available to you. You can contemplate the elements that would define the ideal work for you. Think of the things that you would do for free—fund-raise for a favorite cause, raise orchids, help children with learning disabilities—and put those on your possibility list. Writing down your list is a very good idea.

The energy you direct toward an image of your goal assists coincidence in bringing formlessness into form. Shakti Gawain writes in *Creative Visualization*, "The idea is like a blueprint; it creates an image of the form, which then magnetizes and guides the physical energy to flow into that form and eventually manifests it in the physical plane." Our thoughts have creative power.

In 1985 I complained to my friend Beth, a co-producer on *Days,* that because I was now known as a soap-opera actress, I might never realize my dream of a hit record. She asked me if there was any way it could happen.

"Well, the only way it could happen," I began, "would be if I found a really great song . . . and if I started singing it on the show, maybe it could be tied into a story line as someone's theme song . . . and maybe if the fans liked it, we'd get a lot of mail . . . and I could go to a record company and tell them about our ten million daily viewers."

Because of Beth's prompting, I took my mind off why it couldn't happen and shifted to how it could. Within 24 hours she brought me a song that had been sent to the show. It was "Friends and Lovers," which became my #1 hit duet with Carl Anderson. Every step of my "the only way it could happen" ramblings came to pass.

Inventory

With your intention clarified, scan your life to see what you have and who might help with your intention. I got the idea for a celebrity cookbook from noticing my fellow actors trading recipes. Then I checked with the owners of the show to see if anyone had done a *DOOL* cookbook. No one had. I talked with friends at our local JDF. One board member worked for *Architectural Digest* and recruited colleagues to provide graphic design. In thinking about how to get the attention of the show's fans, I recalled a friend's comment that there are ways "to sell a book without selling it" by giving it away as a donation to a charity. All of these elements—the what, how, and who—were close by, waiting for me to use them.

At first, your inventory list might look painfully small. Don't be discouraged by appearances. You may be thinking about your resources in a limited way. Coincidence taught me that I had resources I hadn't yet come to know. There's always a larger truth than we, with our limited vision, may know. When you make your list, you can add a phrase indicating resources you haven't yet considered or that haven't yet appeared. It could be "this or something better" or "the working of coincidence" or "God's generosity." By acknowledging coincidence, you'll be making a list of *all* your resources.

The bird needs two wings to fly. It also takes two wings for our dreams to take flight: self-effort and grace. We make an effort, and by doing so we invite the other wing called grace to support us. Grace is the activity of love that comes dressed as coincidence.

Shirlee taught me about grace. I met her when I was promoting the cookbook on weekends at JDF chapters around the country. During one cookbook autograph session in Lincoln, Nebraska, Shirlee and her young son Michael approached me for an autograph. Before she and Michael left, she handed me two letters: one for me and one for my sons. I read mine when I returned to my hotel room.

It began, "May I help you carry your burden? I will share with you those anxious moments wondering what the future holds for your son. I will care with you that we work and search and seek until a cure for this dreadful disease is found . . . ." It went on for two pages of the most generous and loving words I had ever heard. I cried tears of relief and gratitude.

Two months later, as my life was changing in irretrievable ways, I received her second letter. Shirlee wrote that during her prayers she was getting messages for me that began with the words, "My Daughter." She explained that God wanted her to send me these messages. This was a little surprising to me since God was not on my list of intimate confidants.

As a child I had heard that God was eternally punishing, but the God of these letters didn't admonish or preach. These letters spoke to me with a kindness and understanding that no earthly lover or parent ever had. They responded to questions I hadn't even voiced, secret doubts that dredged up my darkest mornings, my loneliest nights. No one had ever known so well what I needed to hear. The first "Letter from God" arrived just after I told my husband I wanted a separation. I had not told anyone else about my decision, and since it was not trumpeted in the press, there was no way a woman in Nebraska could know of it. The letter counseled, "My Daughter, let go the fears. Let go the doubt. Let go the envy and pride. I will take care of you. I will love you for all time . . . ."

Leaving my marriage dredged up the same helplessness I had felt when I was a teenager and my parents divorced. Each letter felt like a lifeline, arriving just as it was needed. The letters came every few months for two-and-a-half years, until my divorce became final. It wasn't until I began writing my book about coincidence many years later that I called Shirlee and asked why she began sending me those letters.

She told me, "It was February 1984. I was on my way to a Bible Study class when I suddenly felt as if I were suspended in time. A voice said to me, 'You must tell Gloria that I love her, not to worry about anything. It's going to be all right.'

"I knew who 'Gloria' must be. I had seen you on television. But I remember saying, 'Lord, this is impossible. I don't know Gloria and she doesn't know me.' I heard, 'Wait and see.'

"That night during our prayer time, one of the women at the Bible Study class said, 'I don't know why anyone needs to hear this, but I feel prompted to tell you that Gloria Loring is going to be in Lincoln this Saturday for a book signing at the mall.'"

Shirlee was certain I would think she was "a loony tune," but she listened, came to the mall, and handed me those letters. By trusting the voice within her, Shirlee gave me a great gift: the experience of knowing that I was not alone, that there was a benevolent presence in my life.

Investment
Begin to move toward your desired outcome, even if you have no idea

how you're going to accomplish it. Start where you are, with what you currently have in your life, and you may find that coincidence fills in the blanks. You may need to make a conscious effort to put aside doubts that come up. "Act as if" you are certain that your intention will be accomplished.

Of the most famous scientific discoveries of the past century, the serendipitous ones were not made by random chance but by scientists who used their skill, judgment, and curiosity to pursue a focused quest. My friend Suzie Humphries, an inspirational speaker, concurs: "First you want it, then you expect it, then you act on it." While speaking at a corporate event, she had just finished advising the audience of the importance of "living your life as if you knew what you wanted would happen" when a woman excitedly raised her hand. The woman said, "I did just what you said. I acted as though I knew it was going to happen. I started packing before my husband and I sold our house, before anyone was even interested."

She explained that her husband had been transferred to Texas and had to leave right away to begin his new position. She had stayed behind to sell their home in Iowa. She listed it with a good realtor, but two months went by without an offer. They lowered the price. Still no interest. One night she awoke at 2 a.m. with a revelation she had while sleeping. She sat straight up in bed and said, "That's it. I need to start packing."

She jumped out of bed, gathered empty boxes from their last move, and began to pack. By the next afternoon, she had finished packing half the house. Her husband called and she told him she was packing.

He asked, "Did we sell the house?"

She answered, "Not yet, but we're going to."

One week later the realtor brought over a young couple who needed a home immediately. They inspected the house and said, "We'll take it. The only catch is we need it right away."

The woman, who was packed and ready, said, "No problem. It's yours."

By investing our time, energy, and spirit working toward our goal, we exhibit trust in our connection to a solution and encourage the support of coincidence.

Coincidence and Intuition

That which is, already has been; that which is to be, already has been.
Ecclesiastes 3:15 (English Standard Version)

Intuition is the inner form of coincidence. Coincidences appear to us in the outer world and intuition comes from the inner world. The word *intuition* derives from the Latin *intueri,* meaning "to look within." The Greeks believed that intuition was delivered directly from the gods and the heavens. The *Yoga Sutra 3:33* says: "Through keenly developed intuition, everything can be known." How else to explain that in a commentary on one of the world's oldest scriptures, the *Rig Veda,* the fourteenth-century Indian scholar Sayana describes sunlight as traveling the ancient equivalent of 186,000 miles per second, and yet the modern scientific community only came to that agreement in 1975?

Intuitive guidance from the God-within-us place may speak in clear words such as my inner voice urging, *Tell him about the cookbook.* When your intuitive wisdom is speaking either as a feeling or in words, you might feel the body respond. Even though the guidance may seem unusual, there's often a sense of rightness, clarity, and certainty. One way to assess intuitive guidance is to ask, *Is this the most loving thing to do, for myself first of all and also for others? Will it lead to greater peace and balance?*

Albert Einstein had it right. Coincidence *is* God's way of remaining anonymous. Whether it comes as an outer circumstance or as an intuitive inner knowing, coincidence gives us evidence that we are connected. Coincidence provides evidence that we are linked, to each other and to what we need. It gives us proof of the activity of love in the world. Sometimes it comes as the result of the effort we make as co-creators. Sometimes it comes just because we need help.

Like Carl Jung, I don't just *believe* there is a benevolent power in the Universe, I *know* the sweetness of an attendant goodness that wants only the best for each of us, that wants us to grow and prosper and let go of our doubts. Anytime I need a reminder, I find myself being drawn toward, or suddenly put in the company of, happy reminders.

You are connected to the people and resources you need. As the saying goes, "If you can see it, you can be it." It starts with that moment of inspiration that then solidifies into an intention. It's sometimes at this juncture that we begin listening to the naysayers in our heads or the ones around us. DON'T! Believe me, I had my share of negativity when I came up with the idea for the cookbook. I wasn't a businesswoman or a fund-raiser or a publisher or an advertising firm, but what I was, was inspired! Everything else was provided.

My friend Cheri says, "Love something else more." I loved Brennan more than my fear of failure. Dear friend, love something and someone else more than the voices of limitation within you and around you. Move forward with what inspires you. Don't let anyone or anything stop you from bringing your heart into the world. If it can happen to me, it can happen to anyone, everyone. Perhaps this chapter will, in some coincidental way, be just the evidence and information you need so that you can begin to participate more fully in the creation of miraculous coincidences.

I hope so!

About the Author

Gloria Loring is a singer, entertainer, and host who is known for her energy, commitment, and joy. She is the recording artist of the #1 hit song "Friends and Lovers"; co-composer of television theme songs "Diff'rent Strokes" and "Facts Of Life"; an audience favorite from daytime TV's *Days Of Our Lives*; spokesperson for the Juvenile Diabetes Research Foundation; author of four books for people living with diabetes; a keynote speaker for corporations and non-profits; and one of the few artists to sing two nominated songs at the Academy Awards. As a performer, she toggles effortlessly from classic rock to standards and from Broadway to pop at clubs, performing arts centers, symphonies, casinos, and fairs.

Gloria is currently in the recording studio working on her next album, which will include songs by songwriting legends Burt Bacharach and Desmond Child. She just finished writing a new book, *Coincidence Is God's Way of Remaining Anonymous*, an autobiographical journey into the benefits of coincidence, and has begun work on its sequel, *Life Doesn't Have To Be a Soap Opera*.

Gloria is an articulate champion of bio-medical research. After her son Brennan was diagnosed with diabetes at age four, she created and self-published two volumes of the *Days Of Our Lives Celebrity Cookbook*. Those books, along with her recording "A Shot in the Dark," raised more than one million dollars for diabetes research. She followed that success with two commercially published books, *Kids, Food and Diabetes* and *Parenting a Child with Diabetes.*

To find out more about Gloria's work, visit her website at <u>www. glorialoring.com.</u>

$\mathscr{A}$ World with More Rich Women

by Kim Kiyosaki

The morning sun woke me. I was lying in bed in my rented house on Lanikai Beach on the island of Oahu, Hawaii. The windows were open, and I could hear the trade winds blowing through the palm fronds of the coconut trees in the yard. My mind was already at work. I was thinking about how my day would unfold and then began looking into my future. I said to myself, *I go to work each day, I get my paycheck, I pay my bills, and I spend the little that is left over. And then I go back to work, get my paycheck . . . .*

Suddenly this surprising thought popped into my head, *There must be more to life than this*. Where did that come from? I was 27 years old, single, living in Honolulu, with a good job and having a *great* time! Why did there have to be more? Who could ask for more? Apparently, *I could* ask for more. Something deep inside of me began searching—for what? I had no idea. *There must be more to life* just kept repeating in my head.

At the time I ran the advertising sales and marketing for a small publication in Honolulu that catered to the business community. I owned my car and rented a house with a roommate one block from one of the "Top Ten Best Beaches in the World." Life was very good. Yet it seemed I wanted more. I just didn't know what the "more" was. I tucked the thought away and went on with my life.

Is New York City the Answer?

I could see how my life might take shape in Honolulu, and I decided that the way to experience the "more to life" was to move to New York City. I grew up in New Jersey just outside the city; so while the East Coast was familiar to me, I had never lived in the city. I thought this was an adventure worth pursuing. I began making my plans for the big move.

The first thing I would need to do in New York was to find a job. I can still feel the churning in the pit of my stomach when I thought about sending out resumes and interviewing for a job—again. I hated the thought of it. A little of my past history may give you an idea why:

When I got the phone call with a job offer from the #2 advertising agency in Honolulu, I was ecstatic! I had just graduated from the University of Hawaii with a business/marketing degree. I went to work Monday morning in the media-buying department. Nine months later I was fired. My boss and I did not see eye to eye.

That boss left soon after, and miraculously the agency hired me back in the production department. Within a few months, I was fired again! It was obviously time for a little soul searching. This time I couldn't blame my boss because she and I got along great. I had to face the fact that the problem might just be *me*. My conclusion was simple: I hated being told what to do! The problem was that I needed to get a job, but I couldn't stand it when my boss told me what to do.

Another revelation I had was that I wasn't interested in learning a *job*. I wanted to learn *the business*. I was not content sitting at my desk all day doing the same work day in and day out.

After that experience, I went into advertising sales jobs where I was more or less my own boss, yet the thought that there "must be more to life" still rattled in my mind.

Seeking Out the "More to Life"

Though I still planned to move to New York City, I thought, *Maybe New York is not the answer. Maybe I'm just trading one location for another.* I had lots of questions but very few answers.

One night my girlfriend Karen and I were having a glass of wine in a restaurant bar near my office. That night she introduced me to a friend of hers, Robert. Later that week he called to ask me out to dinner. I declined. I reminded myself, *You're moving to New York City.* Robert persisted for months, and eventually I said "Yes" to a first date.

On that first date, Robert asked me two key questions. First he asked, "What do you want to do with your life?"

Without thinking, I blurted out, "I want my own business."

He said, "I've started several companies. I can help you with that." One month later I had my first business.

The second question was, "What is your life's purpose?" *What's a life purpose?* I silently asked myself. I just looked at him blankly. He explained about there being a higher meaning to life. *A higher purpose for my life?* I thought. I flashed back to that morning in Lanikai. *There must be more to life* echoed in my head. This was my first glimpse of "more to life."

My First Business

Thus began my entrée into entrepreneurship. My first business was planned to last one year. We designed a logo and embroidered it on shirts and jackets and sold the clothing at business conferences and conventions throughout the U.S. The goal of this business was to pay for the travel expenses to attend these business conferences. This was part of my education to become an entrepreneur.

And to this day the learning never ends. Thank goodness no one ever told me at the start, "If you embark on this entrepreneurial path you will be broke, homeless, humiliated, lied about, sued, cheated, and stressed to the max." I've been through all of that and more. And looking back I'm glad, because all of those experiences contributed to the person I am today. Entrepreneurship is a Ph.D. in personal development.

After my first business venture, and plenty of mistakes and lessons learned, I was hooked. Robert and I created several businesses, the most successful being The Rich Dad Company that we own today. Its purpose is to teach people what Robert's Rich Dad taught him about money, which allowed us to "retire" when I was 37 and Robert was 47. The mission of the Rich Dad Company is *to elevate the financial well-being of humanity.*

My First Investment

I began investing in 1989. Following the Rich Dad principles and armed with some knowledge but no investing experience, I tumbled onto a small 2-bedroom, 1-bath house in Portland, Oregon. The plan was to buy it, rent it out, and hopefully make a profit or positive cash flow every month. The Oregon economy was extremely depressed, which meant real estate was cheap. Yet, having never done this before, I was scared to death. I had to come up with a down payment of $5,000, which I did not have. All kinds of frightening thoughts ran through my head: *What if you lose your money? What if the tenant moves out? What if you need a new roof? What if you've made a big mistake? What if? What if?* What I was really doing was looking for any reason not to buy this property so I wouldn't have to deal with all the *what ifs.* Long story short, I did buy that property and it did produce cash flow—a whopping $25 per month.

That first property became the catalyst for all of my future investments. It taught me the fundamentals of rental property. Of course I made mistakes. That was when I learned the most. Mistakes are how we are designed to learn. Can you learn to ride a bike without falling off many times? Mistakes are our greatest teachers . . . if we learn from each mistake we make.

After that first property I simply repeated the process. The more investments I bought, the greater my confidence and my knowledge. Today I own about two thousand rental units, as well as commercial properties, land, paper assets, and commodities. With every deal I do, I learn more.

Rich Woman

The Rich Dad Company started with the CASHFLOW 101 board game that Robert and I created in 1996 because people kept asking us, "How did you become financially free?" Instead of traveling the world and speaking to groups of people, we decided to create a fun and entertaining game that teaches people how to get out of the rat race of life and become financially free the same way we did. The game could travel to places we would never get to and people could teach each other.

We manufactured 1,000 CASHFLOW 101 games. Then we had to figure out how to sell them. We decided we needed a brochure, so Robert set out to write one. It took a little longer than expected; and when it was finished, it was not a brochure at all but a book titled *Rich Dad Poor Dad.* The book had a grass-roots following and made all the bestseller lists. It was the only self-published book on the New York Times bestseller list. (We self-published it because no publisher wanted it.) In 2000 Oprah called. Robert appeared on her show and that skyrocketed the book to international fame.

Robert and I were invited to teach the Rich Dad philosophy all over the world. I would take a few minutes on stage and speak to the women about money. It didn't matter if I was in Singapore, Tokyo, Sydney, San Francisco, London, or Cape Town, after the talk I would be surrounded by women who had the same questions and issues. It was clear that this was a global message women wanted to hear. It was also clear that there were issues unique to women worldwide regarding money and investing.

The Problem

The problem for so many women is that we do not make our financial lives a priority until we have a wake-up call like a divorce, a job layoff, an illness that prevents us from working, or the death of a spouse. Then we come face to face with the reality of our financial life.

Here are some surprising statistics regarding women and money. These are U.S. statistics, but the trend is very similar for most countries.

Forty-seven percent of women over the age of 50 are single. It's likely that the majority of these women have to take care of themselves financially.

Fifty percent of marriages end in divorce. One of the leading causes of divorce is money, and the first year after a divorce a woman's standard of living drops an average of 45%.

Of female Baby Boomers (women in their 40s to 60s) 58% have less than $10,000 set aside for retirement.

It's estimated that only 20% of female Baby Boomers will be secure in their retirement. That means that 80% will not. Given the economy, inflation, and taxes, the odds are that a high percentage of women will never be able to retire.

Two-thirds of women over age 65 rely on a small Social Security payment every month as their primary source of income. What if Social Security isn't around in years to come?

Of the elderly living in poverty, a staggering 87% are women (up from 75% just a few years ago). However, 80% of these women were not poor when their husbands were alive. A woman's husband passes away and she has no clue about her finances. "Mr. or Ms. Financial Helper" comes along to "take care of everything," and the next thing you know she's broke.

(Also consider that women live an average of 7 years longer than their husbands. That figure jumps to 15-20 years longer for Baby Boomer women. Plus, 75% of all women are widowed at an average age of 56.)

These are pretty sobering statistics. They tell me that too many women do not have the financial education needed to truly take care of themselves financially. Think back to what you were taught—consciously or unconsciously, including all the fairy tales and cartoons. Many of us were actually taught to depend upon someone else for our financial well-being: a husband, father, or other family member. And then there's always Social Security and Medicare. How many of us were taught growing up that we needed to depend upon *ourselves* for our financial future and happiness?

Rich Woman Is Born

It was clear that there was a growing worldwide need for women to take charge of their financial lives. It was also evident that there wasn't a woman who was talking—just to other women—about money and investing. I am a businesswoman and investor, and I've been in the business of education for many years. As much as I resisted the task, educating women about money so they could become financially secure and independent became my mission . . . and Rich Woman was born.

The idea of a purpose or mission in life can sound overwhelming and even unattainable, as if it miraculously appears one day through some divine power. That may happen for some people but not for me. I did not choose my purpose. Looking back, I see that my purpose chose me. The more I spoke with women, the more evident it became that there was a need that was not being filled. It made sense, given my experience and life path, that I take on that role; but something inside me resisted. I knew I'd have to write a book, and I wasn't a "writer." I knew I'd be asked to speak publicly, which was not my forte or passion. Yet I knew I could overcome these obstacles. There was a greater looming issue that I was being forced to address for the first time in my life. That issue was women.

I am the youngest of three daughters. My parents always encouraged, "Go for your dreams! You can accomplish whatever you want!" So I never understood women who thought differently. I never saw women as disadvantaged, unequal, or victims. Any woman who saw women in that way was, in my opinion, weak; and I wanted nothing to do with her.

After some serious soul searching, I came to the astounding realization that I actually had a prejudice against women. I had subconsciously labeled women, in general, as weak. That aha moment really rocked my world! This may explain why most of my friends growing up were male and why I worked and mentored with men. It was the encouragement of people pushing me to take on the Rich Woman role that forced me to address this issue that was holding me back, not just from making a commitment to the Rich Woman movement but from embracing the power, the knowledge, and the insights that women offer. It was a process—a process I am proud to have followed through. My life as a businesswoman, an educator, and a woman has been forever changed for the better.

Rich Woman is not just a book, a website, a TV show, or a seminar. It's a philosophy, an awakener, an empowerer, and an educator. Rich Woman is about you and your money and so much more. It's about women living the richer life they want and deserve.

The Rich Woman focus is around money—not simply managing your money but growing your money, taking the money you have and putting it to work for you so that one day, if you choose, you can stop working for money because your money is working for you. I don't believe you can have the richer life you want until you take charge of your money.

One objection I get specifically from women is, "Money's not the most important thing in the world." I can't argue with that. Money may not be the most important thing in the world. On a scale of 1-10, with 10 being very important, how important is money to you today? Remember that number.

On a scale of 1-10, how important is your health, your children's health, your marriage or primary relationship, your or your children's education, your personal peace of mind? My guess is those items all scored near 10.

Money may not be the most important thing in the world *but* it does affect so many things that are important: the quality of healthcare and education, our relationships, and our peace of mind. This is why I made money and investing the primary focus of the Rich Woman brand and philosophy.

Putting Rich Woman into Practice

KIM— My friend Kim met her wake-up call in her 20s. She was working for a start-up dot-com business when dot-coms were in their heyday. The company went public; and everyone in the company was very well rewarded. Kim had a windfall of money, and she didn't know what to do with it. She asked her co-workers, and several told her that they had turned their bonus over to the company-selected money manager; so she blindly handed over her hundreds of thousands of dollars to this corporate money manager. She quit her job, bought a new house and other expensive "toys," and proceeded to have a *very* good time. About two years later she received a statement showing her balance was down to almost zero. Convinced that this was an accounting error, she called her money management firm many, many times. Finally she reached her money manager. He said, "No, there's no mistake. Your money is gone."

Kim was in shock. "How can my money be gone?" she asked.

He stumbled for words. The reality was that this manager and his firm kept trading her account and putting her into different stocks and funds. Regardless of whether Kim made money or not, the manager and the firm did. They were paid lots of fees and expenses while Kim's entire financial life dwindled away to nothing.

Not only was Kim now broke but she was also up to her eyeballs in debt from the house and other goodies she bought using loans. She vowed never to let this happen to her again. She did everything she could to get herself educated about money, the stock market, paper assets, and investing. Today she is very successful with her paper asset investments and she teaches people how to do the same.

TARA— Tara contacted me via e-mail. She was in the military and stationed in Iraq but had two young children at home. She joined the military because she felt that was the only way she could care for her children. But being separated from them was difficult, and she was missing out on all their special moments. When she studied the Rich Woman philosophy, it was the first time she felt she had other options. Her dream is to be reunited with her children and to build her life and a business with her children next to her, not thousands of miles away.

LIEN— Lien is a young woman from Vietnam who is studying Rich Woman because she has taken on a crucial mission for her village in Vietnam. It's common practice in her small village for parents to marry off their 13- or 14-year-old daughters to men overseas. The young girls don't know of other options, and the parents do not have the academic or financial education to realize they have other economic options. Lien's mission is to bring this information back to the young women of her village and educate them and their parents about other options they have so that daughters will not be sold off like slaves.

For many women the wake-up call becomes their call to action. Others fall victim to their situation if they are unaware that other options exist. No woman today need be a financial statistic. Every woman, if she chooses, can learn the skills and gain the knowledge and experience to be a financially secure and independent Rich Woman.

How To Get Educated

There is a world of information available: books, CDs, DVDs, online resources, seminars, local meetings, mentors, and coaches. *The first step is to make the decision that you are going to take charge of your own financial life.* You are not going to depend upon someone else to take care of you financially, and you are going to do what it takes to become a financially secure Rich Woman. Your next steps will flow from that.

The following are three of my "secret keys to success" that I use to stay focused, motivated, and moving forward, especially at those times when I just don't want to.

KEY #1: What you do in your spare time

I believe this is one of the greatest indicators of a person's success in any arena. Women today have little spare time, so making the most of the spare time you have is crucial. Even more important is consciously creating spare time in your day to do what you need to do.

Taking control of your personal financial well-being is very important; but because it doesn't have to be done today, for many women it just doesn't get done. If you don't make time to do it now, you may one day face an urgent financial wake-up call without the knowledge or skills to handle it.

What you do could be as simple as learning a new financial word daily, reading something about money, or figuring out your real expenses and your true income. Before you decide where you want to go, you have to know where you are.

KEY #2: Who you look to for advice

There are so many people on TV, in magazines and newspapers, and online who want to give you advice. But what are their credentials? My friend Kim took advice from co-workers with as little knowledge as she had about money management and investing. Then she trusted the advice of a money manager who actually benefitted from her ignorance.

First you have to know the difference between a salesperson and a real advisor. Kim was taking advice from a salesman. He made money on what he recommended she buy. Many salespeople disguise themselves as financial advisors. They make it sound as if they are giving you solid investment advice geared specifically for you when in reality they are selling you the same thing they sell all of their clients.

Much of the advice you read in money magazines or watch on financial television programs is aligned with their advertisers. If the majority of advertisers and sponsors are stock brokerage firms and mutual funds, then you will probably be advised that these are where you should put your money. They will spin their reporting to tell you why, no matter what has happened, the markets will go up in the future. Beware of the source.

Who do you take advice from? I have one primary criterion: I want to take advice from people who practice what they preach. I want to learn from people who are doing what I want to do. Does your stockbroker buy the same stocks he or she is recommending you buy? Does your real estate broker invest in property outside of his or her personal residence?

A friend of mine wanted to invest in property in Phoenix but was too fearful to actually buy it on her own. We spent several days together finding a property and following through all the steps to the property inspection. Then I had to leave town on business. When I returned, I asked her when she would be closing. She said, "I decided not to buy the property."

I was confused because this was an excellent rental property that would generate about $100 a month in profit or cash flow. "Why?" I asked her.

"Because my friend, Barbara, said it was a risky deal."

"Barbara has never bought a rental property."

"I know, but she's a pretty smart woman."

She may be smart in some things, but investment real estate is not one of them.

Seek out people who have done what you want to learn. You'll be amazed at how willing successful people are to share their knowledge. If the advice comes in written, online, or television form, track down the bio of the person offering the advice.

KEY #3: Surround yourself with people who support your dreams and goals.

So much energy, power, hallucinations, opinions, and decisions are influenced by money. This is why some people say *Money is evil. The rich are greedy. I'd rather be happy than rich.* And then there are those who see money as a tool, a life skill, and a motivator to create great things in the world. This is why Key #3 is very important to me in all aspects of my life.

Jenna struggled in school and in life. She didn't have many friends, and those she had were a bad influence. Jenna was caught drinking, and she was growing more and more rebellious. Yet she was bright and caught on quickly to new ideas that interested her. In order to pass into 12th grade, Jenna needed a C or better on an upcoming math test. She studied hard. I saw her the day after her test, when she got the news that she got a B. She was beaming. That moment her father walked in the front door. The first words out of her mouth were, "I got a B! I got a B!"

Her father replied, "You know, Jenna, if you put more effort into it you could have had an A." And he walked away.

She retreated to her bedroom, closing the door behind her.

That was a turning point for me. I asked myself, *Who are the people I surround myself with? Do they build me up or tear me down like Jenna's father?* I made a conscious decision to get the negative, unsupportive people out of my life. I may see them occasionally; but the conversation is brief, and their attitude and words have no influence on me.

In the world of money and investing you will have people say, "Are you crazy? You can't do that!" Or "Investing is risky. You'll probably lose everything." And "What are you reading that for? Why in the world are you going to that seminar?" Get these people and their negative vibes out of your life! Instead, attract people to you who will support what you want to do, who will encourage you to keep going, and who will build you up, not tear you down. Hang out with people who will push you and challenge you to be more of who you are, not less than—and do the same for them.

You might form a Rich Woman Study Group with like-minded women to support each other as you move toward your goals. If you are married or in a primary relationship, then I trust your partner is that supportive, uplifting person for you. Ideally, building a financially free life is something you and your partner do together. Your partner should be your greatest asset in this whole process. Having a common goal or purpose for your marriage is a vibrant and essential way to keep your relationship alive and keep you growing together.

It's All about Freedom

Money is an emotion-charged topic. It has the power to enslave you and the power to free you. Rich Woman is about women being free. One of the greatest gifts I received once I was financially free was that I had the luxury for the very first time in my life to ask myself, and act on, the question, *What is it I really want to do with my life?* Until that time I was too busy earning a living. Once I had money handled, I was not only financially free but, more importantly, I was free to seek out whatever in the world I am here to do. That is the real reward of financial freedom. It's not about money. It's about freedom. It's about the freedom to be who you are and to do what it is you truly want to do in this world.

About the Author

Kim Kiyosaki is a businesswoman, investor, author, and educator who is helping women around the world take charge of their financial lives. But this didn't happen overnight! In fact, for a time Kim and her husband, Robert, were penniless, choosing to follow their dream of becoming financially free and learn all they could about money, people, and life. Rather than take jobs, they studied and worked to develop a company that would teach people what they themselves were learning.

Today Kim has the freedom to do whatever she wants in life. She has developed the Rich Woman brand and leads a team of inspired women who help her bring it to life. As an author of the *Business Week* bestselling book *Rich Woman*, Kim travels around the world teaching and empowering women to be financially independent. According to Kim, "Women can't be truly free unless they are financially free." Her mission is to teach women about money and get them to do their *first deal*. "It's more than a first step," says Kim. "Your first deal is the realization that you can do this, that you can be a Rich Woman and live a life that is rich in experiences, rich in giving, and, yes, remain rich in relationships too."

To find out more about Rich Woman, visit www.richwoman.com.

The Decision Tree: Making Every Branch Count

by MaryEllen Tribby

Sometimes It's in Our DNA

I had my very first job when I was ten years old, delivering our local newspaper. The papers would arrive in our driveway by 5:00 a.m each weekday. I was up by 5:30. By 7:00 a.m., when most ten year olds were just waking, I had already delivered the newspaper to 34 homes. More importantly, by 7:00 a.m. each morning I had an overwhelming sense of accomplishment.

In 1971 the daily newspaper was the window to the world for most people in my hometown. It brought excitement, intrigue, and tragedy into their lives, making me the conduit between them and the rest of the world. I knew all of my customers by name. I knew their kids' names, their grandkids' names, even their pets' names; and all my customers knew me.

You may wonder who the heck was up at 5:30 to meet and greet me. Well, there were a few during the week, but it was on Saturday that my paper route turned into a party on wheels. The paper did not get to my house until 9:00 a.m. So when I would deliver the Saturday edition, many of my customers were already outside raking leaves, washing cars, or cleaning out their garage. Whatever they were doing, they always stopped to talk.

They told me fascinating stories about their lives, inviting me into their homes and sharing lifelong souvenirs. Whether it was an exotic stamp collection or family photos, I felt honored that they wanted to share those moments with me. They would ask me in for breakfast. I sampled goodies like chocolate chip pancakes, croissants, and crepes—nothing like the oatmeal I was used to!

These people were complete strangers just a few months earlier, and now they were surrogate parents, grandparents, aunts, and uncles. My customers were not only fascinated by this little ten-year-old girl who knew more about what was going on in the world than most of their friends, golf partners, and colleagues, they actually cared about me, and I them.

I later realized the reason I enjoyed my conversations with my customers so much was because there was so little conversation in my home. In fact, it seemed like all my brothers, sister, and I did was listen to my mother complain. Mostly she complained about money, which we did not have enough of, or about her job and how much she hated it. It was because of my mother's distain for her job and her considerable lack of discretion that I asked if I could have a paper route in the first place.

The 5:00 Whistle Was the Devil in Disguise

Like most middle-class kids in the early '70s, we played outside after school, jumping rope, playing ball, or riding bikes. As long as we were within "calling" distance, we could pretty much do whatever we wanted.

The time between 3:00 and 5:00 p.m. was what I labeled my "kid time." It was the only time during the day that I felt like a ten year old, acting like every other kid I knew. Once that 5:00 whistle blew, everything stopped and all the kids scurried home.

By 5:15 my family was seated at our dinner table, prepared for but not looking forward to the habitual rant about my mother's lousy day. It always started with the horrible traffic. A ride that should take 30 minutes turns into 45 minutes because of the number of cars on the street. Even at ten years old I understood the irony of traffic and how miserable the daily commute could be. People would complain about it all the time, yet they were part of it. They were just complaining about themselves.

Then it got worse. My mother would complain about the sick kids. Again, I thought about the irony. My mother was the school nurse; yet she did not particularly like children and she especially did not like sick ones.

One night I interrupted the daily monologue and stated what seemed like the obvious—that if there were no sick children she would not have a job. This did not go over well. Then I took it one step further. I had the audacity to ask why she had children in the first place and four of us at that.

I was prepared for immediate sanction to my room after a good smack. But what I got instead was an epiphany of a lifetime. My mother just looked straight ahead and simply said, "Because that's what I thought I was supposed to do."

That night I vowed to myself that I would never have a job that I did not like and that if I was ever blessed enough to have children they would know they were wanted and loved.

Money May Have Started It . . .

In my ten-year-old mind $1,000 was a lot of money. And if I had $1,000 I would be able to move out. Since $1,000 was a lot of money and if I wanted to move out when I was 18, I needed to start saving now.

The day after the infamous dinner, I asked my father if I could get a paper route. He said I was too young—one needed to be 12 to have a paper route. Since I already knew this from an older kid at school, I was prepared. I said that since my brother was 12, we could register the route under his name but I would deliver the paper and, of course, keep all the money.

My father was impressed with my initiative to earn money. He, too, had started in the wonderful world of employment at the age of ten, but out of the necessity to eat. Even though we had the essentials of food and shelter, he thought I wanted the money for the extras that we rarely got; so he agreed to register the route under my brother's name.

One Dime at a Time

I heard from the older kid at school that his tip was a dime a house. I had 34 houses on my route, which meant I could make $3.40 a week, $176.80 a year; and in 8 years I would have $1,414.40, which exceeded my goal!

Because I had a goal, I delivered that paper every day with pride and enthusiasm. Soon my average tip went from $.10 a house to $.12 to $.15 to $.20 a house per week. I was making twice as much as the older kid!

But so many other things were happening than just making money, things that were much more important, though I did not realize it at the time. For one, I read the paper every day. But since my day started so early, I read it in the evening, which almost made me an outcast with my family. As in so many other families, after dinner, clean up, and homework, it was TV time. I guess watching TV was just easier than talking. But soon I was giving up *Bonanza, Laugh In,* and *The Partridge Family* to read the paper. (Okay, I'll admit it—I put the paper down when Keith Partridge sang.)

Next, I started having conversations with people. I spoke with my customers, teachers, and friends about what was going on in the world. It was the first time I could talk about something other than our local football team score or who was in the *TV Guide.* Most importantly, I enjoyed getting up early and getting my day going. I loved what I did and I got paid to do it.

I did not realize it then, but 1971 not only laid the foundation for my adolescence but for my adult life. It is profound to think that a single statement that caused me so much pain is responsible for my success today.

Find the Right Balance

"I can't believe he called you at 9:00 at night. You don't think that is totally inappropriate?" asked my sister-in-law Connie. When I told her I did not and was happy he'd called, her jaw dropped even further.

We were talking about a business colleague of mine. "Larry" had called to ask if I could speak with his mastermind group on a teleconference later that week. He wanted me to talk about accelerating their businesses growth via multi-channel marketing. Given the fact that his attendee list included people who were my mentors, I was honored to accept.

When I tried explaining this to her, she said, "In my day, when you left the office at 5:00, you were done until 9:00 the next morning."

I thought about dropping the subject, but I couldn't resist the challenge.

I asked her if she'd ever left the office to pick up a sick kid from school, go to a dentist appointment, or meet the cable man at her house. When she begrudgingly nodded her head yes, I knew I had her attention. And I hope I have yours as well. If you think that your work life exists only between 9:00 and 5:00 and that your home and social life exist only between 5:00 and 9:00, you need to make a change.

I recommend that you resolve to make your life better, more rewarding, and more balanced. And I'm going to help you do it. Who am I to talk about balance? Well, I'm a happily married mother of 3 who runs a 25-person business. Over the past few years, I've gotten pretty good at managing all the different aspects of my life in a way that makes me feel happy and proud. The very first step to creating a happier, healthier lifestyle is to realize that "9:00 to 5:00" no longer applies. By giving yourself the flexibility to do business at all hours of the day or night, you are actually better able to enjoy both your work and your family. By taking the following five simple steps, you will be able to break free of the 9:00 to 5:00 shackles.

Creating Balance Step One: Define What a Balanced Life Means to You

Many people think that having a balanced life means spending the same number of hours on work as you do on personal activities. That is just not realistic. To define what will work for you, you need to take into consideration that life is constantly changing. The right balance for you today may not be the right balance tomorrow or next week because over time your priorities change. The one constant in knowing you have a balanced life is the feeling of accomplishment and happiness you enjoy every day.

Creating Balance Step Two: Create Boundaries

Some people may agree with my sister-in-law that receiving a business call at 9:00 at night is inappropriate. But the way I look at it, Larry is good for my organization and for my career. Besides, when I met him at a conference earlier this year, he asked the best way to reach me. I gave him my e-mail and my cell number. So why shouldn't he call?

And keep in mind that I made the decision to take his call that night. It happened to be a good time to talk. Otherwise, I would have let it go to voice mail and called him back when it was convenient for me.

Later that week, I was the keynote speaker on Larry's mastermind teleconference. I got several e-mails from attendees saying they'd purchased the book on multi-channel marketing that I co-authored with Michael Masterson. Others asked if they could promote the book to their in-house list. Had I adopted the attitude that I would do business only from 9:00 to 5:00, I may have lost out on a wonderful opportunity.

I support the efforts my team members make in striving for balance in their own lives. Some of them work evenings and/or weekends, so I have no problem if they need to leave to take care of something personal during "normal" business hours. I truly believe that your accomplishments aren't dependent on how much time you spend in the office.

Creating Balance Step Three: Learn How To Say "No"

No one wants to say "No" to the important people in their lives, but to achieve balance, you are going to have to do it once in a while. We don't have enough time to do everything that we want to do AND everything that everyone else wants us to do. So a big part of leading a more balanced life is to cut down on unnecessary tasks and protect your priorities. When requests or conflicts are set before you, ask yourself: *Is this going to give me a feeling of accomplishment and a feeling of happiness?*

Almost four years ago, my friend "Rita" wanted my husband and me to meet her new boyfriend. He was "the one," as she put it. But when our two-month-old baby, Delanie, woke up on the morning of the dinner, she had a fever. I called Rita and apologized but said we would have to cancel. Rita was irate. She said I was overreacting and asked how I could possibly feel that way given that Delanie was our third child. As I held Delanie through the day and night, I knew I had made the right decision. But I was saddened by Rita's anger—and her anger lasted for weeks.

About five weeks later, Rita called to say that "the one" had dumped her. This time she apologized.

Work decisions can be more difficult. Sometimes you have to choose your family, your health, or your social life over work. And sometimes you have to put work first. For instance, last week a doctor's appointment conflicted with a last-minute visit from one of Agora's top executives. Since that was the only time I could see him and the doctor's appointment was for a simple check up, I didn't think twice about rescheduling.

Creating Balance Step Four: Keep a Journal

The only way to make your life better is to understand what you're doing, what's working, and what isn't. There are far too many things going on in our lives to try to keep it all in our heads, so keep a journal. Write down what you spend time on—everything from the meetings you attend to how many times you go to the gym. Keeping a journal will help you see if you are spending your time in the most productive way and will make you accountable for your actions. It will help you accomplish your professional and personal goals and will make you proud of those accomplishments.

Creating Balance Step Five: You're Not a Superhero

Having a balanced life means being realistic about the fact that some things are just not going to get done. And you have to be okay with that. When my husband and I got married 12 years ago, we both had busy careers. But we still enjoyed decorating our home and keeping it immaculate.

Well, once we had kids, things started looking a lot different. Instead of the beautiful vase I picked up in Mexico on the coffee table, there was a stuffed Elmo. Often while we're making dinner, the kids have all the pots and pans on the floor. Instead of spending my time cleaning up and making my house look perfect, I would rather play with the kids.

This goes for work, too. You may have a dozen projects on your plate and only so much time to complete them. Don't get down on yourself for letting one of them slide so you can spend more time on marketing or caring for your ailing grandmother. Following the other guidelines I've recommended will help you feel confident that your accomplishments are enough, even if you have more goals you want to achieve.

The Balancing Act That's Up to You

People ask me all the time how I run a successful company, raise three small children, travel all around the world, AND manage a household. It's simple to maintain balance; you just need to follow these steps:

Step #1 to a Balanced Life: Having the Right Attitude

We have a choice, every day, regarding the attitude we will embrace. MJ, one of the acquaintances I've made in our info-publishing world, runs a nice little consulting company and has two healthy little boys and a wonderful husband. Yet every time I see MJ at a function and ask about her family, she starts in about how hard it is to run a company and raise two kids and about how much more successful she would be if she did not have to take them to school, soccer practice, and play dates.

I have never looked at my children as a hardship. It is a privilege for my husband and me to raise them and build our lives together. But this positive attitude is not something that magically happened to me.

Early in my career, I interviewed for a management position at Forbes. The competition was fierce. Finally, they narrowed their choices down to two of us: Natalie and me. Natalie had graduated from Harvard, had an MBA from Columbia, and had a reputation for being tough as nails.

The day of our last interview we were both meeting with Steve Forbes himself. The HR director made it very clear that Mr. Forbes was a busy man—that he would ask the questions and we would answer them; that he would spend no more than ten minutes with each of us; and that a final decision would be made shortly after he had met with us.

Natalie and I both wound up sitting outside of Steve Forbes's office at the same time. They called her in first. I heard Mr. Forbes's muffled voice through the door and her muffled reply. Then I heard laughter. Thirty-five minutes later, Natalie swaggered out. Her grin said, "Don't even bother."

Then it was my turn. I went in. I answered Mr. Forbes's questions. After five minutes, he thanked me and I left.

As I opened the door to my apartment, my phone was ringing. You guessed it. It was Forbes. They were calling to offer me the job!

After I'd been there a few months, I mustered up the courage to ask my boss how they made the decision to choose me. Her answer rings true more than 20 years later: "Mr. Forbes liked your attitude."

That single experience helped me understand what is really important and what is not. It helped me learn not to sweat the small stuff and not to get upset about things I have no control over. And that leads me to . . .

Step #2 to a Balanced Life: Making the Right Choices

We all have to make hundreds of choices every day, starting first thing in the morning. Do you eat your healthy high-fiber cereal with blueberries and skim milk or a chocolate chip muffin? As the day goes along, our decisions generally get more complicated and difficult to make.

Last summer, a friend in the industry sent out invitations for a huge networking party. I was honored to have been invited. Everyone who is anyone in our industry was going to be there. This was the event of the year.

I immediately RSVP'd. That evening, my husband pointed out that this event was being held on the first day of the new school year. He encouraged me to go on the trip, assuring me that he could handle the kids that day. I knew he could, but that wasn't the point. My daughter was only going to have one first day of fourth grade and my son only one first day of first grade. And I wanted to be there.

I applied my two-two-two rule, asking myself, *What will be the impact on both sides two weeks from now, two months from now, and two years from now?* If I missed their first day of school, would my kids still be upset in two weeks? in two months? And would the disappointment continue to echo in all of our hearts and minds in two years? I knew the answer was "Yes."

I went through the same process with the networking event. I figured that most of the people at the event would remember I had been there after two weeks; but the majority would not remember I had been there after two months, and none would remember I had been there after two years.

I skipped the networking event and took the kids to school. Of course, I did not just blow off the networking event. Our Internet Marketing Director went and brought back tons of useful information, and I have since spoken with or met with everyone I would have seen that day.

This dovetails nicely with my final point . . .

Step #3 to a Balanced Life: Developing the Right Relationships

I was fortunate to have someone to send—someone who would represent me and Early to Rise, our core values, and our policies. I knew he would see it as an opportunity, and that is exactly what happened. Many of the people he met there told me what a great job he did. Had I not cultivated my relationship with him over the last 19 months, this would have been a lost opportunity for both of us instead of a win-win situation.

Many high-level executives would rather miss out completely than send a substitute. In fact, one sign of a good leader is that the business runs smoothly even when he or she is not present.

I pride myself on hiring and mentoring people who have as much potential as I do, if not more. It is the same with my personal relationships. I have a mother's helper whom my kids love, and she loves them. Every once in a while someone asks me: "Doesn't it bother you that your kids love Nora so much?" No!

Now don't get me wrong, I am not Super Woman. And I have days that are more challenging than others. Sometimes the only reason I can accomplish as much as I do is because I have a spouse who is my biggest fan, who never puts his career before mine. We decided a long time ago that we could accomplish *anything* as long as we were in it together, our goals were in alignment, and our philosophies regarding success were the same.

When people tell me there is no way they can maintain balance between their business life and their personal life because they have so much work to do, I simply don't buy it. Everyone can have a balanced life. You just need to want it—and act to achieve it.

About the Author

MaryEllen Tribby is a CEO, speaker, wife, mother, business consultant, and best-selling author. She is the founder and CEO of Working Moms Only.com, the leading newsletter and website dedicated to empowering the working mom to lead a healthy, wealthy, and more balanced/blended lifestyle. Since she herself is a working mom, MaryEllen lives the life herself. She believes it is her true calling to supply the necessary tools all working moms need to live life the way they dream it.

She has been the publisher and CEO of Early to Rise, where she was responsible for growing the business from $8 million in sales to $26 million in 15 months, and president of Weiss Research, where her leadership moved the company from $11 million in sales to $67 million in just 12 months.

MaryEllen credits much of her success to her traditional New York City publishing career. She ran divisions at Forbes, Times Mirror Magazines, and Crain's New York Business, and her mentors were some of the best direct response marketing and business leaders in the world. MaryEllen is in demand as a business consultant. In addition, she teamed up with Michael Masterson to co-author her first book. Within 10 hours of its release, *Changing the Channel: 12 Easy Ways to Make Millions For Your Business* hit #1 on Amazon.com. MaryEllen is also the recipient of the 2009 BraveHeart Woman's Marketer of the Year Award.

MaryEllen lives in Boca Raton, Florida, with her husband and three children. To find out more about her website for the empowerment of the working mom, visit www.workingmomsonly.com.

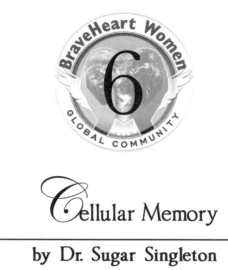

Cellular Memory

by Dr. Sugar Singleton

I am a medical doctor, and I was one of those kids who knew that I wanted to be a doctor from around the time that I could walk and talk. There was never any doubt in my mind that I could do it—that I *would* do it. I decided early on that I wanted to learn something new every day, and I attribute a lot of my success to it.

Every day take little steps toward the dream.

I also take little steps toward my dream every day, and this goal has been important in my journey to becoming a doctor. Now along the way, there were many times when I took a wrong step, times when I was going in the wrong direction, and even a time or two when I tripped and fell down. But each time this happened and I got out of the groove, I stood back up, dusted myself off, and continued taking little steps toward my dream.

I breezed through high school and college. My journey to becoming a doctor, while sometimes difficult and challenging, was never a journey that I questioned until I actually got into medical school. I had been accepted to one of the best medical schools in the country. I was smiling from ear to ear, and I was filled with admiration for my professors and excited about all of my new friends. I remember bonding with the other students over the smell of formaldehyde as we dissected cadavers and laughing as we looked under the microscope trying to figure out exactly how we could tell that that tissue on the slide was liver and not kidney. It was the best time of my life.

When the dream is big enough, the facts don't matter.

One night I was sitting with my nose stuck in a big medical book, just about to doze off. I got jolted back to the present by the ringing of the phone. It was my dad. I've been very close to both of my parents all of my life, so when I answered the phone, I could tell from my dad's tone that the news was not good. He said, "Sugar, the doctors say your mom has cancer and it is very advanced. She has two-to-four months to live."

It took my breath away to hear those words. I felt like I had been kicked in the stomach, and my eyes began to sting with the tears. The phone slid from my hand and hit the floor as I beat my fist into the wall, screaming, "Why? Why? WHY? It is not fair. It is not right. Not my beautiful, healthy mom!" I cried through the night as my heart broke into a million pieces.

The next morning I had a big decision to make: go home to care for my mom and assist my dad in our family business or stay in school and follow my dreams. Of course, I left school and returned home to become daughter and caregiver. I loved my mom so much. I remember sitting at her bedside one day as she said to me, "Sugar, I am not ready to die. I have things that I still want to do." I took her hand, looked her in the eye, and said, "I need you to do one thing for me. I need you to believe with all of your heart and soul that you will get better, and don't worry about anything else."

I was devastated at the thought of my mom dying. I was devastated to be away from school. You've probably heard the old saying about beating the odds. My mom did better than beat the odds. She turned that two-month deadline into almost ten full and fabulous years. The first four years I stayed with her—sitting by her bedside, wiping her brow, bathing her, protecting and caring for her as she had done for me so many times.

I carved out a new life: my husband and I started a new business and we were doing well financially, we had a nice little house, and my mom was doing better. I was working in our family-owned business, and we were blessed with our firstborn child. However, as good as it was, there was something missing. I wasn't living my dream. Somehow deep inside I knew that if I didn't return to school I would carry the burden of wasted potential on my shoulders for the rest of my life.

Whatever this was deep inside of me—call it my conscious, my intuition, or my inner voice—I remember the exact moment that it spoke to me. I was lying in bed listening to the soft snoring of my husband next to me. I had just finished nursing our little baby boy and had returned him to his bassinet. It was so clear and so loud when it spoke that it startled me. It said, *What about me? What about my dream?* Immediately I knew that I had to go back to school, if not to become a doctor at least to let go of the dream so that I didn't wake up someday and ask, "What if?"

I woke my husband up at 2:00 a.m. with these words: "Honey, I have to go back to school." He rolled over and took me in his arms while looking deeply into my eyes. In that moment I understood how much he loved me and how much he was willing to give up for my happiness. He said, "My love, if that is what you want to do and that is what will make you happy, then that is what you will do and we will make it work."

Now in that moment none of this made sense. I was a key player in my family business, and it required me now. My husband, Rick, and I also had a successful business that he really couldn't run alone. My mom's cancer was always looming on the horizon. The nearest medical school was 180 miles away. We had a little baby boy. It seemed totally impossible. But sometimes when the dream is big enough, the facts don't matter.

And so for the next seven years I commuted back and forth to school weekly. During that time we were also blessed with a little girl. I am still not sure exactly how that happened when I only saw my husband once a week, but it sure did! For seven long years I saw my husband and my children only on weekends. I got my heart broken every Sunday night as I would look into my husband's eyes and then get into the car. I would cry for the first hour of my drive and then think about turning around and going back for the next two hours. For seven long years I kissed my babies good night on the telephone. But as I am writing this today, I have two initials after my name that I am very proud of—M.D.

I learned many things during this journey. The most important was to have the courage and the strength to follow my passion, to move forward regardless of the circumstances and the challenges that might arise.

I found my purpose and the true foundation of lasting change.

After I became a doctor, I realized that my purpose and my passion lay in something much deeper than just the routine practice of medicine. Now this was something that in the beginning was difficult for me to digest. If I had just wanted to lead a normal life, I would have become a great medical doctor and been satisfied with that. But there were two things that I learned very quickly. The first was that I found a great deal of satisfaction in working with women. Second, I found so much more value in working with people deeply. You see, sometimes when we just practice traditional medicine, it can become almost a little bit superficial, like a band-aid. We do a really great job of medicating and oftentimes alleviating symptoms or managing disease in our current medical system, but in many cases this is not healing. We may fix what is wrong today but usually never really have the opportunity to find out what is at the root of the problem.

My medical school studies provided me with a very traditional training in Western Medicine, but over the years I've also trained myself in the path of deep healing and energy work. True healing is a more preventive healing, and true healing occurs on an energetic level. I have seen it over and over and over again—women who unknowingly and subconsciously carry unproductive cellular memories in their bodies for years or even decades. These unproductive cellular memories create blocks that hold women back from truly being happy, healthy, and prosperous and from truly being the amazing women that they were meant to be. Therein lies the basis for the deep work that I do with women. Working with women at this depth on an emotional, mental, spiritual, and especially on a cellular level is so much more healing than just treating the end result of those cellular memories.

What is it that holds us back from living our ultimate life, and where does that come from? Where did it get its start? How old were you when the blocks developed? How deep is the root? Where in your body are these blocks held and what if . . . what if those blocks could be released?

What I'm discussing is a compilation of my medical expertise, my interest in healing, which goes beyond traditional medicine, and my experiences as a successful entrepreneur. I am talking about cellular memory and cellular healing. It is the most important work I have ever done, not to mention the most powerful work I have seen done anywhere. This is a big topic for a small space, and there is a lot to this powerful work; but let me give you an introduction to it here.

Consider the possibility that every single cell in our body has the ability to remember. Our cellular memory can store physical, emotional, and mental memories from a lifetime of experiences. We all have cellular memory; we remember all of our experiences—the positive as well as the negative ones. The problem arises when we have not released the unproductive cellular memories in our body. Our energy can get stuck, and blocks may occur in our life. Even though we all have these unproductive cellular memories, the primary reason we aren't healing at this level is because we don't even know consciously that we're holding on to them. So just knowing that these cellular memories and energy blocks exist is very important; and then you can begin the journey toward healing.

Studies have shown that as we age, the DNA helix coils inside of our cells coil tighter and tighter, losing flexibility; this can lead to a decrease in the number of times our cells can divide. Contractive emotions such as pain, fear, regret, apathy, grief, guilt, or shame may also lead to a tightening of the DNA helix coils. The DNA gets choked off and then it can no longer do the appropriate job in the cell. When the DNA is no longer doing its job, this dis-ease in the emotions or in the mind and certainly in the body's cellular memory can eventually lead to true disease in the body.

These unproductive cellular memories, or energy blocks, can cause other problems as well, in many areas of life. They may lead you to procrastinate: Why don't you make those follow-up calls that you intended to make? They may lead to financial challenges: Why aren't you making five figures or six figures a month if that is your goal? Why don't you ask for that raise at work when you know you deserve it? They may lead to communication blocks and relationship challenges: Why haven't you attracted an amazing partner into your life? Why do you keep fighting with your spouse, your co-workers, your boss, or your children? Why do you keep getting no after no after no? What is it, inside of you, that is attracting these outcomes? They may lead to physical challenges: Why are you tired or fatigued so much of the time? Why is it so hard to lose weight or maintain a healthy weight? They may lead to mental challenges: Why do you feel depressed or overwhelmed? Why is it so hard to focus? Why does the little voice in your mind keep saying the same things over and over?

Let's use a computer as an analogy. Who we are, "our beingness," is the hard drive. The experiences that we have over our lifetime will become cellular memories. Cellular memory is the data that we store on the hard drive. Over many years, we have hundreds and thousands of files, or cellular memories, that we have put onto our hard drives. Consider what happens when your computer has a lot of data on its hard drive. What happens to the computer's ability to function? It operates more slowly, technical difficulties occur, it may freeze up, or it doesn't work at its optimal speed or energy. When we clear the unnecessary files, clean the cache, delete the cookies, and do it all in the right way (because we are techies or we know a computer expert), then the computer will operate effectively again. So it all comes down to cleaning up the unproductive files that were on the hard drive in order to restore maximum efficiency to the computer.

In a similar way, if we know how to RELEASE our unproductive cellular memories, we can RESTORE our space for creating and manifesting our intention with a whole new level of energy. Cellular memory release and cellular healing are the true foundation of lasting change.

What are your unproductive cellular memories? Where do they come from? When did they start? What if all of that could be changed? What if there were no more blocks? Who would you be? What could you be? What could you become? Who is the true BraveHeart Woman inside of you who is just waiting to shine for the world? Are you ready to find out?

Cellular Memory

There is no greater burden in life than wasted potential.

Remember, we all have these unproductive cellular memories or files. As women, when we are not being successful, it is often because some level of cellular memory has been activated. Now understand that this is not a conscious thing; it is not something over which you have control. In most cases, you are not even aware it is happening. It is cellular memory coming up in your body, and it is happening on a subconscious level.

My purpose in life is to assist women to completely remove those blocks and limitations that are holding them back from living their fullest and best life. I teach and guide women through the process of releasing unproductive cellular memories. Once they have been released, this sets the foundation for using the tools you need in order to be able to implement a successful plan without having blocks in the way. We all want to be prosperous and lead fulfilled lives. To do so, we must Release the blocks that are getting in the way of both our internal and external prosperity.

Over the years, I have created and tested many methods with which I am able to help women Release layers and layers of negative emotional charge that are associated with the memories that are stored within the cells. Hundreds of women have come through this visceral Release experience during which I have assisted them to Release their unproductive cellular memories and, more importantly, to transform them into positive cellular memories in a way that is deep, practical, and even fun.

Let me give you an example of just one success story. Actually, Release doesn't just work for one or two or even half of the women who participate. It is a visceral experience that I have never seen fail. In my experience, the results are 100 percent successful.

A wealthy professional woman came to Release years ago. She had a wonderful career, beautiful home, successful husband, and great kids. From the outside, one would have thought that she had a great life and that she had every reason to be happy—and on the surface she was. But underneath was a woman who was unfulfilled, who wasn't very self-confident, and who was lacking in internal prosperity.

She carried guilt, shame, and pain in the cells of her body from being raped as a young child. Although she hadn't thought about it on a conscious level in decades, it caused her to subconsciously distrust men, made her hold on to too much weight, suppressed her sensuality, and put her very much out of touch with the "woman" inside of her.

This woman also had low self-esteem from being teased and ridiculed as a young teen. This experience created cellular memories of feeling unaccepted and left out. Although she became quite popular in later years and eventually very successful in her career, she still felt an emotional charge in her body whenever she got into social situations.

She had all the external prosperity anyone could desire, yet the cells in her body carried unproductive cellular memories from three generations of women who had suffered so much loss and anguish that they had forgotten how to give or receive love. She grew up thinking that if she could be perfect, then she would be loved. She drove herself harder and harder to achieve perfection in every area of her life until there came a time when she looked around and decided that it wasn't working and that life wasn't any fun anymore. She thought about taking her own life rather than continue with the pressure and the overwhelming sense of emptiness.

But instead of choosing to die, she decided to Release all of these unproductive cellular memories in order to begin to live again. She traveled to a magnificent estate in Arizona, where she met 25 other professional women from all walks of life who had traveled from all over the world to Release the cellular blocks that were holding them back from living a prosperous and fulfilled life. The environment was empowering, safe, and prosperous. During the three days they spent together, they were given all the tools and training to Release all the unproductive data that was on their hard drives. Once the unproductive cellular memories were released, they had a solid foundation as women, and they could build on this foundation to become more prosperous and more fulfilled.

During these three life-changing days, she experienced very specific experiential and visceral cellular Release processes. She learned how to get to the core of what was blocking her—the blocks she was aware of and those that she wasn't aware of. Then she was given the tools to recognize and Release those blocks in a way that was simple, easy, and fun. She learned about spontaneous healing, and she was able to let go and Release in such a way that the changes that occurred within her body were permanent changes on a cellular level. She brought about change and healing in her body, and the experience was totally transformational.

After releasing those unproductive cellular memories that were running her life and had blocked her for decades, the woman discovered her purpose in life, and then she was able to move forward and begin living a life on purpose. She was passionate about her life and everything that she was here for; and in the years that followed, she started attaining her goals with ease and attracting even greater levels of financial prosperity. Now she is in charge of her life and feels great about where she is going. She has a fulfilling and loving relationship with her soul mate. She loves her body and is completely in touch with the feminine goddess within, is very sensual, and has released all the excess weight that she had carried for years. Today this woman feels peace in her body and is completely fulfilled internally. She is focused and no longer feels fearful as she goes about her day-to-day life. Instead, she exudes confidence and high self-esteem.

If someone told you that it was possible to Release all the blocks that were getting in the way of living a completely fulfilled and prosperous life, Release the blocks that were getting in the way of creating prosperity on both internal and external levels, Release the external constraints and the internal blocks on a permanent level, what might that be worth? What would it really feel like to be completely fulfilled, to love oneself unconditionally, to be very prosperous internally as well as externally?

"Women" carry memories in our collective consciousness.

As women, we all hold unproductive cellular memories in our bodies, both from our own experiences as well as the experiences of our ancestors. These have been passed from generation to generation because most people are not aware of cellular memory or cellular healing. These cellular blocks are one of the barriers that have collectively held women back from more success and achievement.

The collective cellular memory that each of us carries as a "woman" is almost like a cloud or a shadow that is within or over all of us as "women." It comes from thousands of years of oppression, of being owned, of being the lesser sex, the less intelligent sex, the ones who needed to be taken care of, who couldn't own property, who didn't have the right to vote, whose voice didn't matter, who were abused, raped, molested, and tormented. . . and the ones who gave birth, who gave new life. This collective pain remains for thousands of years, even though we may not even consider many of these experiences because they seem so long ago.

We have to begin to understand what cellular memory is and how healing cellular memory release can be. Then what we all must begin to do as "women" is to release our own personal cellular blocks and cellular pain. One by one as we heal on a cellular level and become whole on our own, we will begin to create a mass healing in the collective consciousness of "women." Together we will step out of the cloud and rise to greater and greater success, prosperity, fulfillment, confidence, and peace.

Together, we can make a difference. We can begin the shift.

Women of the world who are personally and professionally successful or who are striving to be more successful and are continually growing in this manner realize that personal empowerment gives them the foundation of success. When we, as successful women of the world, get together in the spirit of cooperation and collaboration, we can change the world.

I am not saying we are going to "save the planet." There is always going to be conflict in the world. And there will always be hungry children. But when we come together as successful women who are continuing to grow and heal ourselves, as women who are investing in ourselves, when we come together, we CAN make a difference. We can begin the shift. We can begin to be the change we want to see in the world.

About the Author

Sugar Singleton, M.D., is a practicing medical doctor, a wife and mother, and a powerful resource for women and their well-being. Dr. Sugar has dedicated her life to helping women break through barriers and transform their lives.

As a cellular memory expert, she conducts regular Release experiences in the U.S. to assist women to release unproductive cellular memories that are blocking them from achieving true success, wellness, and happiness.

Every month, women come together from different parts of the world to spend time with Dr. Sugar. She helps them to gain clarity about the causes of their resistance and to learn the tools that give them permanent transformation on a deep cellular level, enabling them to "release their issues from their tissues."

Dr. Sugar has dedicated her life to being a healer. In addition to saving people's lives in the urgent care, she spends most of her time assisting women to release the blocks that are getting in the way of their true self-esteem, fulfillment, and prosperity. This passion has led her to become the exclusive expert on cellular healing in the largest online community for inspired women, www.BraveHeartWomen.com.

Dr. Sugar is a lifetime member of the prestigious medical honor society Alpha Omega Alpha; she served as chief resident at UNM Hospital; she is board certified in family medicine and has served as vice president of the NM American Academy of Family Physicians. She is married to her soul mate, Rick, and they have three beautiful children.

Dr. Sugar's website is http://TheCellularWoman.com.

$\mathscr{N}$udged by Spirit

by Cynthia Krejcsi

Beginning to Connect the Dots

The day I had my first big nudge from Spirit I was sitting in a counselor's office. I had just finished reading an article he'd given me, and a major truth began to hit home. I was co-dependent—and that was my contribution to the demise of my marriage. Now I understood why I had been attracted to my husband—someone who could be so kind and sensitive one moment and verbally abusive the next. I was addicted to the vicarious excitement and drama that I got from being in this type of relationship. My own life seemed so boring. I always followed the rules, while he freely broke many of them.

I told the counselor that I was an Adult Child of an Alcoholic, but I couldn't see how that had brought me to where I was right now. My father had died when I was only six years old, so how could his alcoholism have affected me? I had no firsthand memories of the stories my older brother and sisters would tell—they were 10, 13, and 18 years older than me. Although I had very few memories of my father, I always felt I was his "little girl." The descriptions I'd hear coming out of the rest of them just didn't match my own childlike memories.

When my father died, I'd reacted according to my parochial school upbringing. Having been told that God had taken my father because He needed him in heaven, I couldn't complain or get angry or feel abandoned. I was very proud when I told my first-grade teacher, Miss Edna, that only two little tears rolled down my cheeks as I stood in front of the open casket;

meanwhile, my 16-year-old sister had become hysterical. I didn't know it at the time, but I was stuffing my feelings way down deep.

It wasn't until I was 28 years old and had finally moved into my first apartment that those feelings surfaced, quite by accident. I was watching a TV movie about a guy who was getting married. His elderly father was becoming very forgetful, and it was getting dangerous for him to live alone. Considering the possibility of having the father live with them precipitated a crisis for the couple.

The fiancé was really upset, sobbing uncontrollably. No, wait a minute— the sobs were coming from me, not the TV. I couldn't stop. I paced around the house yelling, "It's all your fault! You had to go and die! You abandoned me! How could you leave me to take care of Mom?"

My siblings had left home by the time I was 14. They had families and houses of their own. By default, I had been left to take care of my mother. How could I ever get married or have my own life if I continued living with her? But economically, she couldn't survive on her own—and I didn't think I could survive the guilt of leaving her alone.

As a young child, I became very aware of our money worries. We tried not to complain to the landlord about anything for fear that he would raise the rent. So we put up with plaster falling from the dining room ceiling, windows with rotten ropes, and a rickety front porch. We always had an "old clunker" car. My mother used her exceptional sewing talents and worked as a seamstress from home. I baby-sat all through high school and bought my own clothes and eyeglasses. I dreamed of getting out of there, of being successful, of making money. I vowed when I was a teen that I was never going to be in a situation like my mother's—a stay-at-home mom who had lost her husband and thus her livelihood, with no work experience outside the home, four kids to raise, and a huge, palpable fear ever gnawing away at her insides. I'd depend on myself to get what I wanted. I was smart and I worked hard, so a college scholarship and summer job became my ticket to freedom.

I still didn't see exactly how I had "caught" the disease of co-dependency.

The counselor explained that even though my father was gone, family patterns of interaction had already been established and continued to play out. Okay . . . and then I began to connect the dots. I told him that my sister had married someone who was an undiagnosed schizophrenic. He threw a big, heavy ceramic ashtray at her stomach when she was pregnant, hoping she would lose the baby. When that didn't work, he made her give the baby up for adoption, and he concocted a big whopping lie. Just after my sister gave birth, he came over to our house. Sobbing, he told us that the baby had been born with a hole in its heart and had died. He could have gotten an Academy Award with that performance! Nobody questioned his story. At ten years old, I'd been really excited about becoming an aunt, so I was very disappointed and sad.

When I was 12, my sister divorced him and moved back with my mother and me. But her ex-husband stalked her. On several occasions we had squad cars out in front of the house at 3 a.m. My brother-in-law would be all red in the face yelling and screaming, with his foot in the front door so that my mother couldn't get it shut. Then suddenly he became oh so pleasant when the officers walked up to him—a real Jekyll-Hyde!

Now I finally understood—my mother passed her pattern on to my sister and they both passed it on to me! Was it any wonder that I ended up married to a manic-depressive? (I think that term is more descriptive than bipolar.) I spent my life with him walking on eggshells, never knowing if he was going to be depressed for two months straight or suddenly switch over into a manic frenzy of erratic activity. His illness made it impossible for him to hold down a job for more than a few months at a time, so I had all the financial responsibility while he just spent money. When a questionable mammogram threw me into a tailspin, he told me that if I had cancer I'd just have to toughen up and handle it because he wouldn't be able to put up with my being hysterical and needy. While he didn't want me to be needy, it also turned out that he didn't want me to be the one with more power in the relationship—but that was inevitable since I was the one pulling in the money.

Based on further tests, my doctor just monitored my situation every few months, so things settled down at home for a short time. But during the next argument my husband demanded that I finance a trip to Nashville so he could "get his big break" as a country music songwriter (one of his grandiose fantasies). I'd just paid for him to make a demo tape and we had recently moved into a new condo, so I refused. That was when he flushed his wedding ring down the toilet, along with our marriage.

So what did I learn from that? Lots of things, but two really stand out. One was that as much as you would like to, you cannot save another person—especially one who does not want to be saved. Actually, the only person you can save is yourself! And I'd just learned something else from my counselor—I had my own issues with co-dependency and it was time to save myself!

I looked for support groups, and I read everything I could about co-dependency. One book mentioned that co-dependents not only had control issues but also lacked a spiritual life. What did that mean? How could I not be spiritual? I'd gone to parochial schools my entire life. Was being spiritual different from being religious?

This was another nudge from Spirit, and it was the beginning of my spiritual journey.

First I tried the traditional route, going back to the church I'd turned my back on after I got out of college. I made people extremely uncomfortable with all my questions. But I couldn't stifle myself any longer, and so I looked for other avenues. I started reading spiritual books—first discovering Wayne Dyer and Deepak Chopra and then moving on from there. Gary Zukov's book *The Seat of the Soul* threw me for a loop because it made me consider the possibility of reincarnation. The next thing I knew I was at a seminar experiencing my first past-life regression. It blew me away! I started to see how some of my issues in this lifetime were actually related to or repetitions of previous issues. I would "recognize" people who were in my current life, and I realized that many of the issues I had with them originated in an earlier lifetime. Amazing stuff!

Learning to Embrace Change

As my quest carried me further into meditation and spirituality, I became more and more dissatisfied at my job. True to the vow I'd made when I was a teen, I had pushed myself up the ladder of success. I made good money. I could buy myself anything I wanted. But I was disillusioned with the corporate world of educational publishing. There was no humanity, no caring, no collaboration. It was all about the bottom line, back stabbing, and stepping on the other guy to get ahead because there were only so many jobs at the top. After being on the fast track for a number of years, I'd been shoved onto the back burner. I felt dead inside. The company started laying people off; though I was spared, I experienced "survivor's guilt." I wondered when the next layoff might happen and realized that years of dedicated service didn't guarantee safety. Finally I realized that I could either make myself sick from anticipating the change that might be imposed on me or I could embrace change. I could die on the vine where I was, doing the same thing for the next 25 years, or I could be proactive and take charge of my career.

So after more than 20 years with a large publishing company, I decided to take a higher position at a smaller company. For a while that was satisfying. I was able to build departments and teams, and I really enjoyed mentoring new editors and setting up training programs for them. I was at a point where I wanted to give back. This would be my way of leaving an imprint on the next generation. But soon the male-dominated corporate culture stifled me. I attained a fairly high level, but I never felt that I really "fit" because I was going against my natural management style. The crazy deadlines and 60-80 hour work weeks were becoming unbearable too.

Beginning My Career Transition

And so I started to plan my escape. But I was stumped about finding a new career. My very identity was tied up with my job. And I had the limiting belief that I was too specialized and couldn't find work outside of educational publishing. I spent five years searching for my passion and reinventing myself, realizing that whatever work I was going to do in the future had to be in alignment with my new understandings and beliefs.

I had a big breakthrough when I studied Soul Coaching® with Denise Linn. After spending ten days with a small group of people at her ranch outside of San Luis Obispo, I found that I had worked through some major blocks and was experiencing a new peacefulness inside. Although I was certified as a Soul Coach, I still didn't know how I could work this into my career, but I was open. Becoming part of Denise's community hooked me up with all the other Soul Coaches who had studied with her. Several of them had books inside of them that were asking to be written.

A neon sign lit up in my brain! Maybe I could use my original passion of writing and editing for a spiritual purpose. I could write, and I could teach, coach, and guide women who wanted to write. I could help women find their voice through writing!

Making the Shift

Now I knew my passion and my mission, but I didn't know the practical aspects of manifesting this dream. How was I going to set up my own business, build a website, and learn about marketing? The concern I felt about working solely in Spirit was that many of the beautiful light workers I knew lacked business know-how, feeding into that old limiting belief that spiritual workers couldn't be successful or wealthy. I realized that I had to cultivate a prosperity mindset.

The next nudge from Spirit was actually more like a kick in the butt. At the end of 2008 the company I worked for was put up for sale. I figured I had six to nine months before there would be big changes. As head of an editorial, design, and production department, I had a high salary; thus, a new regime might decide to oust me. I actually found myself hoping that I would be laid off. If I had a decent severance package, I'd have money to live on while I established myself in my new life. But there was still that fear, that nagging doubt—how was I going to pull this off?

I started working with a coach and developed my financial baseline and a simple business plan. I built a website and did some free coaching in exchange for testimonials. I joined a coaching support group. When they decided to write a group book, I welcomed the opportunity to become a published author in my own right. Over the years I'd written numerous children's stories, articles, workbooks, and lesson plans; but since I was an employee of a publishing company, I couldn't be listed as an author. This new book would give me credibility and help me attract clients.

I joined one other interesting group in April 2009—BraveHeart Women. I never would have guessed that a mere six months later this community would be the next big nudge from Spirit. In September I was laid off, but that didn't stop me from attending Rise in October. And while I was there, I had the feeling that something amazing was about to happen. I didn't know what. I just knew that I had to learn more about this community. I signed up for Dr. Sugar's Release, and my work there helped me to break through some stubborn limiting beliefs I had been holding on to. That same weekend I also met Ellie Drake. And suddenly the missing puzzle piece fell right into place: the spiritual aspect blended together with a prosperity mindset and practical business sense. And I found myself clicking into alignment.

My life has changed rapidly and dramatically in just the past ten months. That's what happens when you shift into alignment. Occasionally there are still a few vestiges of fear or doubt that creep in, but that is happening less and less, especially since I received this past-life vision that left no doubt that I am on my true path and ready to step into my passion and power:

Lady at the Piano

A young woman is playing the piano. She is wearing a long, black satin dress with a bustle. There is a bit of red on it—a hanky or a scarf. The piano is facing the window so that she can look out on the street as she plays. She is in Europe—Vienna? She is waiting for someone. She is playing a sad song, a lonely song. It is a beautiful, haunting melody. She is very accomplished, but she is unsure if she is ready to perform in front of the huge audience at the theater tonight.

Nudged by Spirit

She is waiting for her mentor to arrive. He will help her calm down. He will reassure her. Why does she continue to need his reassurance? Why isn't she able to reassure herself that her performance will be brilliant? Why can't she see her talent and feel comfortable with it, trusting her ability to feel the nuances of the music as she plays? She knows how to let the music lead her. This is what she does when she is playing at her best—like Michael Jordan playing "in the zone."

So why does she continue to be so fearful that she won't be able to follow through? Why is she afraid that she won't be accepted by the big, important people who own and run the symphony—and the critics? They have been less than complimentary before, when she was young and unsure of herself. She let them distract her from her playing. Nothing must distract her from her focus now. She can't let them and the fear of what they will say or do worry her. She knows she is ready for the performance of her life. She knows. She feels it in her bones. And yet she is still afraid, still tied down by what others think of her.

It was a former teacher who made her feel so insecure, someone who put her down and made her feel inferior and insignificant, as if she had no talent. He harped at her. He made her feel like she couldn't do anything right—not like her current teacher, who believes in her and encourages her to be what he knows she can be.

It had taken her a long time to come back out of the dark, cold recesses to which her spirit had retreated from all the abuse. It was her mentor who was gentle, like a Horse Whisperer, slowly making her feel comfortable and nudging her out of her cave and back into the warmth and light of the world.

So what if THEY don't believe she can do it? She knows in her very soul that she can. She knows that she can feel the music and move along with it. She becomes the music. She is one with it. It takes her along with it and they fly together to the clouds, away from the chatter of everyone below and yet flying high and singing their song for those very same people who just don't get it. It's for them. It's all for them, for their enjoyment, for their enlightenment. *And yet she never feels that she is one of them. She continues to feel how they distance themselves from her. They don't understand the message of the music.*

As she plays, she stops looking out the window for her teacher. The music captivates her and draws her in. Now she feels no fear. She only feels the beautiful music, just like the song of the nightingale. Her hands glide across the keys and she is happy, ecstatically happy. Now only joy fills her soul. There is no room for fear and darkness—only the light and the joy of the song and the oneness she feels with it. She is carried away with it and has gone beyond the day-to-day world to a beautiful place of harmony and peace. Now she is in a meadow, dancing to the music and collecting wild flowers. She hasn't a care in the world. She is safe and protected and happy.

She is so engrossed in the music that she doesn't realize that her teacher has entered the room. He sits down carefully on a chair by the door. He closes his eyes and feels the music too. Ah, such lovely music she makes as her fingers slide over the keys. Her fingers move quickly yet smoothly, like the wings of a hummingbird. She hovers over the flower, extracting the nectar and sharing it with all who can hear. This is what she will do tonight. She will play so sweetly that finally the others will see the world as it really is, not the shell that their illusions have created. She will bring down to them the music of the heavens so that they can remember, so that they too can play this music here on Earth with her, so that they can harmonize and move up and down with the waves of music. Tonight they will fly along with her and her music, soaring up to the heavens. It will be magnificent. This gift will be shared freely with everyone, and they will finally begin to awaken, finally begin to see the truth.

Suddenly the music stops. Slowly she turns her head to him and asks, "How long have you been there?"

"Long enough to hear the melody of the heavens. You heard it, too, and now you are playing it. You know now that you have nothing to be afraid of. I can hear it in your music. It has risen above the world, and yet it has the ability to pull the world along with it, upward, lifting into the heavens.

You have a gift to share with the world. You can help them remember. You can help them see. Listen to the music in your head and follow it where it takes you. Do not be afraid. You are ready. The others will follow as they can. Many will be inspired and captivated by your music, and they will be there with you as you move into another realm. You are ready. You have gone through all the years of preparation. You have perfected your craft. But most importantly, you feel the music; the tempo takes over in your soul and merges you with the song of the Universe. You have earned your wings, and now you are ready to fly upward, unfettered by any cages. No one can pull you down. No one will clip your wings again, for you have turned from the Ugly Duckling into the beautiful, magnificent Swan. You have no more need of me. You can fly on your own."

Joining the Symphony of Souls

Now I invite you to join the Symphony of Souls along with me and all the other BraveHeart Women who have contributed to this book. First, search the world far and wide until you discover your true passion—that special instrument that makes your heart sing for joy. It might be the sweet melody of the flute, the powerful beat of the drum, the exotic strains of the oboe, or the sometimes lively and sometimes regal trumpet. Next, find nurturing and knowledgeable masters to teach and mentor you. Then practice diligently, blocking out all background noises that would distract you in an attempt to turn you from your path, be it negative "noise" from other people or your own inner chatter. Hone those skills, developing your inner voice and becoming an expert at your passion. And, finally, make your debut on the world stage as a member of the Symphony of Souls. Let your voice join together and harmonize with all the other voices and melodies in the orchestra to create a wondrous Symphony of Life. Believe me, the world will listen!

About the Author

Cynthia Krejcsi is a writer, editor, and entrepreneur who has recently transitioned out of the corporate arena. She spent most of her career working in the textbook industry, specializing in language arts and reading materials. Beginning as a proofreader at Encyclopaedia Britannica, she worked her way up through several editorial levels at various educational publishing companies and eventually became a vice president leading an editorial, design, and production department.

A job layoff less than a year ago gave her the opportunity to walk her talk and turn her dream into a reality. Cynthia founded the Career Transition Community to share what she has learned while reinventing herself over the past five years and to support BraveHeart Women in their own career transitions. She also started her own business, Tailor-Made Books, LLC. In addition, she is now honored to serve as editor in chief of BraveHeart Women Publishing.

To find out more about the Career Transition Community, visit http:// CareerTransitionCommunity.com.

The S Factor

by Sheila Kelley

I am an actress and passionate feminine advocate. Over the years I've appeared on *L.A. Law, ER,* and, most recently, *Lost.* When I was about 22, I became fascinated with strippers. I was making a movie, and during the course of filming I had to go to a strip club. Shockingly, I fell absolutely in love with the movement, even though I was uncomfortable with the fact that the strip club itself represented a man's view. I never could have predicted this would lead me on a journey to becoming a whole woman.

In 1999 I made another film about strippers called *Dancing at the Blue Iguana.* In addition to playing a role as an exotic dancer, I wrote the screenplay and produced the film. To prepare for my role, I had to take my fascination to a deeper level . . . I had to learn to strip and pole dance. It *profoundly* changed my experience in life from the inside out. I had discovered my sexual power as a woman.

It was almost as if I'd hit a light switch and life went from a muddy, sepia-colored world to a technicolor world. Everything changed: my sensual experience in the world; my ability to confidently, with absolute pride and ownership, allow my curves and my sexuality to live in every part of my life. The sensation was not confined to my bedroom or in a seedy little strip club. It became a part of my wholeness.

This was a major, mind-blowing experience, and it came from learning that the natural inclination of my body is to move. It came from learning how to move. And it thrived on allowing my body to explore "her" natural inclination to move in large, slow, circular, sensual movements. I learned to really turn on my sensuality in a way that society doesn't believe is okay for women most of the time. I found it very freeing. Cathartic.

While we were preparing for *Dancing at the Blue Iguana*, several of the actresses—Daryl Hannah, Jennifer Tilly, Sandra Oh—and I went around to strip clubs in the off-hours when they were the least busy, and we practiced on the back stages. One time, at The Ice Lady, the professional strippers invited us to come back and try out the movements in the evening. Daryl and I returned, along with all of the crew and the director, art director, and costume designer. We all got up and danced, and everybody in the audience was screaming and throwing money at us. That night, I thought: *I'm going to try this with people I don't know. I'm going to try this alone. I'm going to try this as if I were really my character.* So I did, for several nights. And it was the most difficult, disturbing, and unpleasant thing I've ever done in my life. I was taking something that was priceless—my beauty, my power, my sensuality, my body—and I was dancing on stage for men I didn't know and didn't particularly want to know. It felt very vacant. I realized then that when you give something that is invaluable away for a few scattered dollars on a dirty floor, you betray yourself. And when you betray yourself, especially your body, "she" feels it. She feels everything.

One night, my husband surprised me and showed up at the club. When I got up to dance and they announced my character's name, Sheila Kelley was incognito. As I started to dance, I saw that awful coldness in every man's eyes. But then I saw my husband's eyes, and it was as if there was this fire burning between us, like kismet. It was a moment of complete and utter electric nirvana—the connection between two souls. His love for me, his passion for me, his desire for me were incredible. Suddenly it was about allowing him to partake in the gift of the beauty of my body and my spirit and my sensual energy.

This experience empowered me because I wasn't giving myself away for strangers. I was intimately and profoundly connected to somebody. Our relationship changed, and I got a sense of how imperative it is for a woman to own her body, her sensuality, her femininity, and what makes her uniquely female. This sense of empowerment needs to be cultivated, honored, and valued in a culture that does not currently value it enough.

This experience set me on the path to discover the feminine factor, or what I call S Factor. (The *S* stands for the natural shape and undulation of a woman's body when she moves naturally and at ease.) It fueled my desire to empower women with their sexuality, their body, their femininity, and their female nature. It was an aha moment. And I've had many more aha moments since starting S Factor than ever before in my life.

Earlier in my life, I felt like I was always trying to keep up, trying to get through, trying to live for the future. It was all about when this happens, when that happens. The moment I learned this movement, that all disappeared, and it became about this moment, this moment, and now this moment. When you occupy your body wholly, with no apology, it allows you to live in the moment, no longer reaching for some other moment.

In a global culture that's male-driven, I think it's virtually impossible for a woman to be whole, given that her sexuality is lock, stock, and barrel owned and operated by everybody but herself. Yes, there's more overt ownership of the female body and shame in many countries where women have no rights at all, but there are subtler versions of it in "free" countries too. And when you are able to free yourself from the prison of shame that women live in—their beauty, their body, and their sexuality—and allow these aspects of yourself to become wholesome and integrated into the rest of you, you can reach a collective, holistic, spiritual place. It's a place of being completely in the moment, experiencing everything proudly, fully—a place I had never reached before the creation of S Factor.

People ask, "Do you get all this from strip tease?" They don't understand. And I admit that it is difficult to explain and understand until you do it. It's confusing only when you put a male label on it. I have changed the definition of feminine movement. S Factor is "heightened natural feminine movement." It's important to understand that what is "heightened natural feminine movement" for a woman is "erotic movement" for a man. This is why I was blindsided when I first learned to pole dance. How could something that felt so good have a negative connotation? It was because all I had known was the male definition of it. I had lived my life by that erroneous definition, and I had missed out on an enormous piece of my sexuality because of it. This is why I've helped propagate a new definition of feminine movement using the recognition that I've gotten from S Factor—because sex and ownership of your sexuality is a very powerful tool that every woman should own, especially in a male-driven society.

You've got two sets of eyes looking at two sets of things. With S Factor, a woman is encouraged to really embrace her natural body and her heightened movement in the same way that men heighten their bodies in sports and in their work. And when you heighten what is naturally there and you cultivate it, speak about it, and celebrate it, there's nothing like it.

It's that light switch. I think all women have that light switch in a vestibule closet, and it's been turned off all of their lives. But when you flip that switch on, the walls break down, the world opens up! It's like walking into Oz. You experience everything more profoundly because you've turned on your feminine nature and you're cultivating it. Yes, you're cultivating it in a masculine world, but you are still cultivating it.

It's similar to the "divine feminine" but more badass. I'm a little more kickass, so I like to put a little outlaw in it. You've got to let women be raunchy. You've got to let them get freaky. You've got to let women have a sexual connection with their bodies and theoretically have sex in their body's molecules. In my classes at S Factor, I want you to pump up those 6-inch heels. I want you to put on 8-inch heels. I want you to hyper-exaggerate everything. I want you to own the male creature's eyes. I'm moving toward the universal feminine, but I think I'm doing so with S Factor in a little more of an edgy, earthy way.

When I think "divine feminine," all of a sudden I am thinking about the Virgin Mary. I equate "divine feminine" with being austere and pure. What I'm talking about is the *complete* feminine, and the *complete* feminine has got to have desire and sexuality. She has a vagina! The Virgin Mary had a vagina, whether people want to believe it or not. There's the whole virgin/ whore thing, and I think that the divine goes back to the virgin aspect. Yes, the feminine is divine, but you've got to let her be human. This is about being a whole woman. We're all real. But there is a part of women that's imprisoned. It is the final frontier of the sexual revolution. It is the fourth wave, when we finally free up our sexuality.

Men live fully in their sexuality. It's cultivated into their body from the time they're children—from Little League to accomplishing things in school, to accomplishing things in the world, to being that number one seller on the sales force, to being the number one business man, to being number one, one, one. To score, to hit a home run, to get to first base, to make a touchdown—it's not an accident that those all have sexual connotations. A male's sexuality lives in his ability to physically dominate. That's what we cultivate and integrate in our boys.

Women's sexuality lives in the natural curvature, movements, and sensuality of our bodies; and that is what is hindered in our society globally. And when you free that hindered part, cultivate it, and allow it to become as powerful as every other part of you, there's no stopping you. When that happens for all women, they will be equal to men in every facet, and we will truly become a "partnership" society.

This is huge. And sometimes it's hard for people to wrap their brains around it. We have got to stop letting the masculine eye define who and what we are because we are all of it. We are everything! You have to exude it—but not from the "thinking brain." You have to exude it from your body. When you exude it from the "thinking brain," you start to turn into these cartoon versions of ideal woman. They just slice you and dice you up so that you can be this animated version of what men lust after. I want women to get into their own body and find within their own body the treasure trove of their own beauty—not somebody else's idea of their beauty.

There's nothing more incredible than a woman completely and utterly comfortable in her own sexuality, in her own body, feeling confident. It's riveting. It's real. It's powerful. And it's connected to the core of a woman.

You integrate her sexuality into her emotionality, her intellectuality, her mentality, her social abilities. Every part of her will become integrated.

It's a very hard lesson to learn. It's part of the S Factor Journey. It's why the journey takes about two to three years. We're not just retraining women to get into their body, we're teaching women to see from a female eye rather than a masculine eye, and that really takes time. It's amazing how much different it is when you look at a situation from a different point of view.

My young niece is this beautiful blond girl. She's got the kind of rage and anger that second-wave feminists have. I love and respect and honor the second-wave feminists. I think we wouldn't be who we are today if it weren't for them. But I think there's a certain bent. I know that I had it, and I know that other women had this rage and this anger at men that's just so misplaced. I don't want my man to be a woman. I want my man to be a man. But I want him to be a man who feels like he's got more masculinity than any other man on the planet. That's part of my job. That's what I like doing.

The other day my niece said, "Men, they just get women pregnant. And then they leave their women burdened and lonely. They just spend themselves. Then they get all cleaned up and take off and they're free."

I handed her an imaginary pair of glasses. I said, "Put these on. These are the feminine goggles. These will show you a different way to see what you just said. A man makes love and gives all of his power and his goodness and his beauty to a woman, and in doing so he also allows her the gift of these two souls or enables other souls that are her children to come into the world—her greatest loves in the world. If he chooses to leave this beautiful family that's developing, he leaves lonely and alone and disconnected. And he has spent all of his energy and all of his power in this place.

"Instead of seeing yourself as the victim, think about what you've received. Look what this man did for you—all of his positive energy, all of his beauty, his genius. And in the process, he may even have given you children. If you can look at the situation from this perspective, you just switched the light switch. It's a whole other way of seeing the world."

My niece responded, "Oh, I never thought of it that way!"

So many women spend their time complaining, "Look at what this terrible man did to me. And I'm jealous of his freedom." It's true that once you have children, your life as you know it ends. I will never be the person I was before children. But without them, I also never would have had what I have now. I never would have experienced the kind of love I experience or the kind of companionship or the kind of challenges. If you want to talk about spiritual enlightenment, have a child. Nothing will bring you more into the moment than changing a diaper or soothing a sobbing child. There's just nothing that brings you more into the moment. What a gift!

Having children should heighten the things that are important to you and make what's important to you scream out more loudly. I only have 24 hours in a day, and I've got two kids. They are my number one. My number two is me. He's number three, and he knows it. That's the way I do it. I wouldn't be the mother I am, the woman I am, if I didn't take that time to cultivate myself. And my children see that, and they're proud of that.

My husband cultivates himself with no guilt. I cultivate myself with no guilt. It's so hard to find a mother who will cultivate herself. You don't have to give up on developing yourself, but you do have to retrain yourself. It doesn't come naturally or easily. You have to nurture yourself, your spirit, your feminine the same way you nurture your children.

So how does a woman get in touch with her S Factor—her feminine factor? Getting a woman to occupy her body consciously is one of the most important aspects of S Factor, because our bodies have psychology and emotion. Our bodies are living, breathing, feeling entities on their own. They feel and hear everything we think and say. From this moment forward, treat your body as if it were one of your children.

If your body were your actual child, would you ever feed yourself, tell yourself, or do to yourself the things you do to yourself now? Would you call her fat? Would you say, "Ooh, look at those ugly veins?" Would you say, "Oh look at your gross, disgusting cellulite?" I don't think a good mother, a compassionate, empathetic woman, would do and say those kinds of things to her child. And yet we treat our own bodies harshly and carelessly. Your body hears every single thought. And those thoughts turn into shame, and that shame shuts your body down.

I've done this for ten years now, and I can't believe the things I hear women say about themselves: *I hate my this, I hate my that.* It's as if I sat my daughter, Ruby, down and said, *I hate your hair, I hate your shoulders, I hate your ass. Ooh, you're too fat. Oh, you're too skinny. Oh here, eat all these doughnuts because you feel so rotten.* The things we say and do to our body would constitute body abuse, child abuse! When you start to nurture and love and caress your body, you will change. Your body is just like a child, like a puppy, like any creature that needs love. It just perks up, and the shame can just melt away.

So that's the way you begin, and then you have got to move your body into its natural curvature. You could simply start with just big, huge hip circles in both directions. Bend your knees. Take a big, long, slow inhale. Then start to do a hip circle—but not like you're just dancing to some music. Take 10-20 seconds on one rotation, 10 in one direction and 10 in the other. That will start the curvature of your body, and a little smile will start happening in your body.

Next, begin to look at the world from another point of view, through the feminine eye. If you're going to cultivate the feminine, you've got to cultivate it all. That doesn't mean just your sexuality. That means your sensuality, your emotionality, your communication skills, your eyes, and how you perceive the world. When you live through the masculine eye, you're always living a lie, a non-truth, because it's not your own truth.

When I see a woman in my S Factor class undulating her body, opening and closing her legs, I do not find it sexually arousing. But put any straight man in that room, and he's going to get turned on—vibrantly turned on. He's going to be very lustful. I don't have that experience. And yet, when we as a culture see a scantily clad girl, we say, "Oh how sexy." I think it's really beautiful, but it doesn't turn me on. What I find sexy is Derek Jeter hitting a home run. That's hot. I like to see Michael Jordan striding down the court, putting the ball in the hoop. That is hot, sexy. I like to see my husband working on the stage. It is hot. I love to see him doing his movies. I like seeing men do what they do best. That turns me on. That's sexy. A woman who's half-naked? No, that's not sexy to me. Yet we all say she's sexy. Well, that's a lie. We've been trained to view those things as sexy. It's the difference between the sexes and how they view and define things. We're not the same. And we should never, ever be the same.

Women need to create a culture. Wherever you are, in whatever small town you're in, in whatever large city you're in, you need to create a non-exclusive feminine sisterhood. And if that means you get ten of your best friends or ten women down the block together once a month to do something together, then that's what you do. And you do it within the truth of the feminine eye. Maybe you all go see a movie once a month or you read a book or you do hip circles together in S Factor or you cook a dinner together. But you have to do it with one caveat—you have to put S Factor goggles on as you look at everything you're doing. If you see a movie, the discussion afterwards should center on what was the male point of view and what was the female point of view. If you read a book, talk about the male point of view and the female point of view. It's great to read a male author's book because then you switch that male author's point of view to the feminine point of view.

You know what I've done? I started doing this with my daughter, and now she does it with her books. She writes it all in her books. *The Giving Tree is about the boy and the daughter and the mom. It's about this boy, and everything that he takes from his mother. I'm a tree. There's a tree. And he plays on it, he climbs it, he takes it and cuts it down. He takes it and makes a boat out of it.* Well, because I am so ardent about creating a culture of women, I always juxtapose our story into the female version. So I say, "Okay, that's a daddy tree, and that's a little girl, not a little boy. Now let's tell the story." And so she takes all of her books, and she scratches out *he, he, he,* and she replaces them with *she, she, she.* It's so powerful.

If Holden Caulfield were a girl, he'd be rolling over in his grave! Ruby is learning the first paragraph of *The Catcher in the Rye* as Holdena. So we just take everything and transpose it into the feminine point of view; or we talk about the male experience and then we talk about the female experience: "Well, that's his experience, Ruby. What would happen if it were your experience? How would you experience that same thing?"

If you could go through my daughter's bookcase, you would notice that she crosses things out and rewrites the stories in all of her books. It's brilliant. She's empowered to think about these stories from the female point of view. This is one of my greatest passions. Teachers may not be doing this type of book discussion with the girls in their classes, but that doesn't mean you can't do it at home with your own children.

Everything I've written about in this chapter—the moment of revelation with my husband at that strip club; the realization that I could flip that light switch on; the empowerment I felt when I came to own my body, my beauty, my sensuality, my femininity; learning to look at situations from a new perspective—and everything about S Factor is helping to create a culture of women. It's a culture of women who are whole and complete. If we can create this culture, then we can raise our daughters and also our sons to look at life consciously.

My son has so many friends who are girls, and I believe it's because I've taught him to appreciate that there are two perspectives—the male and the female. It's astounding. Girls are all around him because he is so thoughtful with them. He so loves the feminine and he's so understanding of the feminine because he's grown up listening to me constantly talk about how different we are and yet how complementary.

So start today to create your own little feminine culture—a culture that will grow and bond with and become part of a global culture of all women, just as men have created a global culture of men. It's time to begin. Do it for yourself. Do it for the men in your life. Do it for your children. Do it for your sisters all over the world. Do it so that women will be equal to men in every facet of life and so that our society can transform itself into a true partnership between men and women.

About the Author

Sheila Kelley is a feminine advocate, author, actress, filmmaker, and the founder of S Factor. At the age of 15, she was a classically trained dancer and soloist with the Westmoreland Ballet Company. She attended New York University's famed Tisch School of Arts as a dance major, as well as the New York University Film School.

Sheila began her acting career in television, appearing on *Lost, L.A. Law, Sisters, ER,* and *The Sopranos.* She has also appeared in numerous movies, such as *Singles, Matchstick Men, One Fine Day,* and *Nurse Betty.*

After her role in *Dancing at the Blue Iguana,* Sheila went on to develop S Factor—a feminine movement workout that combines pole dancing, striptease, ballet, and yoga to nurture a woman's natural *S* shape. The S Factor workout promotes health, confidence, and empowerment for women of all ages and body types. Studios offering pole dancing classes are located in major cities around the country, including New York, Los Angeles, Chicago, and Houston. Sheila is the author of *The S Factor: Strip Workouts for Every Woman* and has three S Factor exercise DVDs.

Sheila and S Factor have been featured on *Oprah, The Martha Stewart Show, 20/20, 48 Hours, The View, Late Night with Conan O'Brien,* and *The Tonight Show with Jay Leno.* In addition, various magazines, such as *US Weekly, People,* and *In Touch,* have published articles on her workout phenomenon.

Sheila is married to actor Richard Schiff from *The West Wing,* and they have two children.

To find out more about Sheila and S Factor, visit www.sfactor.com.

Alkalize and Energize

by Shelley Redford Young LMT

Were you like me when you were a young girl? Did you gaze at the glossy magazine covers at the end of the checkout counters when you went grocery shopping with your mom? Didn't we all learn from this that women HAD to be pretty, with perfectly contoured bodies, chiseled knees, and China-white teeth? Do you remember studying the latest fashions that were draped ever-so-teasingly on these luscious role models of ours? Back then I figured that THIS is what I needed to look like to be considered BE-autiful and DE-sirable. My hair had to be perfect, with shimmering highlights. My thighs had to be firm and svelte—without dimples of any sort. I had to have thick eyelashes that beckoned, "Come hither!" Looking at these magazine covers each week steeped a huge, self-inflicted homework assignment within my youthful, girlish psyche—making sure I felt *the pressure* of attaining an AWEsome Appearance!

Regardless of age, the pressures that are placed on women in our society do affect our belief systems about what we need to do to be attractive and successful in life. This pressure not only can motivate us to strive for that "Cover Girl" look, but it can also instill feelings of inadequacy, not quite measuring up, or even giving up before we start! Goals that seem so unreachable can defeat us before we ever enlist to become our best selves. From my experience, I would have to say that appearance is the best way to make a good first impression. And let's remember one of my favorite sayings: *You never have a second chance to make a first impression.*

I live by this motto. When people meet you for the first time, they have split-second judgments regarding how you come across. Do you look vibrant, rested, healthy, athletic, studious, intelligent, or well-groomed? Or do you exude lackluster energy, depression, fatigue, negativity, stress, or self-neglect? People make their initial impressions within the first three minutes of meeting you. What do you want them to know about you from your appearance? Do you feel you have the proper tools and skill sets to become the most radiant you, or are you somewhat resigned to the limited look and feel of your genetic predispositions? Your vocabulary and general communication skills also have a bearing on how you are received by others; but your appearance, like the cover of a book, will give people their first clues about the rest of you—what's inside you.

I want to share some treasures of truth that I've collected along the way. To be at our very best, we need to understand our physiology—our internal chemistry of our bodies. Your physiology affects your health, and your health affects your appearance and energies. This being so, it stands to reason that we should all seek *the best way—the most conducive way to healing and regeneration.* Only then can we live the most abundantly blessed life with true JOY, healthy self-interest, and self-esteem.

We can affect our appearance and our health and well-being by making lifestyle choices that contribute to the *pH balance* of our blood and tissues. I know you've probably heard of the pH factor when it comes to shampoos or skin toners. You might remember that the pH of your Jacuzzi, swimming pool, or fishtank is something that has to be correctly balanced. We all know that our body temperature is set at 98.6 degrees. We don't vary from that number very much unless we get sick with a fever or get too cold and go into hypothermia. To remain healthy and comfortable, we must keep our body temperature around 98.6 degrees.

Our body pH (pH stands for the *power of hydrogen*) is also engineered with a specific setting. It is balanced at 7.365, which is alkaline. The pH scale goes from 1 to 14, with 7 being neutral. Anything below 7 is acidic, and anything above 7 is called base, or alkaline. The fact that we can make conscious, health-minded choices that will keep our bodies in a more perfect state of pH balance is an exciting discovery, especially when we consider how this also affects our appearance, health, and energy levels. I want to tell you my story so you can appreciate the journey I went on to find my "Cover Girl" look and optimum health.

As I said earlier, I wanted to achieve my best womanly appearance. I wanted to remain slim and athletic. I wanted to discover the easiest and healthiest way to achieve my optimum health, weight, and appearance. I had experimented with high-protein diets (which left me constipated, congested, and with bad breath). I didn't want to battle the yo-yo effect of fluctuating pounds. I knew what size I wanted to be. I just wanted to figure out how to maintain that size while feeding myself well, without the starvation techniques that had left me weakened in the past.

Once I understood the pH scale and which foods and drinks were more alkaline, like the human body, it became easy! Unwanted pounds melted off almost magically and I rarely or never got sick. I noticed an energy level that was boundless, and to me *that* was priceless. To look how I wanted and feel vibrantly healthy was such an exciting prospect. Once I grooved into this way of pH balanced living, eating, and thinking, it became second nature to me, and it has remained so—even today. Now I automatically make good alkaline dietary choices because they always guarantee my desirable weight and best energy reserves. I also keep a regular exercise program as a complement to alkalizing. I run three miles every other day and then do Kundalini Yoga on the alternate days to keep myself limber and flexible. I am 56 years young, the mother of 4, the grandmother of 3, and I've never felt better than I do now! To me, this is miraculous, and it's part of why our book publications are called *The pH Miracle.*

How did I first become interested in this pH phenomenon? It all started when I married a University of Utah tennis player named Rob Young. We both started to pay attention to ideas about health and wellness so we could keep Rob at his peak tennis performance. We noticed he played better when we removed dense proteins like meats, eggs, and cheeses from his diet.

He had less recovery time and less lactic acid build-up in his muscles. We experimented with the idea of becoming vegetarians, thinking that would give Rob the best energy edge to win his tennis matches. But we ran into some problems. Once we took out those animal protein sources, we increased the carbohydrate loads with pasta, rice, and potatoes. We also surmised that carrot cake was an excellent choice, just because it contained carrots! Consequently, Rob felt sluggish and fatigued. The fact was, we were now carbo-loading up our diets, and the switch to diet soft drinks wasn't helping the situation either. The artificial sweeteners were not helping us stay fit. Weight gain became a problem, as well as other allergic conditions. We caught colds and had the flu more often. We knew we had to make other changes but weren't sure where to head with it.

After Rob finished his college tennis days, our lives got wrapped up in raising four kids. Eventually, he decided to study more about the blood and tissues, becoming a microbiologist, a Naturopathic MD, and a nutritionist. He perfected a way to view live blood cells (from German research) and started to develop ideas and theories about what diet would be best to maintain pH homeostasis. We also learned during this period that the body has an *alkalinizing buffering system* to assure the pH of the blood and tissues remains alkaline. As a self-preservation mode, the body will go to great lengths to maintain its slightly alkaline fluid environment. If the body or tissues becomes too acidic through diet or stress, it will tap into alkalizing buffering reserves—like calcium from the bones and magnesium from the muscles—to *neutralize acidity* and maintain its delicate balance of 7.365. Our body is so intelligent that it will do this in an effort to keep us alive and well. You may know people who have been able to eat and drink anything they wanted with no ill effect. This would most probably be due to their strong constitutions, including a strong alkalinizing buffering system, a good lymphatic system, and good genetics.

Once we learned the significance of pH balancing for the blood and tissues, we had to discover and research which foods and drinks were acidic and which were alkaline. We could then create a new food pyramid that would contribute to health and vitality instead of sickness and degeneration. Everything we eat or drink metabolizes down into an ash residue, which can be neutral, acidic, or alkaline. Acidic diets high in animal proteins, dairy products, carbohydrates, and fermented foods like alcohol, vinegar, and soy sauce can cause the body to manifest with symptoms of sickness and disease. Other foods that create an acid residue ash are coffee, black teas, soft drinks, baked goods, and even high-sugar fruits like bananas, apples, and oranges. As the blood becomes saturated by these types of food and drink, excess fermentation takes place, giving rise to acidic residues in the blood, which need to be neutralized. Weight gain is a sure sign of being over acidic, as is water retention. As a protective mechanism, our bodies create fat to bind and hold acid residues away from our vital organs. This is why we pack on pounds just under the skin on our hips, thighs, and stomachs. An acidic person can actually look puffy, as the body retains water to dilute acids in the system. Edema and puffy bags under the eyes are typical acidic traits. Skin conditions like acne, ruddiness, and blotchiness are also signs that over acidification in the body causes acids to come to the surface. Even more serious conditions like eczema and psoriasis are manifestations of acids that take a strong hold and erupt through the skin, which is sometimes called the "third kidney" because of its filtering ability. The body can also rob the skin of precious moistures, leaving a person looking parched or dehydrated. Premature wrinkling and aging are more prevalent in people who choose an over acidic lifestyle. Many other serious symptoms can appear in the internal environment of our body's rivers and streams. Eventually they can become sluggish and polluted. If a person doesn't make changes in diet and lifestyle and continues to bombard his or her system with acidic foods and drinks, organs and tissues become affected. Diagnoses such as diabetes, cancer, fibromyalgia, and CFS (chronic fatigue syndrome) are common.

Otto Warburg, winner of the Nobel Peace Prize in Medicine in 1932, stated: "When the pH is wrong, oxygen falls, cells respire in an anaerobic environment by fermentation giving rise to increased acidity—cancer is a result of an ACID environment."

The main thing to consider here is that everything we eat and drink affects the way we look, think, act, and feel. If people choose a highly acidic diet and lifestyle, they set themselves up for proliferation of certain types of microbes that thrive in an acidic terrain. These are referred to as endotoxins and mycotoxins, which have yeast and fungal base forms that can wreak havoc in our systems. Many of you have experienced or heard of yeast infections. Sometimes they are reoccurring. Headaches can also be a signal that the brain is somehow connected to a toxic bowel. This needs to be cleaned up in order to bring relief from inflammation and pain. General aches and pains, such as in arthritis, bursitis, and even carpal tunnel syndrome, involve acidic saturations of the blood, lymph, and affected tissues.

Think of a fishbowl and the fish swimming around in the water. If the fish were to get sick, what would be your first inclination? Would you treat the fish or change the water? Most people would choose to change the fish's water—the environment in which it functions. We realize that the fish needs a properly balanced environment to remain healthy. All of us have witnessed what happens when toxic calamities occur in the ocean. The fish are immediately affected by the change to their alkaline, pH-balanced ocean. Scientists claim that even small changes in the pH of the ocean will affect all life found in it. Think of your own cells as the fish in the fishbowl. Your cells are suspended in an aqueous solution that needs to be maintained as an alkaline environment. Once that inner terrain is compromised by unhealthy choices or extreme stressors, the cells can morph into unhealthy forms. Then we get sick and tired.

Another great discovery we made was that our bodies are alkaline by design but acidic by function. This means that while our blood and tissues need to be kept in a delicate balance of 7.365, every function of our bodies, such as running, thinking, eating, and breathing, produces acidic, metabolic waste products. There is also a scientific ratio that exists concerning how our body neutralizes these acid by-products. It takes 20 parts alkalinity to neutralize 1 part acidity in our systems. More specifically for you chemistry buffs, it takes 20 parts sodium bicarbonate to neutralize 1 part carbonic acid in the body. With this guiding information at our disposal, we then set out to create an "alkalinizing" lifestyle program that anyone with the desire for optimum health and radiance can follow. You simply eat and drink 80/20: 80 percent high-water-content, high-fiber, chlorophyll-rich, alkalinizing foods and drinks (like fresh vegetables from the garden) and 20 percent more grounding or mildly acidic foods such as sprouted wheat tortillas, cooked legumes/grains, or some oily fish or tofu. When you start changing your diet and lifestyle to this 80/20 ratio, you can achieve the ideal weight and radiant energy you've always desired.

Our bodies break down to:
70% water
20% fat (give or take depending on your body type)
 7% protein
1-2% vitamins and minerals
½-1% sugar. (ONLY ½-1% sugar)

To simplify, we could state that our bodies are 70 percent water and 30 percent matter. This is similar to our Earth's composition and also a good way to visualize each plate of food we eat. The majority of the food and drinks we ingest should replace our internal rivers and streams (our blood and lymph fluids) with fresh, alkalinizing hydration. This means food predominantly from the garden and the more chlorophyll-rich, the better. Try to think of your blood as a living, streaming organ in your body that feeds and brings nutrients and oxygen to every other organ and system. Then realize that chlorophyll—*the "blood" of green plants*—is molecularly structured almost identically to our own hemoglobin, an iron-containing protein in red blood cells that transports oxygen around the body. This would mean that chlorophyll might be considered one of the best blood transfusions we could ever get. Some even tout chlorophyll as a blood *purifier.* Even recently in the new *Iron Man 2* movie, you see him swigging on chlorophyll to slow down the toxicity in his degenerating blood.

In the chlorophyll molecule there is a center atom of magnesium that is an electromagnetic sync or, more simply put, the sun-sensitive element in the process of photosynthesis.

Dr. Klinik Bircher-Benner has said: "Absorption and organization of sunlight, the very essence of life, is almost exclusively derived from plants. Plants are therefore a biological accumulation of light. Since light is the driving force of every cell in our bodies, that is why we need plants."

We found that the best way to alkalize was to first drink 3-4 liters a day of alkaline water with a pH of 9 or above. Our choices of the most alkalizing foods was the next step. Moving towards an alkalinizing lifestyle was a process, not an event. I started to implement more alkaline choices while phasing out acidic options. Some of those decisions were as simple as substituting fresh lemon or lime juice for something as highly acidic as vinegar. You may be thinking, "Well, isn't lemon juice acidic too?" It's actually true that if you took some pH paper and tested lemon juice it would test acid; but once the lemon juice is metabolized in the body, the inherent alkalizing mineral salts contained in the lemon juice leave a residue of alkaline ash in the bloodstream. Also, because of their low sugar content, lemons and limes do not ferment in the blood.

Other substitutions took place. I started using avocado and healthy oils like flax seed, hemp seed oil, and coconut oil in place of butter and margarine. A huge mixed green salad became our main entrée and we doctored it up with goodies like sun-dried tomatoes, almonds, pine nuts, and garbanzo beans. I started to use many more dark green leafy vegetables in our diet: kale, spinach, and collard greens. Onions, garlic, and ginger became our natural antibiotics. Our morning smoothies went from sugary fruit and yogurts to english cucumbers, spinach, avocado, red ruby grapefruit, fresh coconut meat, some ice, and a little raw green stevia (an herbal sweetener that is 100 times sweeter than sugar!). We still could have sides of pasta, fish, or cooked grains, but we found that steamed buckwheat and quinoa were better than white rice, baked potatoes, or yeasty breads. We also added the benefits of good mineral salts. The proper salt is vital for your health and helps keep you alkalized. We still splurged on a dessert once in a while, but not every week like we used to.

Once we got rid of most of the acidic foods and drinks from our diet, we noticed improvement in our health and appearance. Those last ten vanity pounds disappeared. My son's sinusitis cleared up. Headaches became rare. We also noticed clarity of thought, better sleeping patterns, and much more energy. Hay fever and other allergies disappeared completely.

It's been one of the richest blessings in our lives to find this treasure of truth. And it makes so much sense. Just eat and drink those foods that are best suited to your body's pH chemistry and watch the dividends appear! We hardly ever get sick. We have energy levels that match what we had back in high school, and we're the same size we were back then too!

The menus in most restaurants can even be navigated to create a beautiful alkaline meal. Here are some examples:

If you're eating at an Italian restaurant, order:
minestrone vegetable soup as an appetizer;
a big green salad with avocado, tomato, lemon juice, and olive oil;
a side of pasta with marinara or pesto sauce, or some fish.
If you're still hungry, order a side of steamed veggies like broccoli.

If you're eating at a Mexican restaurant, order:
a large taco salad without the meat and cheese (and use fresh salsa stirred up with guacamole, lemon juice, and some salt for your dressing);
a side of beans (preferably black beans and some rice for your 20 percent) or a tortilla.

If you're eating at an Asian/Chinese or Thai restaurant:
order a vegetable-based soup, if available (Some Thai restaurants have a good veggie soup with coconut milk broth.);

order a large stir fry or steam fry (with water, if possible) of a mixed veggie medley (leaving out the mushrooms and corn, if possible);
add tofu to the entrée as part of your 20 percent;
use Real Salt or Liquid pHlavor Salt instead of soy sauce;
order a couple of side veggies like spicy green beans and asparagus.

If you're eating at a place like The Cheesecake Factory, order:
avocado and tomato egg rolls with cilantro sauce for an appetizer;
a roasted artichoke (and use lemon and oil as a dipping sauce);
a large mixed veggie salad (and use oil, lemon, herbs, and spices for the dressing);
sides of steamed broccoli and other available veggies of choice.

When you're willing to make some simple changes in the way you feed your body and realize that everything you eat or drink affects your body's delicate chemistry, appearance, and energy levels, then alkalinizing makes perfect sense. It's not a program of deprivation but rather freedom to choose and eat (as much as you want) the kinds of foods and drinks that will be best assimilated in the nine yards of your intestinal tract. You also need to think of that intestinal tract as your literal *root system*—similar to how plants have roots to absorb their nutrients from the soil. You wouldn't think of pouring chocolate milk into the soil of your favorite house plant, right? You'd kill it! It's a fact that everything you eat or drink finds its way into your millions of intestinal villi and microvilli, which are tiny, hair-like structures with the total surface area of a tennis court! Within each of these intestinal villi there exists a vein, an artery, and a lymphatic vessel. It is of utmost importance that you always provide the best possible nutrition so that your root system can absorb the minerals and vitamins that build your blood and tissues.

In our minds, food is no longer just a choice about fat grams or calories. It's about the *life force* of the food and how it energizes us with electrons. Acidic food choices do just the opposite. They introduce more protons into our systems, which takes our energy levels down. The pH Miracle is an invitation to change. Change the way you look and feel, and set out to be the best you! Think about the way you take care of your car. You probably try to put the best fuel in it to keep it running for the longest season you can. Your body is the same! And depending on how many miles you already have on you, alkalinizing just might be your best bet for a long, healthy road ahead! Try it, and don't be surprised if you get a few miracles of your own! Who knows! You may hit the cover of *Cosmopolitan*!

About the Author

Shelley Redford Young, LMT (licensed massage therapist) is the co-author, along with her husband, Robert O. Young, of The pH Miracle trilogy of books: *The pH Miracle, The pH Miracle for Diabetes,* and *The pH Miracle for Weight Loss* (Time Warner publications). She has also published two cookbooks entitled *Back to the House of Health 1 and 2* and along with her son, Adam Young, has published a children's book on alkalizing, *The Doc Broc Stone Hinge Cave Adventure.*

She has appeared on *The Early Show* with Dr. Young and made other TV appearances to share the alkalarian lifestyle and recipes with the public. She has been a keynote speaker at Life Mastery with Tony Robbins and has produced many DVDs, such as *Shopping with Shelley, Hot Rox Lymphatic Massage*, and several cooking DVDs.

Her website offers books, tapes, DVDs, and other products to help people start their own pH Miracle program. The Youngs also hold pH Miracle Retreats and microscopy courses at their Rancho Del Sol in Valley Center, California. They also have extended stay retreats where you can make a reservation to go on the pH Miracle program under Dr. Young's direction.

You can visit their website at www.pHmiracleliving.com.

The Evolution of a Bold and Classy Woman

by Anne Johnson

Becoming Bold

Upon reflection, I can see that my entire life, both personal and professional, has been "male dominated." Bless all the men who have mentored me, taught me, encouraged me, nurtured me, challenged me, competed with me, frustrated me, disappointed me, run screaming away from me, and, of course, loved me! Much of the time they welcomed me into their world. At times, they even tried to make me one of their own. But in reality, I am a woman. My personal evolution and success in life can be attributed to the examination, understanding, and integration of all my bold and classy traits.

There are several factors from my childhood that contributed largely to my becoming a "bold and classy woman"—a woman bold enough to survive and classy enough to thrive in the world of business alongside my male counterparts. I was raised by parents who believed children should be "gender neutral." So, for example, the boys can cook and the girls can do home repairs. Oddly, I am not sure the opposite is true. But, gratefully, it never occurred to me that I might not succeed at something simply because I was a woman. In fact, many times I was successful because of my ignorance. I call it the "I didn't know women didn't do that" syndrome!

My parents, a doctor and a teacher, believed in giving back to the community. They both worked in underserved communities plagued with huge socioeconomic challenges. I understood early on that giving back to the community was not an option but a requirement in life.

My mother's outlook on life, in particular her opinion about nurturing her children, can be summarized in a couple of statements that I carry with me even today. She firmly believed it was her job to "toughen up" her children like a lioness would "toughen up" her cubs so they would be able to stand on their own two feet one day. It became a defining aspect in my developmental years. It was an undeniable message requiring us to be totally independent at an early age.

I was the youngest child in my biological family, and my personal Independence Day came very early. At the age of 15, I was labeled "tough enough" and was informed that "the herd needed to be thinned and I had not made the cut"! Bless my mother's heart. She pushed me from the lioness's den with the expectation that I would survive, and I did!

I have never had a clear understanding of my mother's thinking when she decided I should be emancipated at age 15, but the local attorney was not onboard and solicited one of my siblings to step in and stop the madness. To this day I refer to that brother as my mother/brother. He had always been very involved while I was growing up, and it was not until years later that I realized he and a sister had really done a lot of my parenting as I grew up. My sister went off to college around this time. My mother/brother was young and married, with a family of his own. Another sibling had just returned from Viet Nam and was desperately trying to fit back into society, and my father had moved on years earlier to start a second family.

Although we all visited my mother and her husband through the years, we never lived as a family again. It was years before I began to really understand all the thoughts, feelings, and consequences that resulted.

I moved around, lived with friends, was always working and stayed focused on school. Eventually I was accepted into the first of many "boys clubs" that would dramatically shape my life and my career. I lived on an 80-acre farm for many years with several exceptional "bikers and truckers" who treated me, the only female roommate, like a sister. I took care of the house and the animals and was strongly encouraged by this unconventional family to attend college!

As I worked my way through college I had an opportunity to partner with one brother and buy a couple of gas stations. Owning the gas stations was my first crack at managing employees. By the end of the '70s I had created my first success as an entrepreneur. I started a small business that supported me halfway through the '80s and allowed me to finish college debt free! During those six years I learned to negotiate, ask for the business, and grow the business through referrals!

In the mid '80s I decided to give up self-employment, take a pay cut, and enter the traditional white-collar work force. I had a passion for helping people and championing the underdog. I wanted to follow in the footsteps of people like Ralph Nader and make a real difference. So I contacted everyone I knew and networked my way into a position with a non-profit agency. That first professional position allowed me to do community education, fund-raising, and a lot of public speaking with groups like the National Organization of Women. One night I gave a money management talk to a group of newly widowed women, and I still remember the impact I made as I taught them the basics about money, insurance, credit, and mortgages. I knew then that I had a special gift for educating women, and it became my purpose and passion.

Networking continued to bring me opportunities. I served on advisory boards and was a conference committee chair for some national professional organizations. I developed contacts with large corporations and was contracted as a consultant to work with employees undergoing organizational changes, mergers, and downsizing. I continued the challenging contract work until the end of the '80s. Creatively managing change became my specialty and remains one of my strongest skills even today!

By age 35 I had perfected "tough," and most would agree I was rapidly mastering the art of "bold." I had graduated from high school near the top of my class in 1976 and had immediately followed my passion for horses and the "Great Outdoors" by traveling West to the Grand Teton Mountains. I became the first woman to graduate from Bud Nelson's Wilderness Packer and Guide School in Wyoming. Once I was accepted into his "boys club," that old cowboy and I learned a lot from each other!

The '70s were an exciting, "bold" era. Women spoke out about Viet Nam, Equal Rights, and the Sexual Revolution. I lived communally, traveled by motorcycle, co-owned a couple of gas stations, and had my first taste of being an entrepreneur. I reveled in the historic significance of the times. Intuitively I understood that life as a woman would be forever changed. What I didn't fully grasp back then, however, was the significant shift that was occurring inside women—a shift that was actually taking place deep down inside our DNA on a cellular level! It was not until my work with the BraveHeart Women Global Community that I understood how society and history could really impact and change women down in the core of our being—how the thoughts, feelings, and experiences that we have can be filed away in our cellular memory and alter our actions and reactions to life.

By the end of the '80s I was a college graduate, homeowner, investor, and a charter member of the National Harley Owners Group! The career path I was pioneering included a great deal of public speaking, networking, and fund-raising. I had already been contracted by corporate, private, and not-for-profit groups to creatively manage several challenging and unconventional assignments. Having been married for most of the decade, I also elected to become a "stay-at-home mom" when my first daughter was born in 1988, but I did continue to work a few hours a month.

As the '90s arrived, so did my second daughter. I welcomed her into what I considered to be the most "blissful" time of my life thus far! Two years later I turned 35. It was a memorable year, to say the least. My ten-year marriage was crumbling in spite of the efforts my husband and I made to hang on to the love, friendship, and good times. Despite our shared desires and intentions, we finally decided it was best for all of us to stop living as a family and end the marriage.

Once again I began networking in order to find full-time work. I will never forget the call I received from a sales manager. After we chuckled about my transposing the wrong name after *Dear Sir* on my cover letter to him, he explained how my background and combined experiences were perfect for a career in sales. The community education, public speaking, and ability to creatively manage change were all skills he predicted would lend themselves to my success. That was one moment in time when I just embraced fear and went for it.

Discovering Classy

I believe there are times in life when "ignorance is bliss," and one of those times for me was when I began my career in sales. Looking back, I clearly understand why I was destined to excel in the adrenaline-soaked "boys club" known as sales. I also know why I was able to build a successful career, create a prosperous lifestyle, and honor my ongoing passion to give back to my community by empowering other women.

For one thing, I was clueless, and that put me squarely ahead of the game. Plus, I had no formal sales experience, which meant that I had no bad habits to overcome. Life had groomed me to be tough and rewarded me for being bold. Remember my "I didn't know women didn't do that" syndrome? Well, it allowed me to be competitive and approach the "boys club" as though it was a level playing field that included women too. I also possessed a burning desire to succeed. In addition to motivation and drive, I possessed a willingness to learn.

I've always loved to learn from my experiences. If something didn't work, I examined it, looked at alternatives, and tried something else. I thought of this "bold" trait as "following my curiosity." I had never been able to resist the temptation to follow my curiosity when looking for solutions to problems or asking questions about anything that interested me. It was that exact rather bold trait that contributed so much to my eventual prosperity.

Failure was never part of my vocabulary. Instinctively, I always knew that if I tried something and it did not produce the results I desired then it was not really a failure. It just hadn't worked as I imagined it would! That persistence and "die trying" attitude were a direct result of the tough and bold survival strategy that I adopted when the safety net of my family disappeared. It took years to perfect my bold and tough persona, and it allowed me to survive just fine.

Throughout my career I have consistently been described as "extremely coachable" and "open to constructive feedback." It's the best way to learn, grow, and improve myself. I credit my open attitude and my willingness to learn and adapt to change directly to my early Independence Day. Because I was required to support myself at a relatively young age, I was destined to learn several life lessons the hard way. So very quickly I learned to accept and embrace coaching from people around me who already knew the ropes.

Fortunately, I also realized early in my sales career that the feedback I received from others was their "gift" to me. It was intended to help me get ahead. So I faithfully contemplated and utilized any and all constructive feedback. Incorporating feedback from my mentors, co-workers, clients, and even my prospects allowed me to attain success at a much faster rate. It was certainly better than learning everything by trial and error.

It never occurred to me to feel rejected or consider anyone's feedback, advice, or even constructive criticism as a personal attack. It seemed unproductive and detrimental to allow my feelings to be hurt by any type of feedback or simple business decisions. However, a lot of women unfortunately continue to internalize criticism and take feedback personally.

I believe that bold and classy women do not let rejection define them, but they do allow feedback to refine them! In fact, my ability to manage, or rather ignore, rejection on a personal level was instrumental in my overall success. In order to survive being "cut from the family herd" by my mother, I had to work really hard to reconcile my thoughts and feelings about personal rejection early on. So after a great deal of introspection, I managed to develop a very strong "rejection muscle." I thought a lot about questions like *What made her reject me and not the other children?* Eventually, I figured out that I literally needed to separate myself, my worth, and my value from her decisions. I learned to detach myself from the outcome of other people's decisions once I realized that my personal value did not change based on the outcome of any decision. I always asked people for feedback after they made a decision, whether they decided to work with me or not, buy from me or not. I always asked them how they arrived at their decision. I discovered that their decisions were made based on how well their needs would be met. If my solution solved their problem and they could afford it, then the sale was good to go. The outcome was never about me as a person.

Detachment became even easier once I really accepted the indisputable fact that other people are driven by their own personal needs, desires, and agendas. They make decisions for their own reasons, and there's nothing to gain by internalizing those decisions as personal rejection.

In order to separate myself from the pain of my mother's decision, I told myself that she had chosen me to leave the family early because I was stronger and more capable than my siblings. I clung to that thought and used it to override any lingering doubts I had about her ability to love me the way she loved the others. That was the first time I remember consciously rewriting the internal messages or subconscious tapes that played over and over in my head. The rewrite process actually allowed me to overcome my fear of being rejected by her. I quickly realized I could effectively "change my mindset" and experience freedom from the pain of her rejection. That allowed me to truly detach so that I could communicate in a more relaxed, authentic manner. Ultimately, all the resistance I felt went away, and I no longer feared rejection!

After that, I perfected my "change the mindset" technique because it allowed me to overcome numerous fears and resistance toward a variety of challenges and obstacles. I employed this technique whenever I faced something new—especially as my sales career took off. I would simply "change my mindset" whenever any type of resistance began to surface. I also came to see that other women needed to stop all their negative internal chatter if they were going to excel in business!

My conscious decision to trust the mentors and coaches who graced my life was also one of the best decisions I ever made. I trained myself to stay focused, to listen, and to learn whenever an opportunity presented itself. I was considered quite bold because I asked a lot of questions. Boldly asking questions when I did not understand something or needed further clarification had always paid off for me. I remember convincing myself to feel comfortable about asking for the things I needed, wanted, or deserved. I decided it was "classy" to ask for things like the sale as long as my requests were reasonable. I reminded myself that people always had the option to say "No."

I experienced a defining moment in my career many years ago when a Senior Vice President said, "Good for you. People should learn to ask for what they need. If you don't ask, nobody will just hand it to you"! That feedback made a huge impact on me and on my career. It was a positive endorsement that my "bold yet classy" approach to life and business was an effective one. The feedback stuck with me and reinforced the "permission" I had generously given myself to feel comfortable asking for many things like referrals, the sale, financial commitments, networking and business opportunities. This "permission to ask" became another source of freedom from resistance and fear! It was another giant leap toward giving myself "permission to sell."

I continued to develop new sales skills. Explaining to other people why I was asking them a lot of questions was monumental. When I qualified the need to ask lots of questions up-front for people, then they relaxed. Our conversations flowed more freely; and, of course, sales increased dramatically. Essentially, I refined my "bold" style by incorporating a softer, more "classy" approach as time went on. From that point on I never stopped refining, transforming, and adapting my "bold and classy" style!

Authentic trust and sheer determination provided the strength and courage I needed to embrace my personal fears about selling and overcome my own feelings of resistance. Once I made the decision to embrace and push past the fear, I began to experience success. That success increased and strengthened my self-confidence, and "fearless" became my new "changed state of mind." It was a liberating and empowering revelation!

No doubt overcoming resistance and being liberated from fear opened the door to success for me. It's why "changing the mindset" became a fundamental process and skill set in my personal sales survival guide, "The Bold and Classy Selling Philosophy." It's one of many strategies that I developed as I watched women struggle with resistance to and fear of selling. Open-minded, coachable women can diagnose their personal fears, change how they think, transform themselves, and become empowered by "The Bold and Classy Selling Philosophy." In essence, women can give themselves "permission" to open the door to success and excel.

Bold and Classy Integration

When I re-entered the business world, I had unknowingly embarked on a journey of discovery and transformation in which my bold traits would eventually integrate with the classy selling skills I mastered while building a prosperous career and lifestyle. I credit the discovery and integration of my bold and classy traits to an ability to listen, learn, and passionately embrace change. My initial survival, transformation, and ultimate success in the world taught me the absolute necessity of being an "agent of change" and the power that came with it. My ongoing transformation was fueled by my ability to embrace change. My willingness to refine my bold and classy approach as change occurs has ensured continued success and prosperity. I became an authentic, empowered woman who could give back to her community as my bold and classy selves melded into one who would thrive, especially during times of change.

In retrospect, it seems to me that the pendulum of change swung too far during the initial period of transformation known as Women's Liberation. First women felt oppressed, but then they became overly aggressive. As the Women's Movement gained popularity, "we" essentially adopted masculine attributes in an effort to achieve equality at home and in the business world. Of course, I believe women are entitled to equal rights and opportunities. But I also believe that many of us became too bold to do anything but just survive during the '70s. The aggressive "old school," male-dominated method of selling and living that women tried to adopt did not really suit our feminine nature. That historic shift compounded our confusion and magnified the internal fears and resistance toward selling we embodied at the beginning.

Although society eventually embraced women moving to the forefront in business, ironically we women simply embodied even more internal fear and resistance because acting like men just did not work. We didn't realize that being liberated from our feminine selves would leave us feeling so uncomfortable deep down inside on a subconscious level. As we strived to gain and maintain equality, many women felt compelled to try and leave their traditional feminine past behind. We survived, but it was difficult to thrive comfortably in our own skin while being too bold.

We knew change and transformation were still required because we had not yet found our authentic voice. But the path to prosperity had become even less clear, especially as we realized that being too bold was not the answer. Clearly we could not go back to being resistant and afraid of feeling pushy and aggressive. But having "failed" to transform effectively, we have struggled even more to become empowered, successful women who are comfortable enough to be authentic and authentic enough to thrive!

We have continued to survive, gain equality in life, and be successful in business; but we are at a crossroads once again. There is a new global shift well underway right now. It's one that women cannot afford to sit back and ignore. This global shift in how we do business imposes the necessity for women to consciously evolve, transform, and change. But with this tremendous shift comes huge opportunity!

As our global marketplace and world economies undergo such dramatic change, I am refining my "bold and classy selling style" to ensure that I continue to thrive! I am honored to be part of these changing times once again and filled with gratitude that I have found a home in my sisterhood of the BraveHeart Women Global Community.

Women must be bold, embrace change, and prepare to create another shift at a cellular level and redefine ourselves once again. It is an extraordinary time to be a woman in business. I am humbly committed to empowering all the women who are embracing change, overcoming fear and resistance, and willing to undergo the next transformation on a cellular level.

I am extremely passionate about this amazing historic moment in time and about creating a new vision for women around the world—one in which our bold and classy traits will be integrated and we settle comfortably into our feminine selling zone as BraveHeart Women in business!

About the Author

Anne Johnson is an entrepreneur, business owner, public speaker, former executive sales manager, and motivational coach with a passion for helping women overcome their fear and resistance to selling, have better results and higher profits, and thrive in prosperity. She is president of Bold and Classy, LLC, and is the founder of the Bold and Classy Women Community, a global network of business-minded women who support each other as they learn to be bold about selling while maintaining a classy approach.

As a successful businesswoman selling, managing, coaching, and mentoring in a man's world, she developed the Bold and Classy Selling Philosophy, a guide for women who need to overcome a resistance toward selling. This philosophy supports women who want to identify their individual fears, create new internal messages, transform themselves, and overcome their resistance toward selling.

In addition to being an entrepreneur and business owner, Anne has been a corporate vice president, regional manager, and district manager of sales; a dedicated educator who motivated employees through organizational change; and a public speaker at national sales meetings and conferences.

For more information on collaborating with other entrepreneurs and to join the Bold and Classy Women Community, visit http:// BoldandClassyWomen.com.

$\mathcal{A}$cting on Purpose

by Kathy Kolbe

I was labeled a gifted but severely dyslexic kid and told I should stay away from writing. So I became an author and publisher.

A mid-life car accident robbed me of over 40 percent of my IQ, causing me to be unable to read or write. As I once again challenged my brain to do what others thought it would never be able to do, I discovered the power of the mysterious third part of the brain—conation. Two decades later, I'm creating the protocols for first-time brain mapping of this incredibly overlooked human dimension.

Before a drunk driver smashed into the car in which I was a passenger, I had become fascinated by the way human beings used their minds to get things done (or not). I was well aware of how I could "trick" my own dyslexic brain into accomplishing my goals.

As a young mother, I was intrigued by how many kids, even the gifted ones, didn't know how to use such tricks to overcome their obstacles. Although I wasn't an educator by training, I ran a lab school to teach kids creative problem solving. Then I began writing the tricks in books and games I called Think-ercises™! I disseminated them through an award-winning publishing company I called Resources for the Gifted, Inc.

In the early 1980s, I was in the unique niche of being one of the few female entrepreneurs and public speakers I knew. People from around the country attended seminars at which I showed them how to help kids use such tricks to improve their learning. My journey led to my becoming an adjunct professor of gifted education as well as a consultant to business leaders who began using my methods to improve employee performance.

Why NOT Me?

As a kid, I'd watched how different kinds of tricks worked for different people. By the time I was a young adult, I was immersed in politics, helping candidates predict the patterns of people's behaviors, regardless of gender, age, race, or intelligence levels. Some called me a mystic because it was uncanny how I could watch individuals or groups of people solve a few problems and then predict how they would react in other situations.

I was determined to codify the clues I used to help people achieve their goals and reduce their stress. To do that I needed to figure out the objective reality of what I was observing. After years of developing a language to describe what I saw, I finally decided that there were four clearly distinguishable sets of what I called Action Modes.

I'd learned the skills for writing a mental assessment test from my dad, who wrote the Wonderlic Personnel Test, the first test of cognitive abilities used in selection. It seemed natural for me to write an assessment instrument that showed the pattern of an individual's innate use of these Action Modes—what I came to realize defined a person's MO (*modus operandi*).

I knew instincts were subconscious and immeasurable, so I figured an MO was related to—but different from—instincts. I knew what I was seeing was not measured on IQ tests or tests of personality types. But there wasn't a third category of the mind or brain to put it in. It seemed I would have to create a new category of mental assessment, but I wasn't even sure what to call it. So I called my assessment the "IF"–for IF I ever figure out this category or domain of the mind.

The IF was amazing. It proved accurate by every method I used to test it. But I couldn't sell it to others until I knew exactly what it was measuring. It had to be valid as well as reliable. I delved into the literature of testing and found nothing. Finally, using my dad's old *Roget's Thesaurus*, I found the word *conation*. It was a "Ta Dum!"

But when I contacted leaders in the field of psychology I was told, "Conation is an archaic term not used in modern psychology." Since I knew the concept was timeless, I turned to the ancient philosophers, where I found lots of food for thought. Conation, volition, instincts, drive, self-determination, the Will. Lots of discussion. No accessible conclusions.

I needed to confirm for myself that conation was both different from and as important as the cognitive and affective domains of the mind. I needed to be sure I was measuring something that mattered.

Ten days after I discovered the word *conation,* I was on the way to the hospital. My brain was so badly injured that I couldn't speak in full sentences or recall what hospital I was in. Drugs messed with my affect, so I wasn't sure what I wanted for dinner, let alone what my emotional preferences were. All I could do was operate according to the very instinct-driven conative energy that I had been studying.

Even before I could sit up in bed, I was using my conative energy to develop new kinds of tricks—conative tricks—which I needed for my very survival. I later dubbed them Conables® tricks. They were mental challenges that allowed me to self-manage my MO or natural drive—ways I could get myself back in a productive mental gear.

Although I had all but lost my business, my cognitive abilities, and my life as I knew it, the Conables® helped me use my instincts to retrain my mind and work toward a new goal: helping others learn about their conative MOs and how to use such tricks to unlock their innate strengths. The IF became the Kolbe A Index, an assessment of conative MOs.

Writing a Book

As I became stronger through the use of my conative abilities, I felt compelled to write a book about the significance they could have for others. My biggest fear was that I would die without imparting the knowledge I had gained. That meant I couldn't wallow in the peacefulness of illiteracy. I signed a contract with a publisher—and then had to figure out how to write all over again, and it hadn't been easy the first time!

My son gave me a needed deadline. He got me to promise I would finish the book before he graduated from college. (The accident happened the night before he left for his freshman year.) I used every trick in the book to write it—and turned in the last pages to the publisher the day of my son's graduation. Against all odds, *Conative Connection* became a best seller. Of course, that book didn't stop the doubters. Highly educated people who had never heard of conation were sure it couldn't be very significant.

Unlike writing the business and theory books I've authored since then (*Pure Instinct* and *Powered by Instinct*), I've found personal joy in creating Conables® tricks. Now a grandmother of eight, my mission and my family are intertwined. A son and daughter run Kolbe Corp, with my husband heading up our international efforts. Every one of the grandkids is able to benefit from the awareness we all have of the three parts of their minds.

IQs of a Different Sort

It wasn't always great to have an unusually high IQ. It was confusing. Why didn't other people get it? Why was it so hard to get them to see the point? Being "retarded" (I know the word isn't politically correct, but it's the right word for me to describe me at that time.) was far easier.

Ignorance was easier. At first I didn't care that I couldn't read or write. My doctors let my positive attitude and use of Conables® tricks fool them into thinking the accident had only messed up my body.

I loved just stuffing my company's financial statements in the hospital trash can. It didn't register with me that most of my employees, having been told I might be a paraplegic, thought I would never return to work and so were leaving for better opportunities.

It was easy to see through false praise, phony concerns of wannabe friends (I'd recently been in *TIME*'s Person of the Year article on can-do people, and others wanted to cash in on that PR), and superficial advice. I had no guile and sensed when others were full of it.

I wasn't afraid because I couldn't walk, sit, stand, or even move without human help. A mechanical conveyer belt lifted me out of my bed and onto a gurney that took me to a tank of water, where I was supposed to let its slow movement nudge me into slight motions.

Yeah, but . . . when the timer was set and the door behind the aide closed, I could violate all the rules of not trying to move. I could whistle, sing, and move as fast and as often as possible to my own tune.

During the times I was supposed to be resting, I rigged up personal challenges, trying to beat my own records without allowing anyone to help me. (I had trouble counting past 12, but everything after that was gravy anyway.) It was stupid stuff. But I was well aware of its power to help me be me. When physical therapists wondered why I progressed far ahead of schedule, I knew that trusting my instincts was working.

I was at the very basic level of problem solving: moving so the sun wasn't in my eyes, getting my hands to be able to hold a cup of water, explaining to a nurse that I meant I was too hot when I must have said something that made her think I was too cold.

As I got stronger, I discovered what it was like to take charge of my own destiny. It didn't matter that others doubted I would ever be able to write again or to go back to running my business or that I heard them whisper that I might have to go to a nursing home. The more I figured out my own solutions, the more I knew it was because I trusted my undervalued conative instincts. Each step forward convinced me I had to get well enough to be the advocate for this third part of the brain.

Robbed of my former cognitive abilities, I was dependent upon the very part of me that I'd been so curious about. Maybe I had a positive attitude because I had already come to the conclusion that intelligence was not all it was cracked up to be. So what if I couldn't read the newspaper? I could read body language. I was good at figuring out what people really meant even when some of their words were a mental mystery to me. I didn't have to be highly intelligent to be alert to what was going on around me.

The more I realized what I couldn't do cognitively, the more I realized how much I *could* do conatively. I had been given the gift of a stark awareness of the differences between thinking, feeling, and doing. As a theorist, I no longer had to wonder whether my theories of the power of conation would ever prove to be accurate. I knew I was on the right track. And I was certain the world needed to know what I was learning. Everyone could find greater joy, peace of mind, and a sense of true accomplishment by having the freedom to trust the conative part of their minds.

I was living the proof I needed. I just couldn't figure out why the learned scientific world had been ignoring this essential truth

Back to Basics

I first learned the full extent of my inability to read as I was about to speak to a hundred business and education leaders. The seminar had been on my calendar prior to the accident; but even a few months after the crash, I wasn't keeping a calendar or wearing a watch.

It took me by surprise when my office called to see what type of microphone I wanted as moderator for a statewide symposium for leaders in business and education. I had no memory of agreeing to do this. Rather than cancel, I decided I should fulfill this commitment. Panelists usually resent a moderator who takes away from their time to talk, so I assumed that as long as my body could handle the pain, this would be a piece of cake.

Laurel McKiernan (my new-found friend, a specialist in working with handicapped kids who had generously offered to help me with rehab) was by my side as I entered the hotel banquet room. Dozens of people descended upon me, acting as if they were old buddies. Although some of the voices were very familiar, I had no memory of how I knew any of these people. Some got too close. Even though my cane should have warned them I was wobbly, they expected me to give them a hug. That required movements I was physically unable to make—besides, these were strangers to me.

I was clearly disoriented by the noise and commotion around me. So when I was handed vitas for introducing the four speakers, I chalked that up as the reason for the words on them being a blur. When the letters wouldn't settle down, I asked Laurel to get me to the women's room. There I took the deep breaths I'd learned helped clear my mind. It didn't work. When the letters would not stop floating all over the place, I realized I couldn't read.

"Describe what's going on," she said, having decided long before that when I was ready I would make this discovery.

As I tried to put into words what was going on in my brain, I realized that the physical damages I'd been fighting were far less complicated than the mental ones that were now surfacing. It was as if all the tricks I'd learned to deal with my dyslexia had abandoned me.

"Guess I've got lots more work to do than I thought!"

"Yep," she answered in her no-nonsense, no-pity manner. "And here's where it starts. You need to go back in there and deal with it."

Then we both broke out laughing at the absurdity of the situation. We cracked each other up until there were tears in our eyes—and I was ready to go out and have fun with the situation.

The conference was an effort to get statewide leaders in business and education to work together to improve our low-performing school systems. As the state's Small Business Person of the Year and a publisher of educational materials, I had a foot on both sides of the issue—economic and academic. Now I couldn't even stand on my own two feet—or even read or write—let alone publish anything.

I literally limped back into the ballroom, gave each of the panelists another's vita, and told them to introduce that person by explaining the importance of his or her work to the goals of the conference. When I was congratulated later for coming up with such an innovative way to kick off the discussion, I thought: *Necessity truly is the mother of invention.*

The Business of Helping Kids

A few months later, when I was using books I'd written for primary-grade students as tools to retrain my own mind, I agreed to keynote a statewide conference on innovative approaches in special education. Because I was so severely dyslexic, I'd had to work diligently to find tricks that allowed me to be in gifted programs rather than special ed programs. With my own gifted kids and a passion for creative problem solving, I'd co-founded the Arizona Association for Gifted Education and developed/co-taught Arizona State University's first graduate-level courses on gifted education.

I believed in the need for special education, but not the way it was generally being taught. Rote memory and conative Follow Thru structure and repetition are not the answers for all kids with special needs, be they ADD, autistic, or cognitively challenged. I also was convinced that being intellectually gifted had nothing to do with needing accelerated skills-based programs. On both sides of the IQ scale, the goal should be to foster self-management of mental strengths—which is creative problem solving.

My focus became helping all kids reach their potential by using all three parts of their brains—the cognitive, conative, and affective—long before I knew the term for that conative dimension. I'd changed the name of my company from Resources for the Gifted to Kolbe Concepts, Inc. I also started calling our publications Think-ercises™ activities. Now many education customers could not use federal funds to purchase our products because they were no longer considered "differentiated" for gifted students.

I had made these decisions a few months before the accident. The combination of circumstances led to our corporate income dropping by almost 70 percent. At the time of this speech, I hadn't paid myself for 18 months and couldn't afford to replace the 24 (out of 28) staff members who had left.

It was important to my mission to be at this conference to advocate individualized approaches in special education and to introduce the audience to the conative domain of the brain. Twenty-five years later, I consider my impassioned speech that day to be the best one I've ever given. After a standing ovation, I was elated that several audience members expressed interest in following up on my list of action items for creating the changes. As Laurel and I left, choosing the workout of walking down an open staircase for a couple of floors, we could hear two school superintendents talking from a floor below us.

"What Kathy said really makes sense," I heard one of them say. "I think our district could begin doing some of the things she suggested. It could make a big difference for a lot of kids."

"Yes, but you know she's making a profit off all of this?" said the other.

"Really! Well, I'm certainly not going to be any part of that!" replied the first educator.

That's the moment I decided to change the target customer for Kolbe Corp. I wasn't just going to talk about giving kids the freedom to be themselves. I would role model it.

My instincts told me I had to go to the business leaders who had been in the room. They would understand the bottom-line value of improving individual and group performance.

Working with business leaders, we've reached thousands of kids and have proven the positive impact on them from what is now dubbed the Kolbe Wisdom. As my instincts had predicted, business leaders whose enterprises became more profitable through their use of the Kolbe Wisdom have taken the revelations about conation home to their families, to the school boards on which they served, and to other community programs. As parents, they grabbed hold of the Kolbe Youth Index, filled with tricks individualized for youngsters so they can self-manage their conative strengths.

Educators could get access to the Kolbe Youth Index by applying to the not-for-profit foundation, The Center for Conative Abilities, to go through our extensive training called the Perfectly Capable Kids program.

The Trick to Using Conables®

Not all Conables® work for every person. I create them for the different MOs that are assessed by the Kolbe A Index (http://kolbe.com/A). My personal result is 2685—which means that I begin the creative problem solving process by:

1. innovating unique solutions;
2. then I use my Follow Thru to develop a system or plan of action;
3. next I use my Implementor energy with a tangible model or prop

to both recall and teach what I know;
4. finally, I summarize and simplify my efforts.

To kick myself into conative gear, I use Conables® such as:
- going on Twitter, knowing almost nothing about it, and forcing myself to teach people who I don't know as much as I can about Conation, 140 keystrokes at a time;
- drawing a chart without any idea what it is for and filling in the headings with what at first seem like random words; and
- making lists of words that describe things that puzzle me, then putting them into a logical sequence or method of explaining whatever it is.

I'm extremely grateful that I experienced a period of almost a cognitive void. While I had been confident of my own conative abilities, I needed to gain the confidence that gave me the trust that the Kolbe A Index was truly assessing those strengths in others. It took almost three decades, but I was finally certain that the strengths were indelible and trustworthy. They were worth all the effort it would take to help others discover in themselves.

In order to help people understand what it takes to be confident in their conative strengths, I developed the Kolbe Conative Confidence Survey. Try some of these questions and see whether you are nurturing your own instinct-driven abilities:
- Are there some things you do better than other people would do them?
- If a job is difficult to accomplish, do you keep trying until you succeed?
- Do you believe people when they compliment you on your abilities?
- Does a defeat mean you aren't likely to succeed in the future?

If you answered the first three by saying "Yes" and the last question with "No," you are probably confident in using your MO. If not, it's important to find out why you don't trust this wonderful strength within you. Feel free to contact me at info@kolbe.com.

About the Author

Kathy Kolbe founded a highly innovative corporation 34 years ago (Kolbe Corp) that has achieved sustained financial and marketplace success. As its CEO, she received numerous awards. In addition, she has been a consultant to Fortune 500 CEOs and top people in government, law, education, religion, and sports; advised best-selling authors/management consultants, authored best-selling books on leadership, teams, and human instincts; spoken to audiences in 17 nations, been interviewed on over 300 radio and TV shows, and been featured in *The Wall Street Journal, The New York Times, Newsweek,* and *Money;* trained over 4,000 organizational development and HR professionals on methods she's proven effective for increasing efficiency and productivity in enterprises of all sizes; donated her time for 35 years as chairman of the non-profit Center for Conative Abilities; and owned and operated Resources for the Gifted, through which she authored and/or published over 100 books teaching creative problem solving for K-12 students.

Kathy is currently working with brain scientists on studies that are proving the validity of her discovery of behaviors tied to the previously uncharted conative part of the brain.

To find out more about Kathy Kolbe's work, visit her website at www.kolbe.com.

Coming to Clarity

by Radha Conrad

When I was 18, I married a man I'd met in college. When I was 24, I had my second son. Shortly after that I began to have clarity about many aspects of my own personality that I hadn't had before. As a result, my personal life started to fall apart. I suddenly began to feel deep discontent, which manifested in my body as a terrible pain in my left shoulder.

The doctors could find nothing wrong and didn't know what to do for me. Then one of them asked, "Have you ever wondered why the pain goes up and down?" I took out a little blank notebook and began to write down what was going on inside me as well as in my outward environment before the pain started. I also rated the pain on a scale of 1-10.

Keeping this diary helped me gain clarity about the real cause of the pain. I discovered that when I was in my truth, I was in no pain. Eventually I realized that I had lost my own ideals and what I had believed was important since I had been a child. Basically, I had sold out for financial security. My husband was in the aerospace industry and was earning a really wonderful salary, and I had dropped out of college to marry him.

This was a pretty major insight, what I call now a Clarity Snap. I had always thought of myself as a person who lived my truth and spoke it. It never occurred to me that inwardly my beliefs about the way the world needed to be were very different from the way I was living my own life.

When that clarity came to me, I started to fall apart emotionally. I didn't know what to do with that truth. To speak to my husband about it only created a larger gulf between us because, of course, he took it personally. At the same time, I couldn't speak to anybody else about it because nobody I knew was going through anything like it; or if they were, they kept it secret back in those days. Thus, I had a lot of shame and felt a lot of guilt.

I told my husband that I needed to get help. He could see that I was pretty miserable, so he agreed. Through some very deep work with a psychotherapist, I saw that what was going on in my married life was really a reflection of unfinished business that I had from my childhood. When I was 8 years old, my mother was diagnosed with leukemia; she died when I was 10, in 1950. At that time, people just went on with their lives after a loss, and so I had never really allowed myself to grieve. My three older sisters and my father had never processed my mother's death; so if I got emotional, they got emotional—and they didn't want to do that. They just wanted everyone to feel better and move on. So I stuffed my feelings.

I continued to keep my diary while I went to my psychotherapy sessions. Since I knew that nobody else understood, I kept it to myself. That was good because it allowed the process to keep churning and bubbling, bringing more and more things to the surface. Finally, I did a very deep process in which I buried my mother and went through the grief of her loss. I saw my mother in her coffin, said all the things that I wished I could have said to her that I hadn't, and then closed her coffin. Afterwards, I looked in the mirror, and I looked like a different person.

This created a major transformation in me. I could no longer emotionally be a little 10-year-old girl inside a 28-year-old woman. And with that realization, my whole life fell apart, including my marriage. That person who decided to get married at age 18 no longer existed. She had been a frightened little girl who didn't believe in herself, didn't think she could make it on her own, and needed her husband to tell her how wonderful she was. She lived her life for her husband and children. The only problem was that inside she was empty and hollow. I didn't know that until my life fell apart. Suddenly, I could no longer do the things that I had done before. The dam had burst, and there was no going back.

Coming to Clarity

As I started changing, my husband was in a panic because the woman he fell in love with was gone. I had opinions about the way I wanted things to be, and I didn't agree with certain things and didn't want to do other things. Suddenly, I felt like I was back into integrity and I was literally growing up because of the clarity that I was getting inside.

I started to question my relationships. I became aware that my mind was either the basis for peace and harmony within me or the basis for unrest and disharmony. I could either be caught up in duality—where you're always rejecting something or someone whether inside yourself or outside yourself—or choose clarity. Clarity is a wake-up call to what the truth is, and I could tell by going within whether or not I was in clarity.

Many of my relationships began falling away. It wasn't that I had to get rid of them; we just didn't have things in common any more. My friends needed me to be who I had been, and I wasn't that person anymore.

After ten years of marriage, I wanted a divorce. This was in the '60s, and no one in my family had ever been divorced. I didn't have one friend who had been divorced either. So when my husband moved out, my friends saw me as a threat. When they asked me why such an ideal couple would separate, I explained that my clarity had shown me that I was out of integrity and that I was living my family's life but had no life of my own. That was threatening to them. They were afraid they might start to look at their own lives and wouldn't like what they saw.

So my friends basically dropped away. Most of my family members had nothing to do with me. There was no one to give me the support I needed. I realized that was because I was going through such a major transformation that I really needed to do it alone. I had never lived alone in my life. I went from my family house to a sorority house to being married. And my husband went to work and I stayed at home.

Finally I asked him if he would be willing to give me a year to be on my own so that I could find myself and know who I was. I know it sounds very basic, but I really didn't even know when I wanted to go to bed or when and what I wanted to eat. He agreed and arranged to have a live-in nanny stay with the children, who were then seven and four.

It was a great thrill to realize that I could eat whatever and whenever I wanted and to walk into a restaurant alone. I had never done anything alone. In order to grow up, I had to be alone. I had to know I could be alone, that I actually could survive on my own.

Eight months later, I told my husband that my boys could come back and live with me. That's when I realized how angry he actually was at me. He said, "I'm not willing to keep my word. I'll see you in court!" He had been hoping that I'd want to come back to him after being alone, so now his anger and resentment toward me were unleashed. It was a devastating blow when he tried to get custody of my children.

The judge ruled that we would have 50-50 custody. However, because my children were already living with their father, he thought it would be less traumatic for them to stay there. Other than my mother's death, this was the most traumatic experience of my life. I went so deeply into that experience that I had a realization—a Clarity Snap. What I experienced was that the emotional pain that I was in, brought to the ultimate degree, was no different than the emotion of pleasure.

This was a full-body experience in which my body filled with light. All the anger that I had held, without realizing it, toward God for taking my mother suddenly burst like a firecracker; and I saw that it had no substance. It was just released. In the process, I also released many old beliefs and thoughts that I had taken to be who I was, but that were really locked in childhood ideas and beliefs that were covered over by this anger.

In that moment, I knew what my destiny and my purpose in life were. I was a channel for love and light, and my job was to assist people in coming to clarity so that they also could alleviate the suffering in their life.

Not long after this experience, a friend told me that she was going to a Gestalt therapist. This type of therapy is very "here and now." You take full responsibility for the life you're in, and you begin to see how you're getting the life you want or how you're creating the life you don't want.

When I met with the therapist, he asked me if I realized that I was naturally doing Gestalt therapy with people. I had never heard of it. He offered me the opportunity to go through intensive training during which he would "teach" me what I had already been doing. If he could teach me how to officially do this therapy, I could earn a living at it. He insisted that I begin working with people instantly and take my work to him so he could critique it. I was attending three groups a week, a workshop every weekend, and three private sessions a week. At the end of three months, he said, "There's nothing more I can teach you. You've gone way beyond me."

The year was 1973, and I decided to start all over again and move to Maui. My older son had made my ex-husband's life so miserable that he asked if I'd like to have him live with me. Soon my younger son moved back too. And so just as my life had fallen apart, it came together again. But now I was a whole, real person who was being her true self.

Within a month of moving, a psychiatrist who had seen my ad in the paper called and invited me to the Maui Health Clinic to sit in on the group. Then he told me to just jump in and work with anyone I wanted to work with. Two months later he announced that he was moving back to the mainland, and he recommended that all his clients come and work with me. And so my practice was handed to me!

I knew this was happening because everything I was doing was in alignment with the truth. I was living my truth. As long as I went within and asked the questions and sensed in my body and followed my breathing, I knew that clarity would arise to my consciousness and I would know what I needed to do. My Clarity Snaps were wake-up calls or aha moments that would guide me, enabling me to shift consciousness.

If we don't shift our consciousness, we might hear the truth a million times and yet not be able to live it or take the appropriate action steps in the world. The Clarity Snap helps us shift. It turns a light bulb on: *Oh, you mean I'm doing that? I didn't know I was doing that.* And only then do we have the freedom to choose to do something differently.

Clarity is part of our essential nature. It's not something you have to achieve; it's something you tap into that's always there. Yet too many of us ignore our clarity. We can never be in integrity with someone else if we're out of integrity with ourselves. It's difficult to create prosperity if deep down inside I don't believe I deserve it. It's difficult to live my purpose if I have so much fear and tension in my body because I'm repressing this subconscious information that I'm afraid I can't deal with.

When I'm working with people, I hear them on the deepest level—not only what they say but also what they are not saying; not only what they say they want, but what they want on a deeper level. When I ask, *Is this what you're saying?* the person will answer from the exact depth at which I'm asking the question. This is what brings about the Clarity Snap. I'm not talking to the repetitive thinking mind; I'm talking to a place within the person. And I'm really training the person to go there independently.

When you get a Clarity Snap, you feel lighter, freer, more relaxed. If you follow your breathing and you sense in your body, your body will tell you what is true and what is not true. Your body never lies. It will tell you when you're in clarity or when you're caught in duality.

There are five areas in which women most need to gain clarity: prosperity, self-image/weight, purpose, communication, and relationship. We're going to look at each of these areas to see what it looks like when you are in clarity vs. duality. It's important for you to know that self-acceptance is a catalyst for clarity and self-judgment is a catalyst for duality. If you're learning to accept yourself, this is a process that will take you to a state in which you are in acceptance.

1. Prosperity

Clarity allows us to become aware of the abundance that is already in our lives and to be grateful for it. So the basis for creating prosperity is acceptance and appreciation and gratitude for what is.

Duality is filled with rejection of what we have and where we are in the hopes of improving our finances through making us feel wrong—that we didn't do enough, we should have done more. Duality uses fear to motivate us to do more.

2. Self-Image/Weight

Clarity shows us our true value is intrinsic to who we are. Who we are is greater than any idea of what we think we should look like. Clarity shows us we are the one observing whether we like or dislike our body image.

Whether I think I'm thin or fat, whether I think I'm the greatest or the worst, these are ideas, and those ideas change. For example, I think I look fabulous in this outfit and have the perfect body, but I go on vacation and put on some weight and suddenly I feel like I'm fat and ugly. My acceptance of myself is always conditional. I have to meet certain criteria in order to be acceptable. There is always an internal judge evaluating me.

Our true self-image is not impacted by how much we weigh, by how long our nose is, by how many wrinkles we have, by what age we are. If you base your value and your worth on things that are going to change, then your suffering is guaranteed. Clarity shows us who we really are, and it's always greater than any idea of what we think we should look like because who we are is not determined by how we look.

Duality devalues us when we don't live up to our ideal of perfection, which changes. If Renaissance people suddenly materialized, they would say, *These people must be starving!* It's a cultural thing, and it's based on the time in which you live and on what you look up to. We're influenced by TV, magazines, and movies. We judge ourselves against things that aren't even real—models have cosmetic surgery and their photographs are touched up. So we base our ideal on an unreal self-image, and we use that to beat ourselves up. Duality causes us to reject ourselves because we don't look the way we believe we should and to degrade and verbally abuse ourselves to motivate us to change our body image.

3. Purpose

Clarity will show us what is blocking our ability to know our life's purpose. So in my case, what was blocking me was my anger at God for taking my mother away when I was a little girl. Most people want to live their own purpose, but they don't understand that they can't do that until they have the Clarity Snaps to show them what's blocking them from the natural outflow. It's our job to remove the blocks so that who we are can bubble up. Clarity with purpose shows us how to stay on purpose to reach our goals.

Duality causes us to judge ourselves as inadequate to have a purpose or as not knowing enough because our purpose hasn't been realized yet. And this makes us reject our efforts to stay on purpose and reach our goals.

Clarity will always bring you to see where you are in the moment. If you're following your purpose, you're doing everything you need to. And if clarity shows you this is an area that is actually at odds with what you want, it's only to enhance your ability to allow that to dissolve.

4. Communication

There are three ways that we communicate:

- *Assertive communication* is asking for what you want in an effective, clear, and open way.
- *Aggressive communication* is based in fear and duality and creates negative results. It always comes from anger inside of us that we're acting out.
- *Passive communication* is also based in fear and duality and it also creates negative results. It comes from insecurity, from believing that you don't have the right to get what you want or you'll never get what you want anyway, so why even bother? Thus, when you start to ask for what you want, you ask for it in a way that gives you the least chance of getting it.

Clarity allows us to be assertive—to ask for what we want in an effective and clear way. *Duality* makes us manipulate, which is a roadblock to clear and assertive communication, because we don't know any other way. We're afraid that if we ask clearly for what we want, the other person will think badly of us.

Both aggression and passivity are reactions to our inner communication saying that we do not have the right to ask for what we want or say how we feel. Whenever we're caught in aggressive or passive behavior, we're trying to manipulate the situation. If I can be angry at you and bully you into doing what I want, then I don't show you the fear that's causing me to act out in that way. I don't have to show the real me or my vulnerability.

5. Relationships

Clarity shows us how we're creating a loving and supportive relationship or a toxic one. Clarity also shows us what action steps we need to take to create the loving relationship that we desire.

Duality focuses our attention on our differences, making others wrong. It sabotages our ability to accept ourselves and the other person as we are. Duality allows us to righteously reject other people.

Clarity creates purpose, self-acceptance, unconditional love, clear communication, loving relationships, the ability to recognize who you truly are, and the appropriate action steps to take. The inner action steps come first. An inner action step would be realizing I'm tight in my body and that I want to breathe in and come to clarity. Then my clarity shows me something I need to do. Maybe I really need to affirm that I love myself unconditionally. That's also an inner action step. Then the inner action steps will motivate the action step in the world, whether that's saying the affirmation out loud or writing the affirmation or going for the job interview I was afraid of.

Only when we first take the appropriate inner action steps can we come from that place of clarity inside and take the outer action steps. If we take the outer action steps first, we will not be able to maintain them. That's why some people say, *I don't understand. I was doing everything right, everything was going great, and then all of a sudden everything fell apart.*

Duality creates blame, fear, judgment, low self-esteem, competition, where somebody has to lose so I can win. Duality creates comparison and competition, whereas clarity creates collaboration. Duality will always lead me down that path of competition, comparison, and rejection, while clarity will allow me to appreciate the truth of who I am, which will naturally allow me to appreciate the truth of who other people are.

When you're in clarity, you don't feel threatened by others. You know who you are and you know that they can be allowed to be who they are. That doesn't take away anything from you; the more people succeed, the more you enjoy their success. They're examples of how you can do it.

You have clarity when your mind and your heart are in the same place. That's why it's your true nature. It has all the intelligence, but it has all the love, the kindness, the compassion as well. And that's how it shows you what you need to see. It's never a judgment. It has in it the ability to motivate you and shift your consciousness because it's the unconditional love we all want. And it literally teaches you how to be what you know.

Clarity has never failed me. That's what brought me to do this work and to name my community the Sisterhood of Clarity. I know that if women develop their clarity, then the rest of the qualities that we have developed through the centuries will be more effective and we will shift our consciousness. I have felt for a long time that the only way the consciousness of human beings can shift is through clarity.

To be part of this new world, we have to stop blocking our truth, stop living in duality and thinking that we're not good enough. Once we are in clarity, we're on the same level as everyone else. It's time for us to take our seat as women next to men so that the yin and the yang are both present.

If I can appreciate a man for who he is and appreciate who I am as a woman and know that together we make a whole, a complete picture that can address the issues that need to be addressed so that the consciousness of humanity can be raised, then we can accomplish anything.

We also have to be aware that we each have yin and yang inside of us and that sometimes it's appropriate to dip into one and sometimes the other. We don't have to repress any side of ourselves. Even if you have the most wonderful loving attitude in the world, without strength, you cannot accomplish; without will, you cannot accomplish. In order for women to inspire action in the world, we need will; we need strength. That doesn't mean that these qualities do not come with love and caring and compassion. Clarity is the way all these qualities come together. And clarity is the way to shift the consciousness of human beings and thereby change the world.

About the Author

Radha Conrad is a transformational counselor, trainer, speaker, wife, and mother. After completing the usual two-year course in Gestalt therapy as a three-month intensive, Radha went on to earn her master's degree in counseling psychology. In 1973 she went into private practice with her own company, The Institute for Self Recognition, where she provided all aspects of counseling.

Radha is a member of the National Speakers Association and has been a public speaker at numerous churches, organizations, and colleges. From 1976 to 1981, she served on the staff of a private high school, where she formed and led Life Mastery Skills groups for teenagers. Over a two-year period, she led a series of successful workshops for women called "How To Be a Woman of Independent Means," which dealt with women coming into their power and becoming more effective in the business world. She has also conducted management training for executives and has lectured at conventions on topics such as success, leadership, clear communication, stress management, self-esteem, and creativity.

Radha developed special exercises to help people free themselves from their past to live a life filled with love, power, and success. Her first publication, *Self Recognition*, provided a comprehensive set of exercises for those already immersed in the process of transformational work.

Radha created the Sisterhood of Clarity Community to assist women in developing their clarity and to enable them to shift their consciousness. To find out more about her community, visit http://SisterhoodOfClarity.com.

$\mathcal{E}$mpowering Our Children

by Audie Perove

It was Easter weekend, and I was eight years old. I thought it was going to be such a happy day with a new dress to wear and an Easter basket filled with chocolate and decorated eggs, but then the unthinkable happened. My father, who adored me as much as I adored him, had a massive heart attack and died.

It was commonplace back then to have "viewings" in the home. However, I was still taken by surprise when I came downstairs and walked into my living room the next morning and saw my father's casket there. Feeling confused and sad, I panicked inside; but I didn't question what was happening or make a scene. Later in the day, four or five girls my age came to the visitation with their parents. Since I was only eight, it was difficult to sit quietly and look somber, so I went outside to play with the other kids. It was such a release to be able to laugh and play—until one of the other kids asked me how I could even think about playing when my father had just died. That made me wonder, *What am I doing? Why AM I having fun when my father is lying dead inside the house?* I feel sure my insecurities and self-doubt began on that day.

After my father died, I felt totally lost and alone. Technically I wasn't "alone," but it felt that way to me. The security that I had known had been abruptly taken away from me. Before my father's death, my brothers and I had enjoyed a comfortable life—one of limited new experiences but one that was loving and stable. My father had owned a lucrative trucking business;

but when he died, the income was suddenly gone and so my mom had to go to work outside the home. She was faced with the stark reality that she was now the breadwinner of the family. She had no professional training of any kind. Although she was a fantastic cook, all she could find was a job washing dishes at a local restaurant.

Since my mom had her new role to deal with and my two older brothers were adjusting themselves, I didn't want to add to their burden. I didn't realize back then that it was okay to ask for help; instead, I tried to handle my emotions on my own. My family was doing their best, but they had no idea what I was going through because I kept my feelings inside. For me the loneliness was unbearable. I craved connection and guidance and security—all the things that build self-esteem in a child—but I didn't see how I would ever be able to experience those things again.

My mother and I never really talked about the family's financial situation. I sensed that she was struggling to make ends meet, but she always sheltered me from whatever money worries she had. Mom always made sure that I had whatever I needed before she bought anything for herself.

The other thing we never talked about was feelings—neither mine nor hers. When I was younger, it was so easy for me to show her affection. One morning when I was in first grade she forgot to kiss me goodbye when she dropped me off at school. I actually left the schoolyard and followed her down the street until she saw me and stopped to give me my hug and kiss. But after my father died, she didn't show me much physical affection. Looking back now, I think it may have been too painful for her to allow herself those feelings anymore. I knew she was grieving, but she kept it to herself. Years later my aunt told me something that my mother had confided in her. After everyone was in bed and she knew no one would hear, my mother would sit in her rocking chair with tears flowing down her cheeks, wondering how she would ever be able to manage. At the time, I didn't understand the sudden lack of affection, though; and because she stopped giving me hugs and kisses, I shut down too. I thought that was the way it should be. I was always a good kid and never wanted to make waves or be the cause of anyone's discomfort, so I accepted my new way of life.

Actually, I'm not really sure how I did feel about all of this at the time. What I do know is that for years afterwards I had trouble trying to identify my feelings. Because I hadn't been able to share my feelings when I was growing up, I had a hard time trying to know, much less describe, what I was feeling and why. Yet something positive did come out of my pain. When I had my own children—Ben, Lauren, and Alex—I made sure that our relationship always included open communication as well as shows of affection. I've always given them hugs and never hesitated to say *I love you.*

Part of my problem as a child was that I didn't ask for what I needed. I never told my mother or my brothers how lonely I was. My brothers were having their own challenges adjusting. My oldest brother was finishing college, and my other brother was just starting college. They were dealing with our loss on a totally different level than I was.

And so I pulled more tightly inside my shell. I didn't talk much, and I remember feeling like I just wanted to hide. My intentions were to not stand out in any way, shape, or form. I had friends, but none that I could confide in. Maybe that was because I felt I'd been criticized by my friends about playing when my father had just died. But I didn't start to come out of my shell with people until I was in my 20s.

Although I had trouble relating to people, I always had an affinity for animals. And at this time in my life they became my life. I felt a soul connection to all my pets. They gave me joy and comfort and filled the void in my young life. Dad and I shared a love for animals, whereas Mom just tolerated them for our sake. Yet after he died, I fondly remember how my wonderful mother recognized my need and never said "No" to the constant parade of pets that I would bring home. I think that was her way of letting me know that she understood how much I missed my father.

A few months after my father's death, I was diagnosed with rheumatic fever. Under doctor's orders, I was confined to complete bed rest. Since we lived in a two-story home, the stairs were a definite issue. My older brothers were a great asset to me. They were always there to carry me wherever I needed to go. During my very long recuperation time, my school-bus driver, who was aware of my love for animals, stopped by one day and brought me a puppy to keep me company. I was elated when my mom said it was okay to keep him.

I also would mysteriously win the church-bazaar raffle every year; and, of course, the prize usually just happened to be an animal. One year it was a cat, another year a dog. If there was an injured animal anywhere in the neighborhood, it found its way to me too. I just loved to "doctor" them. Add these to the strays that I picked up on my own, and you can see that I had quite a menagerie! At one point, I wanted to become a vet, but I was concerned that I wouldn't be able to handle the inevitability of sometimes losing an animal no matter what I did to try to save it. Another obstacle that stood in my way was my lack of self-confidence; I was afraid I wasn't smart enough to become a vet. Actually, the feeling of not being smart enough or good enough has been a major stumbling block for me throughout my life.

Even as I considered writing a chapter in this book, I was plagued by feelings of inadequacy and self-doubt. I experienced a lot of "static" and anxiety: *Who am I to be telling my story? What do I have to share that's worthwhile? I can't write. I'm not smart enough to do this. I'm not good enough. My story isn't going to inspire anybody. How am I ever going to be able to express my feelings in a way that will get my point across?* And then it dawned on me—these are all indicators of a limiting belief mindset. And this is what I've been doing to myself my whole life—talking myself out of taking on a challenge, passing up opportunities to grow and learn new things, tearing myself down, making myself feel stupid. In that aha moment I knew that whenever you are closed to something, whenever you resist, you are in fact keeping grace from coming to you. Grace embodies everything with which I resonate: peace, joy, love, gratitude.

Then I realized that the answer to my problem was not in pushing my anxiety away and pretending it wasn't there; rather, the answer was to feel what I was feeling and to trust in myself to know that it would be okay. Once I allowed myself to do that, I began to get momentum. Little by little, my thoughts began to settle down and become clearer, until I was finally able to transfer them to paper. At first it didn't seem natural, but then I remembered that some action is better than no action, and so I persevered. I stayed grounded in the present moment, and soon I found grace sitting at my side.

I know now that everything happens for a reason and just the way it is supposed to happen, even though it may not seem that way at the time. The lessons I learned when I was a child were guiding me to where I am now. At the time, I wasn't very adept at interacting with other human beings, but I was able to connect with animals. Thus my experiences with animals served as a bridge to show me how to connect with and relate to people. Isn't it ironic that what I lacked as a child is where my strengths lie now?

Animals are put on this Earth to teach. God in his infinite wisdom has masked this learning experience that they give us with big, brown eyes; soft, cuddly fur; and wagging tails. Yet through caring for them I began to learn about responsibility, relationships, communication, trust, honesty, and unconditional love. The similarities between humans and animals in these valuable life lessons are countless.

These furry friends taught me many lessons in a hidden sort of way. It was when I had children of my own that I was able to put into practice what I had learned. Like children, pets can sense trust and honesty, and they give unconditional love. Have you ever noticed how young children can look into your eyes so deeply that you feel they can see your soul? Their world is so pure and open. They definitely are living in the moment.

After a few years of working as a dishwasher, my mom was able to land an accounting job at a local car dealership. She was good with numbers and was a self-trained bookkeeper. As things got a little better for us financially, my mom and I began, in a small way, to help some of the needy kids in our town. Even though we didn't have much ourselves, my mother was very generous. When I was ten, we started spending time with kids who were neglected. When you live in a small town, it isn't too difficult to find out who they are. Sometimes we'd buy a small gift for a child who didn't have much. Or we'd give away the coins my mom had saved. Helping kids who were less fortunate was a way for the two of us to bond. I loved taking care of the younger kids—my shyness seemed to go away when I was with them—and soon I started to think about having my own kids one day.

Looking back, I also realize we were doing something else by sharing what we had with others: we were creating a wealth mindset. Given our actual financial situation, it would have been all too easy for us to constantly feel that we were lacking in abundance. But by giving to someone who had less than we did, we actually invited prosperity into our lives.

As I mentioned earlier, I didn't start to come out of my shell until I was in my 20s. I have my loving husband, Dave, to thank for all his assistance and encouragement. He is my soul mate. He not only loves me, but he believes in me; and he has never wavered in his commitment to instill that same belief in me. It took me some time, but I finally share his belief in me and I am forever grateful for his support and devotion.

My mother passed away ten years ago, but after years of hard work she was able to leave each of her children some money. My inheritance was enough for my husband and me to take a vacation, so we went to Maui for our 25th anniversary. As we were driving around the island, we rounded a corner and were mesmerized by a glorious rainbow. We enjoyed looking at that rainbow for 45 minutes. It looked like it was in 3D, and I felt as though I could almost reach out to touch it. It is a picture forever imprinted in my mind. When we got back home, I mentioned the rainbow to my aunt, who told me it must have been my mother's gift to me. Mom knew how much I loved rainbows, so she gave me one!

Five years ago my husband retired after having quadruple bypass surgery, but I wasn't quite ready to sell the pet-grooming business that I'd had for a number of years. Although it was back-breaking physical work, I still needed my "fix" of being around animals every day. For the most part, I did all the work by myself; but eventually I realized that I might need some assistance. That was where Cindy came in.

As it turned out, Cindy helped me with my business and I was able to help her come out of her shell. When she started working with me, Cindy was extremely shy and had very low self-esteem. (She reminded me of someone I knew quite well!) Her husband was very controlling and constantly put her down, telling her that she couldn't do anything. He even came with her when she interviewed for the job and wouldn't let her talk when I asked her questions! But I followed my gut and hired her anyway, and a great collaborative team was born!

We were much attuned to each other, and Cindy shared my affinity for animals. I started to understand how important it was to let someone help me. And as Cindy told me all about her life, I shared my story about my own childhood issues with self-esteem. I did everything I could to counteract her husband's influence, helping her see that she was a caring, capable, and reliable person who was very good at working with animals. Eventually, Cindy became self-confident and courageous enough to rise above her situation and take charge of her life.

Seeing how Cindy blossomed once she was able to develop self-esteem, I began to think about how important it is to grow up with healthy self-esteem and how debilitating it can be for you even as an adult if you don't have it. Self-esteem eluded me as a child and for many years after that. The lack of self-esteem consumed me in such a way that it was paralyzing. Everything that required my emotional or mental energy was predicated by negative, self-doubting thoughts and self-talk. It didn't matter if it was something small or something of great importance—I missed out on countless opportunities because I lacked the self-confidence to "go for it."

Supporting Cindy as she transformed her childlike demeanor into healthy adult self-esteem was one more step in allowing me to realize that I have a passion to empower children to believe in themselves by assisting them to develop self-esteem and nurturing a "can-do" attitude in them that will make them unafraid to dream and to know that they can accomplish whatever they set out to do.

Cindy helped me realize something else—the importance of teamwork in getting things done. I'm sure it was partly because of my lack of interaction with other children when I was growing up that I had never seen how valuable it could be to team up with another person to get a task accomplished. I always preferred to "go it alone." But Cindy showed me that working with good, positive people helps you attain your goals more quickly and efficiently. Having other people on your team gives you some additional attributes and strengths that you might not have all by yourself. When a team pulls together, the whole is truly greater than the sum of the individual parts.

I finally did decide to sell my pet-grooming business, and for six months afterwards I felt as if I was going through a devastating withdrawal from seeing my beloved animals every day. Cindy is no longer a part of my daily life, which I greatly miss; but it truly warms my heart to see how she has grown. And I am very happy to report that she is now the owner of a very successful pet-grooming business. We both have learned a great deal from each other, and she will always hold a special place in my heart.

Although I was never unhappy in our home in Pennsylvania, whenever I went away I realized that I was much too attached to my house. So I determined that this mindset was no longer serving me. When the opportunity presented itself, Dave and I decided to change our lifestyle; and we started traveling around the country in our RV, basking in nature and the outdoors—another great love of mine.

In thinking about my life now, I'm reminded of Eckhart Tolle's book *A New Earth.* He talks about raising our level of consciousness by being in the present moment and explains that the way to achieve this is to surround ourselves with nature. I feel that I'm making up for lost time from my childhood, when my experiences were very limited. I yearned to be in nature, but I never had the opportunity to do so. Now I "collect" sunsets, taking pictures of them wherever we go. And of course I am always on the lookout for rainbows!

Right now we're located in California; and although we are enjoying our beautiful surroundings, we may decide to get our RV on the road again soon. Who knows? We are going with the flow, and it's so liberating!

But wherever we travel, we will remain dedicated to helping kids because they are our future. Collectively as a society we have dropped the ball with our children. Now it's necessary to build momentum on a grand scale to help them build self-esteem and develop a healthy self-image at an early age. If we can also model how to develop a wealth mindset, no matter how much material wealth they have right now, as well as show them the power of teamwork to achieve their goals more quickly and efficiently, we will go a long way to assist children in avoiding the limiting beliefs that so many of us grew up with. If we can do this, we will be giving them invaluable tools to help them reach their true potential. We will teach them to not merely survive but to thrive.

About the Author

Audie Perove is an entrepreneur, wife, and mother of three amazing children. Her family constantly inspires her with their creativity and compassion for people and animals. As a child, her pets were her best friends, and what she learned from them has assisted her in building her own self-esteem. For 16 years Audie owned and operated a successful pet-grooming business in Pennsylvania, which gave her the opportunity to care for and interact with her beloved animals, as well as hone her business and people skills.

A few years ago Audie and her husband, Dave, had the opportunity to change their lifestyle and get closer to nature. They started traveling around the country in their RV and have been enjoying breathtaking sunsets and glorious rainbows ever since.

Audie's passion and purpose in life is to build self-esteem in children. Her life's journey consists of paying this forward for our children. After all, they are our future.

To learn more about her community, Our Children: Strengthening the Future Generation, visit http://OurChildrenCommunity.com.

The Path of the Warrior Caregiver

by Janie Pighin

I was born the third daughter to parents who wanted sons and who did not know how to show any physical or verbal affection to their children. Raised on a small farm in southern Alberta in Canada, at a young age I had many opportunities to care for orphaned kittens, piglets, and calves. Although I did not know it at the time, my dysfunctional upbringing and this early caregiving on the farm would form the foundation of my life.

When I was 19, I married a farmer who was an alcoholic. By the time I was 24, I had three children—a son and two daughters. My second daughter, Jacqui, was referred to as a "premature overdue infant," since she was two weeks overdue and only weighed five pounds, seven ounces, at birth. When she was three months old, Jacqui was registered with the CNIB (Canadian National Institute for the Blind) as completely blind. When she was six months old, I was told she would probably not walk, she might have trouble talking and eating, and she could be deaf. When she was nine months old, I was given the diagnosis that she had cerebral palsy.

I ran though the gamut of emotions, from the normal mother reactions of *Why me?* to the anger reaction of *This is not fair!* to the guilt reaction of *What did I do wrong?* But then, without my realizing what I was doing and without any help from any support group, my early caregiver days turned me into a Warrior Caregiver, and my special caregiving days began.

Jacqui needed a lot of time and care. She was also a determined little girl who required a tough-love upbringing. There were many appointments with specialists in Calgary, over an hour's drive from our home. I took her to physiotherapy classes at the Children's Hospital in Calgary twice a week; and when she outgrew that program, I put her into a nursery school in Calgary three days a week so that the mobile physiotherapy team could continue to work with her. At the same time, I learned to teach her how to roll over, how to crawl, how to stand up, and how to walk. Together we learned how to sit on a chair. I broke down the seemingly simple task into its smaller movements and positions and modeled them for Jacqui. There were many tears as Jacqui struggled with her fear of falling and I pushed her to succeed. Every accomplishment that Jacqui mastered was a miracle to me. I took nothing for granted. I clearly remember when she said her first words, took her first steps, reached for an object (which confirmed to me that she could see), and turned her head when her name was called (which confirmed that she could hear).

Determined to raise Jacqui the same as my other children, I refused to make any exceptions for her just because she had limitations. She would learn how to improvise to get tasks done. I would make her live in my world. I was NOT going to fall into the self-pity trap that happens so often to parents with handicapped children.

One of the biggest challenges was getting people to accept her for who she was and not to treat her differently from any other child. Finding a baby-sitter who would look after her was very difficult because everyone was afraid of her seizure activity. No one wanted the responsibility of dealing with a seizure while she was in their care.

Although I tried to participate in meetings with other parents who had children with similar conditions, I would leave these group sessions feeling worse than when I arrived. Then I realized the reason why I felt so uncomfortable with them was that we had different mindsets. I was not falling into the mindset of "poor me with this little handicapped girl." I had already discovered that this little girl was given to me for a reason, and my plan was to push her to achieve as much as possible and still give her the ability to set her own goals and reach for the stars. I was not content with the clinical diagnosis of my child. I felt that she had abilities, and I wanted her to have the opportunity to live her own dreams. I just had to find ways to pull out her abilities so that she could have the life that I dreamed of for her.

My days were spent juggling my time between attending to Jacqui's needs, handling my son's requirements for his half-day kindergarten classes, and finding a sitter for my other daughter on days that I had to drive to Calgary. While doing all this juggling, I also managed to find time for me. During this time I began to realize that my husband and I had drifted apart and that his alcoholism prevented him from participating in our children's upbringing. He had fallen into the "poor little girl" syndrome with Jacqui; and even when I reminded him, he would not treat her as a normal child.

When Jacqui was four, I enrolled her in a full-day nursery-school program. Then I packed up my three children, left my husband, and moved into a little rental house in town. My husband's family was well-known in that town, and I was unable to get a job. It was not my lack of skills but rather my last name that was the reason no one would hire me. I decided that I would have to move and that my best option was to go back to school to prepare for a career that would generate enough income to raise my children. I only had a high-school diploma, so now I needed to upgrade at a college level to obtain my matriculation in order to qualify for university.

After being turned down by several colleges, I was finally accepted at a college in a small town three hours away. Once again, I packed up my children and our few possessions and moved. Jacqui was now going into first grade, and my fight with the education system began. At that time, handicapped children were always pulled out into special education classes, but I wanted Jacqui to be integrated as much as possible into the normal classroom. Eventually I organized a meeting with all of the education agencies involved with her education planning and implementation, and I convinced them to develop an individual education plan that allowed Jacqui to remain in the normal classroom for at least part of her day.

During this same time I realized that I needed to improvise a way to remain in control since Jacqui was always trying to gain the upper hand.

As the caregiver, I needed to stay in control. Jacqui knew just how to push my buttons. One of her favorite ways was by slamming her bedroom door. No matter how many times I told her to stop, she just kept it up. When I couldn't take the constant banging any more, I removed the door.

Shortly after the move, I read a newspaper article about mothers of handicapped children and how and why we are chosen. It reminded me that this child had been given to me because I knew how to help her succeed in life. I clipped the article and hung it on my fridge, where it stayed until it became yellowed and brittle. If I was having a bad day and wondering *Why me?* I read it and reread it. It was my most important tool to jolt me out of a funk. I still have this article today in a special keepsake box.

Although it took me five years, I completed my management degree while still finding the time to take Jacqui to physiotherapy and handicapped riding classes and the other children to all their extra-curricular activities. We lived on student loans, and I held several part-time jobs. Although we did not have much, we cherished and appreciated the little we had. We enjoyed each other as a family and laughed a lot.

When Jacqui was 12 years old, I married a man who had lost his wife in an automobile accident. He was raising his three children by himself. We combined our families, sold his house, and bought a house in the country. Jacqui struggled with the new arrangement and had even more trouble adjusting when her new half sister arrived a year later.

Brittnie was born with abnormally shaped brain ventricles, and we were told that she would not walk, talk, see, or hear. Now I had two handicapped children to raise. I remember standing in the doctor's meeting room staring in disbelief at all the pictures of her brain. I knew then that I would raise this child the same way that I had raised Jacqui and that I would push this little girl to live in my world, just as I had pushed my first handicapped daughter. She, too, would learn how to improvise to make things work; and I would once again marvel at the miracles.

When Brittnie was only six weeks old, my father passed away after a short and courageous fight with cancer. I now had my mother to care for, which required still more juggling to accommodate her schedule. Mom decided to leave the farm and move to town. My sister and I spent many hours in preparation for the farm auction sale, sifting through years of treasures that my dad had kept. Today my mother is eighty-two years old and is still living on her own. We are blessed that she still has her mental faculties, is able to get around with a walker, and enjoys relatively good health.

Brittnie did not require the same tough-love upbringing as Jacqui, although years later I learned about her outbursts of anger when we were not home. Every accomplishment—even those that most parents take for granted, like walking and talking—was truly a miracle to me. Brittnie lost the ability to balance, and therefore she would never be able to ride a bike, skate, or go horseback riding. But I knew that she could hear and see.

By the time Brittnie started school, the pull-out policy had changed. Handicapped children were mainstreamed into the regular classroom. This turned out to be problematic, as she slipped through the education system with conditional passes and modified classes. Suddenly the school realized that they could no longer provide an education for her. She sat in the library for almost one semester, and I had to become involved in order to get her back into the education mainstream.

I have witnessed many miracles with my two daughters. Brittnie will graduate this year. Although she reads at a second-grade level, Jacqui has her high-school certificate. She now lives on her own, manages her own banking, pays her own bills, and does her own shopping and cooking.

When Brittnie was 16, her father was diagnosed with diabetes. This required a huge lifestyle change, and he wasn't very receptive. I stepped in as a caregiver, only to be received with negativity and criticism. I learned to accept that I can only put the right food in the cupboard; it's up to him to eat this food in the correct proportions at the proper time.

My husband chose to ignore his diabetes and his doctor's advice. Eight months later, at 56 years of age, he had a heart attack that required the insertion of a stint into his heart. From then on, I had to juggle my time between Brittnie, my mother, Jacqui, my other children, my career, and my husband while still finding time for me. Once again, he chose not to listen; eight months after his heart attack, he underwent double bypass surgery. He still plays Russian roulette with his life today, but I know that I have given him the best care I possibly could. I cannot change his life for him. I love him dearly and I can only enjoy whatever time we have together.

There were many times when I almost slipped into the Victim Caregiver role, and it took strong determination on my part to keep pulling myself back into the Warrior Caregiver mindset. The Victim Caregiver model is more accessible than the Warrior Caregiver model, and many times it would have been easier to slip over and join the majority. For whatever reason, I've chosen to remain a Warrior Caregiver.

Sharing this information on how to become a Warrior Caregiver is of the utmost importance because too many have fallen into the Victim Caregiver role. A large number of the Baby Boomers have become part of the Sandwich Generation, caring for our parents while still raising our own children. All too often, we fall into the Victim Caregiver group. Victim Caregivers are overwhelmed with the amount of time and effort caregiving requires; as a result, they have become very bitter. They are fighting contradictory emotions, knowing that they love the ones they are caring for but being angry at these loved ones for demanding so much of their personal time. Having fallen victim to their circumstances, they do not feel that they can take on anything more. They question why they have to do all this caregiving and wonder why someone else cannot take on some of this responsibility. They begin to direct their negative feelings towards the people they are caring for. They feel sorry for themselves, and they let caregiving consume all their energy.

I'd like to share with you the 11 steps I've developed to help you transform from Victim Caregiver to Warrior Caregiver. These steps seem relatively simple when you read them. However, they require complete dedication plus a willingness to change your direction and your mindset.

If you see the importance of transforming from a Victim to Warrior

Caregiver, you will learn to stop feeling sorry for yourself. You will feel less drained, which will give you the energy you need to not only be a better caregiver but also to take on additional responsibility with ease. Your relationships with the ones you are caring for, along with the others close to you, will flourish as you move into the Warrior Caregiver mindset.

Steps 1 through 6:
The first six steps are for the person who is giving the care.

Step 1: Acknowledge what hurts. Clearly identify everything that causes hurtful feelings in your life. Write out your list and share it out loud with those close to you. Anger is acceptable once you have acknowledged it. Then you must learn to manage that anger. Acknowledge that you will have feelings that shift from anger to guilt and then back again. Accept that even though the ones you are giving care to may not be able to positively acknowledge your care, you must accept that they do appreciate what you are doing for them.

Step 2: Learn how to avoid being controlled. Too often we allow the ones we are caring for to control our lives, not even realizing that we plan our days around their schedules. This just turns us into victims of our own calendars. We need to take back control of our lives and work caregiving into our schedule rather than making it our schedule.

Step 3: Learn to manage the guilt that you feel. You might have guilty feelings that you experience when you are unable to be a full-time caregiver. It might be the guilt that you feel when you are angry at the ones you are caring for when you allow them to disrupt your life. It's important to get control of and manage the guilt in order to have a guilt-free conscience going forward as a Warrior Caregiver.

Step 4: Become an effective juggler. We have to learn to juggle our time between our lives, our immediate families, and the ones we are caring for. We cannot let our caregiving time overtake the time that we need to spend with others and the time we need just for ourselves to do the things we want to do. We need to be able to juggle our time so that we stay in control and do not fall victim to being controlled by others' demands.

Step 5: Make sure that we do not become the forgotten caregiver. We do not want to become a forgotten caregiver because too often the people around us take for granted that we will do all the caregiving and that no one else has to worry. Then we become forgotten, and no one even acknowledges the work we do both for others and for ourselves.

Step 6: Find the gift. It truly is a gift to be able to be a caregiver to others while still maintaining and living your own life. You can find this gift and you can share this gift with the ones you are giving care to and to your own support group. It is a gift that keeps on giving, and it is essential to find this gift in order to move from victim to warrior.

Steps 7 through 11:

The next five steps are intended to help you understand and work with the ones you are giving care to.

Step 7: Develop effective communication between you and the ones you are caring for. This is an important key to transformation. Lack of communication is what starts the inner negative feelings. This leads to guilt for having these feelings, which builds up to outright anger directed at the very one you love and are caring for. There needs to be an empathetic connection between you and the ones you are caring for so that there is no fear of communicating your feelings to each other.

Step 8: Neutralize the relationship. It is not "us" and "them." It is just "us." We need to accept that we are all in this together and that we can work together to achieve the goals that we have set out. We can create a win-win relationship between ourselves and the ones we are caring for. This will in turn create harmony as we go forward together to reach our mutual goals.

Step 9: Help the ones we are caring for to express their emotions. They may not be able to do this effectively, so we may have to help them come to terms with their apathy and to have the courage to acknowledge their own anger. The ones being cared for will strike out at the ones closest to them since this is safe ground. We as caregivers need to be able to come to terms with the fact that the anger may not be directed at us but that we are the ones who will have to be able to effectively deal with the behavior and show the appropriate reaction.

Step 10: Practice tough love. Tough love is being able to separate yourself from the person you are giving care to so that you can still love that person while helping him or her to get better. Tough love involves letting the person improvise to find the solution rather than always providing the solution yourself. Tough love requires patience on the caregiver side while giving guidance and direction to the one being cared for. Warrior Caregivers do not fall into the trap of letting the circumstances and the solution direct their actions. They only provide guidance and a helping hand to complete the task. Warrior Caregivers will acknowledge the accomplishments and will celebrate the achievements. Warrior Caregivers teach with tough love, since this method brings out hidden potential in those being cared for.

Step 11: Foster independence. We as caregivers want the ones being cared for to be as independent as possible. But Victim Caregivers do everything for the ones they are caring for. It is faster and easier, plus they do not have to watch someone they love struggle to come up with a solution. Warrior Caregivers encourage independence and work with the ones they are caring for to see that they reach their full potential. Warrior Caregivers have the energy and the resources to find the time to provide solutions while they are encouraging independence.

Sometimes a Warrior Caregiver ends up in situations that require a quick fix. That's when it's helpful to have a Warrior First Aid Kit. You may need an "emergency blanket," which is something that you can quickly say to yourself when a loved one has unleashed his or her anger at you. Rather than reacting negatively, you can respond with a positive and thoughtful response. You might want to print off some affirmation "bandages" and hang them on your fridge. When you are having a bad day or a *Why me?* moment, you can easily read these and remember that you are a Warrior

Caregiver for a reason. You might want to use "safety pins" to help you come to peace with the one you are giving care to, or you might need to use the "tongue depressor" instructions to hold your tongue when you would normally react with a defensive verbal response. These are just a few of the tricks in the Warrior First Aid Kit that can be used again and again when moving from a Victim to a Warrior Caregiver.

Women are programmed to be caregivers, and the model that we have been given to follow is that of Victim Caregiver. It is the model in which we do everything for all of those around us. We fall into the victim model without even realizing that it is happening. Women naturally want to care for everything and everyone. When caregiving becomes overwhelming, women fall into the victim mode of making excuses and using caregiving as an excuse not to take on more. We allow caregiving to take over our lives; and we become tired, overwhelmed, and unable to do more. We are unable to see beyond our caregiving duties to realize that we can make a difference in the world by changing our perspective.

As women, we need to change our mindset and break away from the group victim model. We must leave behind the old mindset of "poor me." We must change our perspective and gain the self-confidence to look at caregiving in a new way. We can no longer be afraid to be a caregiver because caregiving is a large part of the lives of those of us in the Sandwich Generation. We must break free of the old model in order to take on new challenges, preparing to overcome these challenges and grow from them. It is this growth that allows us to move forward. We must break through these victim thoughts, replacing them with positive Warrior Caregiver thoughts and then applying the warrior philosophy to our own circumstances.

Becoming Warrior Caregivers will give us the energy to take on more. Learning how to become Warrior Caregivers at the personal level will enable us to take all this thought and philosophy forward to share with others on a professional and global level. Stepping up to the challenge of becoming Warrior Caregivers will ensure that we can become part of this global voice. Taking on the Warrior Caregiver philosophy that we have incorporated into our personal lives and applying it to our lives globally will empower us to walk forward together as a group.

Warrior Caregiver women will join the movement of women who make a difference in the world. Walking together as a strong and united group, we will raise our collective and collaborative global voice to speak with energy and power. Our success at becoming Warrior Caregivers at the personal level will allow us to fit into this larger group model. Warrior Caregivers will be leaders on the global front and will have the power and the energy to successfully take on new challenges to make a difference worldwide.

About the Author

Janie Pighin is a financial consultant who has successfully owned and operated her own consulting firm for over 15 years. Married to her second husband for 19 years, she has one son and three daughters, along with two stepsons and one stepdaughter. Janie currently has five step grandchildren and is still hopeful that there will be more grandchildren in the future. She and her family live on a small farm near Nanton, Alberta, Canada, where she has also operated a successful dog kennel and dog-breeding facility for the last 15 years.

Janie became a member of the BraveHeart Women Global Community in February 2010, after attending a Release retreat led by Dr. Sugar. Recently, she has changed the direction of her life, fulfilling a lifelong dream by starting her writing career. Her Warrior Caregiver Community on the BraveHeart site is a place where members can share their personal stories and access all the Warrior Caregiver material, including the complete Warrior First Aid Kit.

You can visit her website at http://WarriorCaregivers.com, where caregiver information and expert analysis is regularly posted and updated.

From BoTox to GlowTox!

by Dr. Kim Silvers

Growing up in a small town in upstate New York in an average, boring middle class family, I knew from about the age of ten that I wanted out of there in a big way. My parents say they knew I was driven and intelligent the day I brought home a paper from kindergarten with one wrong answer and cried inconsolably.

I didn't know I was different from anyone else until the other kids at school started to make fun of me. Not only was I smart, I was also quiet and introverted—the perfect target for mean kids. Even though my intelligence caused me some emotional pain for being singled out as different, I am thankful every day that I was smart enough and strong enough to know that my education would be my salvation. My good grades eventually earned me a scholarship—my ticket out of that small town.

As a pre-teen with an active imagination and big dreams in a small town, I didn't have many role models. I looked at magazines and watched TV shows like *Dallas* and *The Love Boat* and dreamed of glamour, travel, living in a fancy house, and having exotic friends. And I read.

The BookMobile, our local mobile library, stopped right across the street from my house, and I never missed it. How I loved mysteries! I now believe my love of mysteries played a part in drawing me to science and unraveling the secrets of the human body.

I was in junior high school when my father suddenly became ill. One day this strong man started to lose his balance and get a little wobbly. Soon his legs were paralyzed, and he couldn't walk on his own. He was abruptly whisked to a hospital, and I wasn't allowed to visit.

He had test after test, but the doctors couldn't determine what was wrong. We didn't know if my dad would ever walk again or even if he would come home at all. My mother began to worry how we would pay the bills if my father died or couldn't work. As the full weight of all this uncertainty and fear bore down on me—the little girl who believed in the infallibility of both her mommy and daddy—I was completely crushed.

Luckily for my father, the doctors finally made a diagnosis of Guillan-Barre Syndrome, which is an illness that attacks the nerves. The good part about this particular illness was that it would eventually subside. The bad part was that there really was no treatment except to watch and wait.

As I witnessed the turmoil this disease caused in my family, as I watched my father crawl around on the floor and drag himself up the stairs with his elbows during his long recovery, I made up my mind that I would never experience that kind of fear and uncertainty again. And nobody else in my world would ever experience it either, if I could help it.

I noticed how much power the doctors held in that scenario—the power to save my father, the power to make or break my entire family. And it was then that I decided I would become a doctor to fight these types of illnesses. I set my mind on becoming a medical scientist, a physician who does basic research to find the cures to disease.

Flash forward four years through a competitive undergraduate program to prepare me for medical school, then two years of medical school and five years of research . . . by that time my focus in research had shifted from the brain and nerves to cancer. I wanted to be a part of finding a cure for cancer. My work involved understanding how environmental toxins can cause changes in the body that lead to cancer. I believe that work was meaningful in terms of making a miniscule contribution to science and understanding the human body. But there was no joy in it, and definitely no glamour.

By that time in my life, I was in my late 20s, with no partner and no children. I had been in school consecutively my entire life since the age of four. I was working in a lab with no windows, doing research on rat livers. I will spare you the details; but suffice it to say, it wasn't pretty. While some of my medical school colleagues would spend their summers backpacking in Europe or volunteering in Africa, I was in a fume hood using radioactive compounds and cancer-causing chemicals. Positive results were slow and few and far between. That young girl who had dreamed of travel and a full life with romance, glamour, and excitement was nowhere to be found. It wouldn't be an exaggeration to say that my young spirit was broken.

Finally, it came time for me to go back and finish my last two years of medical school. This is the period when you're allowed to work with real people and when you're exposed to different areas of medicine. This is the point at which you get to decide what kind of doctor you want to be.

I knew in my heart I couldn't deal with contributing to someone's death (or even witnessing people die on a regular basis), so I narrowed my search to more low-key specialties. I also factored in the choice of lifestyle I wanted. I was already older than my colleagues because of the research; and by this time I was newly married, and I knew I wanted a family AND to be able to be home for them.

I chose dermatology as my specialty. I still fight cancer through education and early detection. Most of my patients are glad to see me because I don't have to deliver bad news—at least not very often. I not only help them with their diseases but I also address issues that raise their self-esteem. And I get a lot of variety in my day, seeing patients from babies with eczema to retirees who need skin cancer surgery to the occasional mystery rash that re-ignites my love for detective stories.

So I set out to become a dermatologist; and true to my personality, I was determined to be the best dermatologist I could be in every way. While attending meetings during my training, I took note of which dermatologists were wearing the expensive suits and name-dropping celebrity clients into the conversation. I was impressed when one meeting schedule was completely changed so the dermatologist could attend the Oscars.

I came to understand that behind every beautiful face there was a great dermatologist. And to the young girl in me who wanted the glamour, who had spent so much time in non-glamorous situations, that was very appealing. I made the decision to look to those cosmetic dermatologists as role models and began to learn the tools of the trade. I went to the seminars, took the courses, learned the marketing, and began to attract patients wanting my expertise. I officially bought into the cosmetic mindset.

The next chapter of my life is a lesson from the "be careful what you wish for" school of hard knocks. I built a dermatology practice, not entirely cosmetic, but I spent a fair amount of time doing BoTox and lasers and fillers and peels. However, I had a hard time "selling" the treatments, which is a basic part of being in business. Women would look at me and ask me to tell them what they needed. I could have said a little of this, a little of that, to the tune of thousands of dollars. (It's called "cover your overhead with one patient" in the trade.) But I just couldn't bring myself to do it.

At first, I beat myself up about not being a good salesperson, and then I came to the conclusion that I didn't become a doctor to be a salesperson. I became a doctor to heal people. The selling and fake stuff just didn't resonate with me, and it was not inspiring nor fulfilling to my soul.

It was then that I began to change my conversations with my patients. One day a professional woman came to see me for a skin cancer exam. She was well-spoken and well put together. During the exam she said to me, "I'm beginning to get these wrinkles around my eyes." She didn't say it with much concern or conviction. I got the feeling that she was saying what she thought she was supposed to say to her dermatologist. I think some women are programmed from the magazine and TV ads that say, "This product will make you carefree and you will look ten years younger—ASK YOUR DERMATOLOGIST!!"

I went with my gut feeling; instead of launching into all the ways we could deal with the wrinkles, I said, "Those lines are from smiling."

This took her back for a moment, and then she said, "Well, yes, I guess I do smile a lot."

And I replied, "Then I guess you must come by them honestly."

That cinched it. She thanked me and said she was happy she came to see me. I felt really good because I addressed her problem AND I made her feel better about herself. That is what a healer should do.

The final aha moment for me involved my daughter. She is in seventh grade and just beginning to feel pressure about her looks and clothes. One afternoon when she was in my office after school, she saw some products on display and asked, "Can I have one of these and take some for my friends too?" My first thought was *No, why do you need that?* Of course, I think she is already beautiful. But I was really thinking about the chemicals and the fact that these so-called "cosmeceuticals" are not really regulated by the FDA. I wondered what they would do to a growing body.

And then I began to think about what kind of example I was setting for my own daughter and all other teenage girls. What kind of role model and facilitator of negative self-image was I being by emphasizing these external beauty treatments? Did I want my own daughter to go down this road of chemicals and treatments and be focused on the external; OR would I rather have her grow up comfortable in her own skin, confident and strong? Taking it one step further, I began to wonder why I would offer something in my office that I wouldn't give to my own daughter.

The protective mother instinct and the cancer-fighting scientist in me kicked in and that was it—down came all the displays and the drug company propaganda! From now on, if someone had a direct question for me, I would answer it, but I would not promote any specific treatment or product.

Then came another unexpected fork in my road in both career and life. I had my glamorous job but I was miserable and working very hard, too hard, at it. I felt like I had sold out.

I had my big house but lived alone in it half the time since my divorce. I didn't feel I was contributing much to the world. I felt angry most of the time because I thought I got a raw deal after all that hard work. I started dreading the next bad thing that would come my way. I started doubting myself and my decisions, and I started to live in fear. Mostly, I began to fear death and that my life would be cut short and I would have nothing to show for it. Talk about living in the negative!

And then I had my life-altering spiritual experience. As such things do, it came to me at the exact time it was needed, as if on cue. It came out of the blue when I wasn't looking for it or expecting it. I had no other choice but to accept it as sort of a wake-up call and get my act together.

I was at a conference, and one of the speakers was doing an exercise in shamanic breathing. I wasn't expecting much. At the time I didn't even know what the work *shamanic* meant. I just followed along because I had paid for the conference, and this was part of the program. So there I was breathing, listening to this New Age music, and my body started to tremble. First it was my arms, then my legs, and then I felt this swoosh of air or electricity—I didn't even know what it was—enter my stomach from the left side and then travel up to my head and cause my whole insides to shake.

As you might imagine, this was quite scary! For a few minutes the physician part of me thought the breathing had caused hyperventilation, which had led to a seizure. I thought about someone having to call 911 and what a big scene that would cause. I thought about missing the whole rest of the conference. But on some deeper level I knew I really was fine, and I actually felt a strange kind of calmness.

When the speaker was finished, I was still shaking. I could barely walk, but I managed to grab him in the hallway and ask about what had happened. The words he told me changed my life. He said, "You have just awakened your inner shaman."

Because this was such an intense experience for me and because I am by nature a very curious person, I did not let it go at that. I began to study. I sought out spiritual teachers. I learned that the shaking was energy, or spirit, or life force. The shaking is the oldest form of healing on the planet.

I began to practice the shaking as an alternative to meditation, which really wasn't doing much for me anyway. I explored energy work and spiritual concepts. I tried to "test" this method on myself as I would an experiment, thinking that it was a fluke and it would stop working and I could go back to my cynical scientific life. But it has never failed me yet.

One of the most important lessons I learned during this journey, and I will credit Dr. Bradford Keeney for teaching this to me, is that to be a true healer you must have an open heart. I was used to living in my brain, approaching my patients and my own life like a puzzle to solve. I struggled to understand the how and why of everything. I was a compassionate physician, but I listened with my brain and not my heart.

I had to learn to LET GO of the mind and just accept that something wonderful was out there for me. I didn't have to know what it was or have a plan for how to get there. I began to wake up every morning looking forward to what I would learn that day. I accepted every challenge as a gift.

I opened my heart to my patients and they definitely noticed. I started to get hugs and more laughter. I heard stories and fears and questions that had never surfaced before. I even received a few cards. Here is one example:

Dear Dr. Silvers,

I wish to let you know how grateful I am for your consultation and treatment of my skin condition. The healing feels to be holding, thank God.

I am getting ready to leave for Greece some time in the near future, and I can't help savoring the sense of freedom that came with that healing! I need to confess that in your person I found not only a skilled and excellent physician but also a kind and generous and gentle human being. God bless you! With many, many thanks—

Sincerely,

CAV

The GlowTox Method

As a result of my professional and life experiences, as well as my new-found spiritual path, I created a new concept that is both a revolution and an evolution in skin care. I call it GlowTox.

It's an approach to life—a philosophy of sorts—that promotes the nurturing of our inner selves in order to achieve real beauty from the inside out. If you are happy, confident, and fulfilled on the inside, your radiant essential beauty will shine through your physical body no matter what that body looks like and no matter how you choose to cover it. Your soul is what determines who you are, not the external features that our society so loudly emphasizes. Injections, magical lotions, and potions are all different masks that actually hide your true inner glow.

Why do we feel it is necessary to cover ourselves up with these types of masks? In my experience these are the main reasons:

- We are scared to show our true selves to the world for fear of judgment, rejection, or even ridicule.
- We're worried we will not be accepted for who we are.
- We feel we're not _____ enough (fill in the blank: *young, pretty, thin, interesting*) as we are.
- We buy into the belief that our looks are our most valuable asset, and we protect them at all cost.
- We're worried that once we remove the mask there will be nothing behind it. How awkward would that be?
- We are afraid to stand out as unique and different.
- We think the media knows more about beauty than we do.
- We care more about trends and fads than honoring our bodies.
- We focus on one little detail of our skin so we can ignore the big picture that we are really unhappy inside.

The culture of the beauty and fashion industry deftly and expertly feeds into these base fears and creates advertising campaigns that further erode our sense of self in the interest of luring our dollars from our pockets.

Here's an enlightening true story: A woman came to me with an allergic rash that was painful and itchy. We determined that the possible culprit was a new cream she had used. I treated her for the rash and sent her on her way. Two weeks later, she was in my office again for the exact same rash. Thinking I'd missed something the first time, I asked her what she was using on her face. She sheepishly told me it was the same cream.

"Why did you use that again?" I asked.

Her answer: "Because it is Chanel!"

Unfortunately, this isn't uncommon! I have all but given up hope of treating allergies on the eyelids because so few women will give up the products that cause it. So they use something that is harmful because it's in a magazine or pitched by a celebrity or they got a good deal or it's a brand name. We shoot our faces full of plastic (excuse me, "bio-engineered microspheres") to look younger or look a trendy way.

A dermatologist once told me that he could tell which women were from Northern California and which were from Southern California just by their lips, because the acceptable "look" was different. Is this really where we want to focus? A fully empowered woman in the modern world does not use a mask to hide anything. She lets her inner glow shine proudly!

We need to believe in this concept for ourselves and our daughters.
- We can support each other to feel comfortable in our own skin without all the extras.
- We can believe we are worth more than our looks.
- We can empower ourselves to follow what we believe instead of what's popular at the time.
- We can nurture our inner selves and thus transform the world.

So where do we go from here?

Ten million cosmetic procedures were performed in the United States in 2009, to the tune of $10.5 billion. I will pick on BoTox because its parent company, Allergan, prides itself on promoting that it is the most common cosmetic procedure performed in the U.S. Over 3 million people per year have at least one BoTox treatment. This is serious "Big Business," and it is funded by a drug company with a big marketing budget. In fact, just as I was writing this piece, I saw a marketing advertorial—an ad disguised as a news article promoting its new line of fillers, all to make you look younger, for a mere $400-$500 dollars per treatment.

Let's take this a little further: If 10,000 of those women getting BoTox treatments were enlightened enough to give up their treatments for a year (that is 4 times a year at a conservative estimate of $300 per treatment) that would be $1,200 per woman and would collectively amount to $12 million saved annually! That's enough money to buy science books for 200,000 elementary school kids. It would fund an after-school enrichment program (including snacks) for 180,000 of our brightest students. Or it could pay for 300 music teachers in our schools. As mothers and leaders of social change, what is our real priority here?

Many women reading this chapter may not use BoTox, so here's another example to put this into perspective. I recently shopped at the cosmetic counter of a major department store without giving away my occupation. I was sold an average of 5 products, requiring 4-6 steps twice a day. Do you have time for this? I know I don't. The average price for these regimens was $200. Assuming you would need to refill at least 4 times per year, that is a total of $800 per year, without counting the time involved in all those steps.

What do you really need to take care of your basic needs? How about a mild cleanser and a moisturizer with sunscreen? You can add an over-the-counter anti-aging product. The total cost would be about $120 per year. Now think about the impact those dollars could make in the world around you. What might happen if you stopped spending $800 per year on skin products and instead focused on a balanced diet, regular sunscreen, and letting your inner light shine?

I'll leave you with a final thought. Do you know what happens if you overdose on fillers and BoTox? First, your face looks like one of those puffer fish and everyone really does know you had "something" done. And although it's not likely to happen, if you do too much BoTox, you could end up not being able to support your head on your own neck. In that case, you'd have to have both a breathing tube and a feeding tube.

Do you know what happens if you overdose on GlowTox? The treatment is instantaneous and the results are long-lasting. People smile at you when you walk down the street. They open doors for you and tell you funny stories while you are standing in line at the grocery store. Wonderful synchronicities appear. It happened to me, it happens for my patients, and it can happen to you too. Give it a try. Ask yourself, *What face do I really want to present to the world?* You might as well face it—it's your life!

About the Author

Dr. Kim Silvers graduated from Case Western Reserve University in Cleveland, Ohio, with an M.D. Ph.D. and did her residency training in Dermatology at S.U.N.Y. at StonyBrook on Long Island. She moved back near her family in upstate New York when her children were born. Three years ago she was able to open her own private practice in Ithaca, New York, and has not looked back since. She is now focused on learning alternative healing techniques to add to her practice and will open a new Center for Health and Regeneration within the next year. This unique practice will help clients to maintain optimal mind and body health by combining the latest techniques in energy medicine and science.

Dr. Kim spends her free time exploring life with her two children, learning the guitar with her son, and tending her gardens. She is also currently working on *The GlowTox Method*, a full-length book and workbook.

For more information on GlowTox support groups or Dr. Kim's private practice, visit www.ithacadermatology.com. For more information on GlowTox, visit Dr. Kim's community at http://GlowToxCommunity.com.

$\mathcal{F}$ree Your Soul™

by Dr. Pamela Zimmer

Born Conscious

My first seven years on the planet were rather bleak. I was sure someone made a huge mistake placing me here. I used to envision a large elevator descending from the sky with me in it. The doors would open, letting me out . . . on the wrong floor! I would look up to the heavens and inform whoever was listening of their mistake in letting me out in the wrong world! It was all to no avail. I seemed to be stuck here against my will!

Before we come into bodies, we are in a dimension in which our Souls are conscious and powerful. We make plans about coming to the planet in a body. We feel there's nothing we cannot handle and that we will use all situations to create more with deliberate intention. We embrace the challenge of being submerged into the density of this world, along with its seemingly unforgiving nature and the fact that everyone here has free will to operate as they please. But things may not go according to plan after all.

Our problem is that once we come through the birth canal and into the physical density, we begin to forget who we are and all the fantastic divine plans we made. And the more we experience the feeling of being physical, the further away we get from our Soul-Selves.

My experience was unique. I was *born conscious* and remained that way! I remembered who I was on a Soul level, the hugeness and expansiveness of being a Soul, and my connection to the Universe and all the energy around me. I kept expecting to see a reflection of the beauty and light my Soul contained, but all I saw outside of my Soul was ugliness and darkness. I thought I was coming into a heaven-on-earth world, since that's what my Soul was vibrating to, so I could not understand what I was doing here in this world. Instead of celebrating my arrival here, I felt alone and miserable. I knew I didn't belong here.

I had no idea how to integrate the expansiveness of my Soul into the physical density of my body and this world. Rather than allowing my Higher Self to be expressed, my physicality resisted the stark contrast; and I just felt completely out of alignment with my Soul's consciousness. I lived in a state of miserable resistance to being here, feeling isolated and remaining tightly confined and contained inside a body I didn't seem to fit in.

Unhappy in my home environment because of the unhealthy dynamics, the lack of real love, and the major dysfunction I experienced there, I couldn't wait to leave the house every day to go to kindergarten.

Things changed, however, when I got to second grade. I had a teacher who I thought was sweet and charming, and she became the first adult in my life whom I admired and desired to emulate. So when I was falsely accused of cheating by a classmate and this same teacher decided to punish me and make an example of me in a very humiliating way, without ever asking me what my side of the story was, I was devastated. I felt totally betrayed by her. Then I realized that she really didn't know me at all and was just as disconnected from her true self as all the other adults were!

Although I was just seven years old, my Soul-Self saw the complete injustice of the situation. Protecting me from the potentially destructive effects on my psyche, my Soul-Self turned me internally to stone so I would be totally detached emotionally from what was happening.

The traumatic effect of this episode changed me. I had been unfairly treated, unjustly punished, and had to turn to stone to protect my inner self. I could never allow myself to connect with another teacher. Now I was more miserable than ever being here on the planet. I just wanted out!

That's what I thought about . . . how to leave here. There was no place I felt safe. I was completely alone with these thoughts and feelings because

I knew no one would understand what I was experiencing. I felt trapped here. I contained the conscious Soul of Humanity but had no idea how to translate that into my physical experience to transform my world. So if I couldn't free my Soul, what purpose was I serving by remaining here?

A Life-Changing Vision

That's when I received an extraordinary metaphysical vision that forever changed my life. This two-part vision ultimately revealed to me my divine purpose and my mission on Earth.

In the first part of my vision, I was sitting up on my bed in the middle of the night when a strange-looking being from another planet suddenly appeared next to me. I was startled but not alarmed, as I only felt warm, loving energy coming from him and knew I was safe. We communicated telepathically. He presented a map of the galaxy and pointed to one of the very distant stars, noting that was where he came from. Intuitively I had the sense that he had the power to travel and materialize without a vehicle.

He conveyed that they knew of me on his planet and who I really was; they were aware of my plight here on Earth. He invited me to join them on his planet. He said it was totally up to me to decide if I wanted to accept or not. Nothing would happen until I made my decision, and I could take all the time I needed. Then he projected into my mind's eye a vision of me sitting on a throne surrounded by circles of hundreds of these beings, all identical to him. They were honoring me, showing me appreciation, and loving me unconditionally. It seemed like I was a queen on his planet! When I asked what I would have to do there to earn such royal treatment, he said that all I had to do was be me, that I was enough and was worthy of such great love and admiration exactly as I was. He said he would return when I reached my decision. With that, he disappeared as instantly as he had appeared.

I pondered this decision long and hard. What would be the effect on me if I stayed? What would be the ramifications for myself and others if I left? While other seven-year-old girls were playing with their Barbie® dolls, I was making the most monumental decision of my life.

I became aware that God was the source of this vision and that it was sent so I would have to make a deliberate choice. Now I understood that God cared enough about me to want to empower me with my own free will by allowing me to decide for myself whether I wanted to remain here or not.

Although the beings in my vision were beautiful and loving on the inside, their outer appearance was quite unappealing; and they all looked identical. Human beings appeared beautiful and were appealing on the outside, inviting in their visual variety. However, on the inside there left much to be desired. Yet my Soul knew that what I was seeing was not their higher truth. Ultimately, I decided to stay here to see it through, with the hope that one day I would get to experience the full potential of the human race.

Having made my choice, I received the next part of the vision. Once again, I was sitting up on my bed in the middle of the night when the same alien appeared next to me, telepathically revealing his awareness that I'd made my decision. He told me I had chosen well and that now I could finally feel that I was here on Earth in accord with my own free will rather than against it. He understood that I wanted to see things through with other human beings in the hope of having the best of both worlds here on Earth— the internal beauty of his and the external beauty of mine. He also relayed that after enduring many years of pain and suffering, I would ultimately find the way to manifest the world transformed into the heaven on earth that was my Soul's vision when I first arrived—a world of unconditional love, peace, and joy, where we were all free to be! He said he would not return, since my decision was final. With that, he once again evaporated into thin air.

In that moment, I was endowed with the full faith of my Soul-Self in connection with the Universe. From that point on, despite what I saw or experienced in contradiction to my higher truth and divine purpose of manifesting a world of unconditional love and true humanity, I would stay strong, never wavering from my path. It is the memory of this divine, otherworldly vision that has provided the foundation of faith that supports me and keeps me here in alignment with my true Self, experiencing high

SoulEsteem™ and serving my Soul so that I can serve the Soul of Humanity.

Raising SoulEsteem™

Throughout my childhood and adolescence, I felt very unsure of how to actually be me here on Earth. Although I was conscious of my Soul-Self and internally lived in a world in which I was fully empowered, I was unable to integrate that sense of confidence and knowing into my external beingness. Even though I felt insecure on the outside, I realized that I did have high SoulEsteem™ on the inside. I continually honored and valued my Soul-Self and my connection to the Universe regardless of what was going on around me. This enabled me to listen to my inner voice, rely on my intuition, and believe in the higher truth that informed me through my Soul and the Universe. Fortunately, having high SoulEsteem™ saved me from much of the conditioning of this world. I simply saw right through most of the thought patterns, as they stood in direct contradiction to my Soul's truth.

My personal experience led me to realize that it is essential for women to develop high SoulEsteem™ so that they can begin living more authentic lives in alignment with their true Selves. And since having high SoulEsteem™ saved me from succumbing to so many of the conditioned beliefs and illusions imposed on women, then reversing those conditioned beliefs for women will allow them to raise their SoulEsteem™.

Although a myriad of beliefs have been imposed upon women since the beginning of time, I have selected the four most prevalent ones that have been key in keeping women unconscious about who they really are and unaware of how powerful they can be, as individuals and as a gender.

External Beauty

The conditioned belief of External Beauty is a myth that has long been perpetrated upon women everywhere. When you look in the mirror, what do you see? Most women see their flaws and imperfections. That is because they are looking at their outer physical image and judging it against an arbitrary set of standards that was imposed upon them. We as women feel compelled to adhere to a standard of beauty that was determined by where we were raised as well as by the culture into which we were born. We begin to internalize these arbitrary standards that were initially imposed upon us, and eventually they take over as the set standard of beauty to which we aspire.

When I was growing up, I was physically self-conscious. I felt awkward in my body and couldn't find too much about it that pleased me. Even if someone told me that I was pretty, I could not relate to it. However, every time I caught a glimpse of my inner self, my Soul-Self, a true and abiding beauty was revealed to me. I began to see it, feel it, and know it on a very deep level. I came to understand that this was the real beauty to which we women should aspire—not some arbitrary standard of beauty designed to objectify us and keep us from realizing our true inner beauty.

How can we reverse this conditioning? We begin by changing the way we look at ourselves in the mirror. Instead of scanning your face and body for its flaws and imperfections, gaze deeply into your eyes—the windows to your Soul—and begin to perceive the inner beauty that emanates from your essence. Tell yourself out loud, *I AM beautiful*.

The more you engage in this exchange with your inner Self, the easier it gets for you to summon forth your sense of your true inner beauty and the more natural it becomes for you to emanate that beauty and light to others. And therein lies the key to exposing the myth of External Beauty and raising our SoulEsteem™.

Nothing makes a woman more beautiful than the belief she is beautiful.
-Sophia Loren

Unworthiness

Unworthiness affects our gender throughout the world. All forms of unworthiness that have been imposed upon us as women serve to devalue us, informing us that we are not good enough the way we are and, therefore, we are not deserving or worthy of everything that we desire.

The accumulation of repeatedly being devalued in some way, beginning when we are small and continuing into our adulthood, takes a toll on any feelings of worthiness we may still have. As women, we end up feeling that we are not enough and there's not enough we can do to be enough. This leads to that deep feeling of unworthiness in each of us that we now have to overcome. How do we do that?

We face it, we embrace it, and we replace it. We face it by understanding that we are operating in a state of unworthiness and that we are probably settling for far less than we actually want or deserve. *We embrace it* by accepting ourselves where we are, with the new understanding that we were systematically conditioned to believe that we are less than we truly are. *We replace it* with these new thought patterns: *I am here; therefore, I am worthy and I am enough. I am a woman; therefore, I am worthy and I am enough. I am a human being; therefore, I am worthy and I am enough.* This creates a solid foundation of worthiness in each of us while raising our SoulEsteem™ as individuals and as a gender.

False Modesty

False Modesty, which stems from fear, is another conditioned belief that has been instilled in women. In this state, women are asked to dim their light, or even hide their light, in some way that prevents them from shining in their full empowerment.

We learned as young girls that we are not supposed to boast about our attributes, talents, or gifts. We are supposed to be the best we can be and to strive to be great at everything; yet we're not to talk about it because that would be conceited and unladylike! But women need to feel comfortable about honestly expressing their genuine attributes that come from a connection with who they really are in their higher selves. We need to give ourselves permission to stop being falsely modest. You may find that other women take issue with you when you compliment yourself out loud, but that is due to their own discomfort with praising themselves.

Did you ever want to express some fantastic thing about yourself and yet held it back because you didn't feel free to share it? It's time for women to reverse this condition. How can we do this?

Start by first really getting in touch with those assets that you own inside yourself. What gifts do you actually have? What talents do you possess that you can feel good about and that you can own?

Next, gaze deeply into your eyes in the mirror, making a Soul-to-Soul connection, and state each one of those attributes, gifts, and talents out loud. Start by declaring, *I own my power.* Then begin to list each one of those aspects that make you feel fantastic and fabulous, that depict the unique individual that you are.

I guarantee that if you do this exercise every single day you will begin to shift your energy and raise your vibration. From now on, when you go out in the world, you own your power. And you feel that you truly have these attributes with you always, whether you choose to express them out loud or not.

Your playing small does not serve the world. There is nothing enlightened about shrinking so that other people won't feel insecure around you. We are all meant to shine . . . . And as we let our own light shine, we unconsciously give other people permission to do the same.   -Marianne Williamson

Competition

Competition is another belief that has been imposed upon us. We are raised in a world that is highly competitive; throughout our lives, competition is encouraged. It starts in our home, when we are small children vying for our parents' attention or competing to be acknowledged over our siblings. It continues in school, when we are pushed to get better grades than our classmates. When we're adults, we compete with others for jobs.

One major area of competition among girls is competing for boys. It starts when two girls are interested in the same boy and compete for him as if he is the prize. Unfortunately, this trend continues into adulthood!

First of all, it does not serve women well to view a man as a prize. Instead, consider your own Self as the prize! Second, competing for that "prize" actually takes you out of alignment with your true Self. And that is the real point I'm making. All women are actually disconnecting from their authentic Selves when they go into any kind of competition. Competing puts them in a race to prove that they're better than another; they are the winner, and someone else becomes the loser. Based on whether they win or lose, their self-esteem either gets raised or lowered. It just does not work for us. Actually, it works against us.

What can we do about this? *We can face it, we can embrace it, and we can replace it! We face it* by realizing all of the ways that we actually do compete in our lives, often with other women. Then *we embrace it* by first accepting ourselves where we are, with the realization that we have had this sense of competing imposed upon us, making us feel that it is something we must do in order to succeed in this world. *We replace it* with the understanding that there is actually a right place for each one of us. As unique individuals, we each have our own right place that serves our highest and best interests. Your right place belongs to you, and my right place belongs to me. There's no competition for it, because it was uniquely and perfectly designed to support who you are, allowing you to be all that you can be.

Imagine a world in which we each can be fully realized in our own right place without ever feeling threatened that somebody is going to compete with us to take it away. That is part of my vision for a transformed world!

Free Your Soul™

I've focused on the impact that these conditioned beliefs have had on women and how they were intentionally imposed upon us by design in order to weaken our gender and prevent our full empowerment. Any conditioning we succumb to as women has the effect of imprisoning our Souls, but our Souls long to be free. That is why it is crucial that we reverse the effect of these beliefs on our systems, that we release them from our minds, and that we replace them with the authentic truth that our Souls contain.

The result will be an automatic raising of our SoulEsteem™, allowing us to value and honor our Soul-Selves, our essence, our higher truth, and our connection to the Universe. As women, it is most important that we develop and raise our SoulEsteem™ as this is key to acknowledging our authenticity and becoming who we truly were born to be. With high SoulEsteem™, we are able to tune in to our intuition and listen to our inner voice, the guidance that comes from our Higher Selves. We become more purposeful and in alignment with who we are and why we are here. We flow with consciousness and intention as we carve out our path to our greatest joy, highest ideals, and most liberating freedom.

We ultimately free our Souls when we free our minds from all the conditioned beliefs that were imposed upon us as women in this world, in modern days as well as ancient times. We then replace that flawed conditioning with our own authentic truths and begin to express these from the Soul, trusting the process and having faith in our Soul-Selves to bring us where we want to go. In order for women to fully participate in the next stage of co-creating and manifesting our transformed world, it is crucial that the conditioning of our gender be released and replaced with our inner knowing.

If you've ever wondered what kept blocking you from realizing your true desires and living authentically, this is your wake-up call. It is time to start operating consciously and in alignment with your Higher Self so that together we can, in unity and harmony, free our minds of all conditioned beliefs that have been imposed upon us as a gender, free our hearts by opening them to unconditional love, and free our Souls so that we can ultimately live in a world of our own creation, a world that vibrates to the essence of who we are, a world that allows us to be the Divine feminine beings we truly are, a world that expresses the Soul of Humanity!

So let's join together to bring about our complete liberation . . . and have a Soul-gasm in unison!

About the Author

Dr. Pamela Zimmer combines her Ph.D. in metaphysics and parapsychology with her degrees in psychology and education to serve as a psychospiritual therapist in the Human Relations Center for Women, which she founded in 1989. She is also the author of *Sex, Lies and Sabotage,* a book that takes women from relationship sabotage to relationship transformation. Dr. Pamela draws from her deeply personal and spiritual experiences as well as her Soul's vast knowledge of the truth beyond the illusions to help women begin to recognize their authentic Selves, free of the conditioning that has long impacted them.

Having been born conscious and highly intuitive, Dr. Pamela saw the world through the eyes of her Soul-Self. And what she saw in the outer world was in total misalignment with her inner world. She realized early on that she would have to find the way to manifest her Soul's vision for a transformed world that resonated to a much higher vibrational frequency. This then formed and informed her higher purpose of creating heaven on earth.

To further expand her vision on a practical level, Dr. Pamela founded the Free Your Soul Community, a place where women can learn to free their minds of all the conditioned beliefs that have been imposed upon them, free their hearts by opening them to unconditional love, and, ultimately, free their Souls by raising their Soul-Esteem™ and consciously and intuitively expressing their higher truth as fully liberated women.

To find out more about Dr. Pamela's work, visit www.DrPamela.com or e-mail her at info@DrPamela.com. To find out more about her community, go to http://FreeYourSoulCommunity.com.

The She Optimal Adventure

by Dr. Angela Sorensen

It has now been three hours of waiting, waiting, waiting. My seven-year-old son, Danny, was scheduled for a brain MRI and we were still waiting to get called back for the procedure. He had experienced a possible seizure and demonstrated an abnormal reflex, which needed further evaluation. Danny was patient but restless because it was his birthday and he wanted to get out of the hospital and start his celebration. Feeling bad for Danny, the nurses gave him a big container of jellybeans, which he accepted with a big grin.

We were finally called back, and Danny underwent the MRI. Then we were asked to stay because the radiologist might want to do a few more scans. *Why?* I wondered. But I was not concerned. Danny had a few more scans taken, with contrast. Once that was done, we were asked to stay awhile longer so copies could be made of the scans. Then I was instructed to take them to our pediatrician the next morning. When I asked what this was all about, I was told that I would have to wait and discuss the findings with our pediatrician. By now, we had spent at least six hours at the hospital.

When we got home, I got a call from our pediatrician, who was also a good friend. She warned, "Are you sitting down?" She told me that based on the MRI scans, it looked like Danny had a brain tumor and would probably be in surgery the next week. I couldn't breathe. I felt paralyzed. Panic set in. *This has to be a mistake,* I told myself.

During our subsequent visits with the neurosurgeon and pediatric neurologist we learned that Danny definitely had a brain lesion. But it might not actually be a tumor. Thus, the neurosurgeon decided not to do surgery immediately but monitor the growth of the lesion instead.

We repeated the MRIs every month for three months. Danny helped make the process easier to accept as he followed through with the monthly IV process and MRIs, which can be very scary, with such strength and without complaint. Most kids require sedation during the procedure, but not Danny—he wanted to be alert and awake! While he was lying down in the MRI machine, I would stand by his feet in his range of sight. I would talk with him to reduce his anxiety from the strange noises and remind him to lie still and not to move his head. The staff remembered him and said things such as, "This is the brave boy who never flinches with his IV and doesn't want to be sedated." That always made Danny feel good. He would sometimes reassure me since he knew I was nervous.

After three months without any active lesion growth but also no resolution, the neurosurgeon suggested that Danny undergo a brain biopsy. When we explained this procedure to Danny, he left the room and returned after ten minutes with a drawing of what he understood was to happen during the biopsy. It was an amazing cross-section view of a head with a brain inside, along with a hand holding a needle that reached the "spot" in his brain. We gave the picture to the neurosurgeon, and he has since used it in his PowerPoint presentations.

The day of the biopsy was incredibly stressful. Afterwards, I stayed overnight at the hospital. Danny wanted me to snuggle in bed with him. That was tough to do with his IV, but I did it. Unfortunately, after he went through the rigors of the biopsy, his findings were inconclusive.

When Danny returned to school, his classmates asked about the shaved part of his head and the bandage. He innocently told them, "I had surgery on my brain," which resulted in kids teasing him about something being wrong with his brain.

A few months later, we had another scare. Danny was playing dodge ball at school and a new kid accidentally pushed him into a concrete wall as they both tried to retrieve the ball. Danny's forehead was cut to the bone and resulted in quite a bloody mess. The school called me to come get Danny and I thought, *Not his head!* When I arrived in the health room, Danny was lying on the table. He said, "I'm okay, Mommy. Don't worry." As we left school to go to the ER, we passed by the boy who had pushed Danny. He was crying. Danny told him, "It's okay, I know it was an accident."

Danny had a CT scan to make sure his skull had not been fractured, which could cause an infection of the brain. This was no big deal for Danny after the MRIs he had endured. At our next appointment with the neurosurgeon, he said it was a good sign that the trauma had not caused a seizure, so I guess there was a positive aspect to the incident.

One major challenge for me was to avoid being overprotective of Danny. This could affect his self-esteem, since he'd probably interpret my desire to keep him safe as my thinking he was incapable of doing things. Being a neuropsychologist who worked with adults experiencing problems with their thinking abilities related to brain conditions, I was well aware of the worst-case scenarios. So I knew too much and was challenged with trying to keep things in perspective and not let my imagination run wild!

My husband and I only shared Danny's medical status with a few people because we were concerned about teasing and others making assumptions about him that might not be true. We wanted him to be treated just like any other second grader.

I had grown up in a health-conscious family. My mother was quite sneaky in getting us to eat well. She would add various "goodies," like wheat germ, to recipes she made. Thus I understood good nutrition, was very active, and pushed myself to be the best I could be and to attain various goals. Being a psychologist, I was very aware of the effects of stress on one's physical, mental, emotional, and spiritual well-being. But nothing can prepare you for the news that your child likely has an inoperable brain tumor, so initially it was a challenge to function. I knew that I had to be physically and mentally strong, with optimal energy and a positive focus, to best support Danny and deal effectively with the unknowns ahead. I couldn't think about the potential negative "what-ifs," because I would drive myself crazy and feel more stressed. As a mother, I also needed Danny to be as healthy and strong as possible so that he could be resilient and meet whatever physical, emotional, and mental demands he might face in the future. Typically, the more cognitive reserve one develops prior to a brain insult or condition, the more cognitive ability is available to draw upon; however, that is dependent upon the insult and some other factors.

When a person is under stress, energy levels are drained much faster than normal. So it was necessary for me to take better care of myself, for my sake as well as for Danny's. He was depending on me to help him through this tough time. I couldn't take care of him if I didn't have the energy reserves to keep myself mentally strong and physically healthy.

Danny has internalized his own sense of being optimal and is doing very well. He is a healthy and happy 14 year old, a very good student and a high-ranked chess player for his age. He stopped playing chess for a while due to teasing about being a "chess geek." This really disappointed me because I wanted him to have the mental stimulation provided by the game of chess, but I did not want to force him to play. After a few months, he missed chess and wanted to play again, despite the teasing. I was thrilled. He is physically fit and prides himself on his "six-pack" abs and being able to do the most pull-ups in his class—at least 30. He also has healthful eating habits. His classmates make fun of his lunches, which may include almond-butter sandwiches, fruit, water, V8® juice, and Greek yogurt for more protein. One of his teachers even asked him why he didn't make his own lunches so he could include more yummy items. He was quite surprised when Danny said that he requested to have these items in his lunch.

Danny's lesion has remained stable. No one would know that he'd ever had any medical scare. His current follow-up plan is a repeat MRI every other year. In fact, our neurosurgeon told us that he is unsure about the original diagnosis, although he is unable to give a definitive diagnosis. Thus the lesion is no longer a factor in how we live our lives. Danny is not "out of the woods," but if something were to occur, I am confident that we will be resilient in dealing with the circumstances the best we can, as a family.

My desire to pursue an optimal lifestyle began after Danny's diagnosis. Though already health conscious, I realized how much more there was to being optimal. I felt a transformation in me as I reflected upon my life and learned a new sense of acceptance of what is and to move forward from that place. If you fight something like this, it will cause more stress and resistance, sapping your necessary energy stores. That's not to say that you can't feel a sense of despair. I felt that way at first. It's normal and to be expected. I honored my feelings, but I didn't allow myself to stay in despair too long because that might pull me down. There is actually much to appreciate and celebrate, even in potentially dire circumstances.

I've grown so much through the process; yet I still have much more to learn and experience as I still have many insecurities and fears. It is a continual personal evolution as I strive to be more optimal in various aspects of my life. I'm passionate about pursuing a life of optimal vitality. It is not always easy, and I sometimes falter. The journey has its ups and downs, but it is worth the effort required to advance from "good to great."

We all face bad news when life throws us a major curve ball. Some bad news can be incredibly overwhelming and paralyzing, but how we choose to deal with our struggles and life circumstances is what's most important. Our choices impact the course of what is happening and the path we take in allowing for optimal growth in ourselves and our life.

Creating the She Optimal Process

I no longer work as a neuropsychologist. Although I am very grateful for who I am and for my life, I know that I can BE and FEEL even better, and so can you. I created the She Optimal process because it has become my purpose to inspire and encourage other women to enjoy optimal vitality—the feeling of physical and mental aliveness. Vitality is approaching life with excitement, positive energy, and a sense of adventure.

I developed the She Optimal process around eight Os, or qualities, that I believe are foundational to living a life of optimal vitality. These eight Os are rather all-encompassing and can incorporate other important aspects as well. So why are these important? If you want to be happy, healthy, prosperous, satisfied with your relationships, of greater service to others, and able to fulfill your personal destiny, then you must be optimal. The philosophy behind the She Optimal process includes eight Os:

1. How to apply the key factors to **Optimal Longevity,** such as mental stimulation, physical and emotional health, and meaningful connections with self and others, including collaborating with your purpose in life— This includes living fully and with passion, seizing opportunities, making healthy lifestyle choices, maximizing energy, and having a high quality of life lived within your years.

2. How to cultivate **Optimal Acceptance,** including accepting what was, what is, and what may be— This also includes accepting and forgiving yourself and others and "letting go" of negativity so you can appreciate what is, move forward, and live in the present. It is also about being a supportive and compassionate friend to yourself, as you can't truly love others until you accept and love yourself.

3. How to recognize your **Optimal Resourcefulness** and become aware of its untapped potential— This includes accessing inner and outer resources to overcome challenges, fostering an "I can" attitude to increase confidence, recognize appropriate options, and develop self-reliance. It also incorporates wisdom and an optimistic approach to life.

4. How to learn the art of **Optimal Curiosity,** which allows you to be curious and open to explore new experiences— Curiosity is key to creativity. It fuels the imagination and promotes the mind to ask questions that unleash creativity. Curiosity inspires new experiences, problem solving, lifelong learning, self-awareness, and greater appreciation of our world.

5. How to tap into **Optimal Authenticity,** which is how you stay true to yourself and your values— Being transparent may cause you to be more vulnerable, but having the courage to do so will allow you to be stronger and more aware of who you were meant to be. Communicating with authenticity allows you to create more meaningful relationships. When you share your true self, others will appreciate your honesty and

imperfections and likely trust you more. Being authentic is also related to self-acceptance, in being satisfied with who you are so that you can express yourself openly rather than hide behind a façade. It provides you the freedom to just be "you" as you learn to close the gap between who you are and how you show up in life and live life the way you were meant to live it. It is through relationships with others that you grow, create, gain courage to move forward despite fears, get in touch with your authentic self, and live your truths.

6. How to practice **Optimal Responsibility** to support your courage to follow through with your commitments and visions— This implies accountability for your behavior but is also "response-ability," the ability to choose your responses in any situation and direct your own life. Even in tough times, you can still choose your attitude.

7. How to enjoy **Optimal Celebration** of yourself and your small accomplishments along the way— Make it a priority to celebrate who you are, what you've done, and what you want to encourage more of in yourself and your life. What you appreciate in yourself and your life becomes more valuable to you, and you take better care of the things that you appreciate. It is especially important to celebrate when you are experiencing significant struggles, as appreciation can bring about a better attitude and increased resources to find creative solutions.

8. How to pursue **Optimal Integration** of body, mind, emotions, and spirit, which are interconnected— You are a holistic being who functions best when these four areas are in harmony. To perform at a high level, you must manage your energy in these areas and take time to rejuvenate.

Later I added a ninth O to the She Optimal process—**Optimal Looseness**—as I was finding myself getting too serious about myself and my life. I needed more spontaneity, playfulness, and joy. My training and experience as a psychologist had better developed my left brain, the intellectual and analytic side, rather than the right brain, which is more involved with creative abilities. Using both sides of the brain in harmony

184

is important for successful change. The logical left side plans how to get from point A to point B, solves problems, and analyzes what is and is not working; the right side keeps you motivated.

Being optimal is a personal process; it is different for everyone based on individual interests, backgrounds, and experiences. It does not imply perfection. Your own She Optimal process is based on your personal circumstances and responsibilities, such as family and work. So be your best, depending upon your situation. This is not a set "one size fits all" program, but these guidelines are valuable for anyone and everyone to follow and apply as they feel appropriate.

I believe that we can hardly afford NOT to live an optimal life! Choosing to be optimal and committing to practice virtues that are most important to you—such as love, courage, and wisdom—will increase your level of happiness, which is actually the ultimate goal in life. It has been shown that people who feel a connection to something larger than themselves or are involved in meaningful service to others and the world are happier in general. In turn, happy people tend to live longer and healthier lives and have better relationships and social support.

She Optimal and the Movement for Change in the World

There are important advancements to be made by women in the world, including beautifying our surroundings, promoting wellness, providing community services, and alleviating human and environmental suffering. Women care about the state of the world and need to take action to improve human rights, conservation, sustainability, mental and physical health, education, compassion for others, and peace across the globe.

Female leadership is more collaborative in nature. By pulling resources together and appreciating different backgrounds, perspectives, and skills, women complement each other and make joint efforts more effective. Women can share what they know and encourage diverse and healthy debates. We share many more similarities than differences with women all over the world. Although healthy competition has advanced society and elevated our standard of living, too much competition may be detrimental. Incorporating healthy competition by encouraging excellence in another's achievement may be inspirational and progressive for all.

How is being She Optimal important for making positive change in the world? Transformation occurs within relationships with oneself, others, nature, and the divine, which are all interconnected. Gandhi stated that we must become the change we want to see in the world. So change begins with the individual, but it is through relationships with others that you truly learn about yourself. A She Optimal woman knows that she can and will make a difference in the world. If she doesn't yet know her unique purpose, gifts, and talents, she will discover, pursue, and realize them. In addition to identifying what she is good at doing and being, she must identify what makes her feel energized, since she may be good at some things that do not interest her. If she does not feel qualified, ready, or that she has anything to offer, she cannot use that as an excuse. She can definitely play a part! Teddy Roosevelt said, "Do what you can, with what you have, where you are."

As the She Optimal woman personally develops aspects of herself and becomes more optimal, she can own her voice and feel more confident in her abilities. She will have the energy and resources required to work toward living her passions and closing the gap between what she is currently making happen in her life and her actual potential. She can focus on positive and purposeful activities that support visions for self and others, rather than being limited by her own problems and circumstances. She will feel less overwhelmed by challenges, be more resilient during tough times, and be more creative in her problem solving. She will also be more optimistic, forward thinking, and focused on possibilities.

Many women feel unfulfilled or question whether they are living up to their potential. These women are seeking guidance from mentors to support their growth towards personal, social, and economic empowerment. A She Optimal woman can become a caring, enthusiastic, and engaging role model for other women. She will demonstrate the importance of physical and mental health, meaningful connections, acceptance, resourcefulness, curiosity, authenticity, personal responsibility, and celebration. Others will be attracted to her integrity, vitality, courage, compassion, and creativity.

A She Optimal woman can also play active leadership roles within her personal sphere of influence and join other women in their quest. She Optimal women can create a ripple effect by influencing positive change within ourselves, our families, our communities, and ultimately on a global scale. By forming meaningful partnerships with other women who share similar values and visions, we can create greater momentum to progress toward our goals. It's important for us to be supportive of each other, as women may not speak out unless other women back their efforts. Together we can grow a network of committed and capable women who have the desire and conviction to lead and expand positive change. We now have the technology and resources for global communication. However, we must be optimal to fully participate, serve, and contribute.

In our leadership roles, we must know what we want changed or improved in order to devise a well thought-out plan of action for desired results. We need to be curious and ask appropriate questions to find innovative and creative solutions. In defining our goals, we can apply our various skills, gather information, and evaluate what is working or not working so that alternate plans can be created and implemented as necessary. We want our efforts to be as effective and far-reaching as possible.

We have the responsibility to speak up for future generations and to generate ideas and plans for purposeful change to create more humane conditions and help our planet heal and flourish. Many before us have made sacrifices and had the courage to challenge current social paradigms. They overcame their doubts in order to address common difficulties while looking past differences. They moved forward with ingenuity, innovation, and optimism to make necessary changes for the betterment of humanity. We must do the same. It is your choice as to how you would like to serve on a personal and collective basis. Identify what issues would be most meaningful and fulfilling for you.

Let's be optimal together! It will be an adventure! I know I am worth it, and you are too! We, as She Optimal women, can collaborate to create and accomplish extraordinary things for ourselves, our families, our communities, our nations, and our planet!

About the Author

Dr. Angela Sorensen was raised in Washington state, where she received her Ph.D. in clinical psychology. After completing her internship in health psychology and a subsequent post-doctoral fellowship in neuropsychology, she worked as a licensed psychologist/neuropsychologist in Colorado, Washington, and Tennessee. She currently lives in Tennessee with her husband and two boys. A few years ago, she decided to explore real-estate investing, coaching, and community service positions.

Angela is passionate about pursuing a life of optimal vitality. She founded the She Optimal Community to connect with and encourage other women who have the desire to achieve their optimal potential and approach life with a sense of adventure and opportunity. In the She Optimal Community, Angela discusses her own struggles and how she overcame them. She also shares her knowledge as a psychologist, physician's wife, athlete, mother of two teenagers, and a gracefully aging woman.

Angela developed the She Optimal Process, which includes eight Os, or qualities, that she believes are the foundation to optimal vitality. Living more optimally will foster health, happiness, prosperity, satisfying relationships, and active participation in life.

To find out more about the She Optimal Process, visit her community at http://SheOptimal.com.

$\mathcal{B}$ecoming an Elegant Femme: The True Story

by Tara Marino

It doesn't really matter, you don't really matter, someone else can do it. It still didn't feel right; she had always sensed something more. She knew deep inside she was special. She knew she was meant for great things. The feeling sometimes welled up inside, too much for her to bear, and then she would silence it: *Stop! Enough! Who do you think you are?* But it would arrive again many times throughout her life—beckoning, calling, the pain almost unbearable. The calling was not quite clear, but the message was the same—*you are meant for great things.* It seemed too big, too much. It grasped her heart. What was this purpose? Why her?

Now quickly the memories started to flood her mind. Who was that girl? Where was she? She knew the purple tutu was a hit as she lay smiling face down on the freshly cut green grass. Ripe blackberries ran across the back fence of their country suburban home near upstate New York. Her fingertips matched the color of her new favorite possession. She was the oldest of four siblings, which often left her exhausted as her eight-year-old little body went from playing cowboys and Indians to directing the family musical. Being in charge came easy to her. She loved the attention—oh and she loved this new purple tutu! All things feminine attracted her. She had an eye for style and design at such a young age. Even then she knew.

She was always the good little girl and loved pleasing her parents. Teachers adored her. There was a combination of princess and warrior in her that no one could deny. She was Grandma's Girl, and it broke her heart the day they left for California, leaving Grandma behind. Girls at school teased her relentlessly, saying she had long monkey arms and hair like a lion's mane. It was not uncommon for her to walk home from school crying four days a week. She did not know it then, but something about her intimidated others. She just never felt like she fit in.

High school opened up a new culture of awareness, and she quickly stepped into the popular scene. Perfection held her tightly. She managed straight As and boyfriends, and the pressure of body image started to set in. Slowly a fear began to creep in—the fear of never being good enough and needing to keep up an image. She avoided swim competition so that she didn't have to worry about not coming in first. The idea of failing seemed too painful; she always wanted to make sure she would succeed.

At age 17 she found herself pregnant—her perfect-little-girl image in jeopardy. Feeling alone, scared, and abandoned, she judged herself harshly. The disapproval on the nurse's face cut her to her core. She said, "You should have been more responsible, you pretty little thing." The guilt of beauty ran deep. Did she deserve this? Was this a punishment? She continued to associate being feminine and beautiful with pain, guilt, and weakness. Something inside was fighting. This did not seem right. She was terrified and had an abortion, an abortion that haunted her so deeply that she punished herself for ten years with an eating disorder. She felt confused about her place as a woman—the power, the beauty, the responsibility.

She drifted back to the moment and THE memory that had changed her as a woman FOREVER.

The pale yellow colors of the nursery walls had been carefully chosen. The natural fabric of the rocking chair was soft and soothing, the dark cherry wood of the sleigh crib perfectly aligned next to the changing table that housed cloth diapers arranged in neat little stacks. Copper pails were filled with wipes, binkies, and the cutest little blue socks she had ever laid eyes on. It was all planned, all determined, all anticipated. She asked for strength, strength to be the best mother, the best woman she could be. It is often said that God will not give you what you ask for directly but give you the opportunity to prepare for what you ask for. This was no exception.

She had it all planned. She quit her job and was prepared to make motherhood her life. It made so much sense. Being responsible for someone else's life seemed easier than taking responsibility for her own. Her own purpose seemed too unclear, too difficult to figure out.

On the morning of February 4th, the day before her 25th birthday, the labor pains began. She meticulously put on her Chanel makeup. The black overnight bag made her smile as she filled it with her chic black sandals and her new black nightie for after the birth of Mason. The only inkling of intuition that crept into her mind was an eerie feeling that her life would never, ever be the same.

After 13 hours of labor ending in a C-section, her 5'5" body felt worn out, but her heart was full as she held her baby boy in her arms. The full, sweet lips, so much like his papa's, the sweet smell of his skin. He was her salvation. Now the world made sense. She had found her purpose.

The next week remained a blur as Mason began to have problems breathing. Although the doctors assured her she was overreacting, something deep inside her told her different. Countless trips to the NICU and meetings with specialists confirmed that Mason had pneumonia, but doctors assured her that his weight was sufficient and he would recover.

On February 10th she found herself by the crib of her firstborn, singing to him sweetly, knowing that this was his path. In a strong and calm sense of silence she told him it was okay, he could go. She picked up her son and held him in her arms as he quietly passed away. She was filled with thoughts of irony knowing he took his first and last breaths with her.

The next year was filled with the comforts of Xanax® and red wine and dreams of motherhood. Conversations with her own mother would echo in the stillness of her mind: "Things like this don't happen to us." The memory of her abortion at age 17 haunted her almost every night: *This is my fault. I deserved this!*

The beauty of the gift hidden under the question of "why me?" and the incorrect assumption that having another baby would heal the pain led to detachment. The feeling of failure set in. The red scar across her stomach screamed of her insufficiency: *You are not good enough!*

She began to counsel other woman who had experienced similar loss. The feeling would return. She could see the desperation in their eyes. The loss of a child was the situation they were facing, but a true loss of self was the real culprit. Woman after woman was the same. All felt punished, neglected, and unloved by themselves. This sense of loss ran even deeper than the loss of a child—and many women could relate to it.

Two years later she had two healthy baby boys, a gorgeous home, and a life most women dreamed of. Yet she still felt empty. The guilt of having it all and not being happy was a burden for which she was unprepared. She loved her children, yet she felt lost. She had no idea who she was anymore. The voice returned: *I want more. I am meant for more.*

How could she even think this way? Her children were the most important thing to her. Why was this not enough? Her day was filled with dishes, play groups, and cooking. It seemed so simple, yet she did not allow herself to enjoy it. She felt guilty for having it, guilty for wanting more, and so angry inside. She had lost herself completely. Her purpose burned deep. She had something more to share.

The moment came unexpectedly as she prepared a fabulous Italian dinner. As the two year old leaned on her leg and she balanced the one year old on her hip, the constant piles of laundry and the never-ending to-do list caught her eye. Her husband arrived home 20 minutes late, and THAT is when it happened. She lost it. Tears of fear, frustration, and solitude streamed down her face. Running into the bathroom, she looked at herself. She had not showered in two days, her hair was in a ponytail, her baggy sweats and loose T-shirt were light years away from the feminine woman she had once been. *What has happened to me? Where did I go?*

She felt dizzy, yet so aware that something needed to change. Locking herself in her room, she began to journal, leaving her screaming kids and a confused husband on their own for dinner for the first time. Thoughts streamed forward onto her journal, images. She began to sketch. Something inside her shifted. She began to uncover the woman inside.

On page after page she began to challenge every belief she had ever had, every inbred thought about what it meant to be a woman, a mother. Thoughts and images raced through her head: her aunt putting her on the scale at age 12 to see if she had gained weight after a trip to Europe, the perception of a young girl now connecting pleasure with deprivation; feeling confused and ashamed of her own beauty because her modeling career made her sister feel uncomfortable and so modeling school was stopped; her own mother struggling to raise 4 kids, always taking care of everyone else, never having time for herself; the constant struggle for money growing up, hearing that you have to work hard, it's not supposed to be easy. Was that really the way it was supposed to be? Images of beauty, grace, and ease flashed into her mind and were challenged by society's views of what it meant to be a woman. But she wanted more. I wanted more! Yes, I am she!

An inner knowing began to emerge—a silence, a calm, a quiet, beautiful voice I would recognize later as my Indie. It was impossible not to see the shift I had experienced. I started to wake up and put on beautiful lingerie and do my makeup. Something inside ignited—my Frenchie. I went out and bought myself gorgeous yellow tulips! I connected with a long-lost side of myself. I felt beautiful and sensual for the first time in years. I didn't feel guilty or ashamed. I began to enjoy my life.

I was piecing myself back together. I had to reach deep, back before the ideas of what it meant to be a woman were implanted inside me. I remembered the little girl who loved the purple tutu and playing cowboys and Indians. I didn't have to choose. It was all part of me. I had disowned pieces of myself. I began to recognize three different aspects of myself. When I connected with each one of them throughout the day, I felt whole and complete. There was a powerful business side, a sensual feminine side, and a spiritual side. I realized I had shut myself off from them.

Stepping into my power, I brought organization back into my life. I felt enhanced as I contributed to the family and began my own business. My husband took notice, and a feeling of appreciation surfaced. I started to fall in love with every aspect of who I was and began to give myself permission to experience myself. I let go of victim mentality and started setting healthy boundaries—something that was unheard of growing up in my house! I activated my authentic voice and started to speak my truth.

Through self-compassion I was able to receive joy, grace, and prosperity. Through the opening of a raw heart, I was given the insight to design a program that supports women in allowing themselves to become the women they were meant to be.

The FemmeType formula was created from my own experience and journey as a woman desperately trying to do it all and always falling short, struggling with a career and blocking prosperity, only to find that once I let go, prosperity flowed easily. Aligning myself with my true gifts and coaching women to do the same is my purpose.

Once I had transformed my own life, I began to see women around me who were crying out for the same transformation. Feeling lost, overwhelmed, and confused by the expectations they felt from society and themselves, so many women were disconnected and in pain.

As I started sharing the FemmeTypes with other women, I began to see the impact of this unique system. One woman in particular stands out. She was a young executive who had everything going for her, yet she felt disconnected and unsatisfied. She had been taught that she needed to work hard and that taking a masculine approach in the world would get her what she wanted. She often worked over 60 hours a week, was always on call, made great money, and felt awful about herself. After she learned the FemmeType formula, everything changed for her. She started to think about herself as a woman and about what she really wanted to share with the world. She started to feel beautiful again and step more into the feminine power of her Frenchie. She used her New Yorker to organize and strategize about everything she wanted and challenged her beliefs about money and how "hard" it was to make. She began to listen to her Indie and heard the whisper she had long ago silenced. Twelve weeks after we worked together, I got an e-mail in which she said: "I am leaving for Peru on June 19th, and

Becoming an Elegant Femme: The True Story

I will be volunteering at a children's orphanage for a few weeks as well as building homes in rural Peru. After volunteering, I will be going on a ten-day hiking expedition across the Andes, experiencing Machu Picchu and then hopefully spending time in either Argentina or Ecuador. I am officially leaving my job and looking forward to having balance again in my life."

Today I still use the FemmeType formula myself to course correct. I run a global business and am a wife and a mom of two. You can bet I still feel overwhelmed at times! If there is a day that I miss my Frenchie, I can start to feel it immediately. In the middle of writing this chapter I found myself feeling stretched and uncomfortable. I immediately got up, put on some lip-gloss, and turned on my iTunes. I then spent 15 luxurious moments dancing around my kitchen, teasing my husband with my not-so-smooth dance moves and reconnecting with my Frenchie.

Your automatic response as a woman dictates the way you feel about yourself and what is possible for you in the world. As women, we are taught by our culture and by our parents what is expected of us and what is possible. We have seen our mothers, aunts, co-workers struggle with balance. What did you hear growing up? Does any of this sound familiar?

Women cannot be feminine and powerful. Women do not make as much money as men. Money is something only men are good at. Being sensual is being slutty. Religion will save you. Believe in this or you will suffer. You will be punished. Being feminine and emotional is weak. Taking care of yourself is selfish. You must put everyone else first.

I have always been an all-or-nothing kind of girl. I like my cake and, well, you know the rest. I hate to settle, and I hate being restricted. I want what I want when I want it. I am impulsive. I have come to know and learn to love these things about myself. I now love all of me. Does this make me selfish? No, it makes me conscious and aware of my power as a woman.

Circle any of the following you heard growing up that affected your view of what is possible for you as a woman:

Beautiful is selfish.

Pretty women do not make money.

Moms are there for their kids.
Balance does not exist.
You are selfish!
Sexy is slutty.
You asked for it.
Men make the money; women take care of the children.
Women run the household.
You cannot have it all!
Nobody is perfect.
You can't have your cake and eat it too.
There is never enough.
You are never satisfied.
Nothing ever makes you happy.
You are high maintenance.

You probably heard more than a few of those, and thus you may feel lost and confused, suffering in silence and trying to make sense of your life.

As women, we are multifaceted creatures, yet we try so hard to fit ourselves into one mold: a mother, a sensual woman, or a balls-to-the-walls businesswoman. Why can't we be all three? I believe the only way you will find joy in this journey is if you allow yourself to be all three.

How do you know if your FemmeTypes are not in sync? They're out of sync if you: feel overwhelmed and burned out; are run by your to-do list; feel like you are doing more and still not getting the results and the prosperity you desire; struggle with body image and your relationships; lack purpose and feel empty inside; question your personal style.

When your FemmeTypes are not in sync, you can benefit from the FemmeType Formula. Women have three women that live inside. These are the FemmeTypes. Women will feel unbalanced and sabotage their desired results if two or even one of the FemmeTypes are not in sync. If you are denying ANY of these parts of yourself, you will suffer.

The New Yorker is the business side. She is the powerhouse, and she harnesses masculine energy. This is who you plug into when you want prosperity, results, and leadership and need to get things done. For the majority of women, the New Yorker is overwhelmed, burned out, and exhausted. She is trying to do everything for everyone else, and this is where we see classic victim mentality and martyrdom. This is where I was after I had my two healthy boys. Never did I use my voice to request what I needed. Instead, I used the classic silent treatment. I was angry, hurt, and depressed, feeling empty and alone staring at my milelong to-do list and endless piles of laundry.

The Frenchie is the sensual, feminine side of you. This is the side responsible for external style, body image, relationships, AND the way you internally feel about yourself when it comes to beauty, grace, and femininity in the world. Most women are neglecting the Frenchie. For the most part, she is a distant memory. Women have been taught that this side of them is a luxury when in fact she is a necessity! This is the feminine side that adores taking care of herself. She feels confident and alive and ENJOYS life. Do you know your Frenchie? Have you lost her? Take a look at your relationships with yourself and those around you. How do you feel about your body? All of these are good questions for your Frenchie. If you are neglecting your Frenchie, I guarantee you your New Yorker is in overwhelm and blocking your prosperity. You are not enjoying life the way you could be. Start honoring this side of you and see what happens. Connect with the beauty, flow, and ease of life without feeling guilty and see what opens up for you. My clients find this to be the most effective part of the system!

The Indie is the spiritual side of you. The Indie is NOT a forced religion—actually, it is nothing external whatsoever. Your Indie is your intuition as a female. She is the precious, peaceful side of you that speaks softly and only once. Are you listening? When was the last time you were able to pull back and hear her? This is not about meditation or prayer. Although these are ways you can honor your Indie, they are not where you find her. The Indie is inside, the inner you, the inner knowing, the place inside that whispers *I am good enough, I am meant to do something big in* *the world. It is me, I have been chosen.* She is there to support you and guide you. She is unconditional in her ways, but she is often overpowered by the New Yorker. In today's society she becomes an afterthought, when in fact she should be your first point of counsel. She is in tune with your feelings; she knows when something does not feel right. Women have been taught to block her out, not to believe what we cannot see lest we be ostracized for this powerful force within us. Your Indie will guide you. She supports your New Yorker, helps her think clearly, intentionally, and strategically. Your Indie is the cradle in which your power as a woman is held.

Here are some steps you can take right away to step back into the woman that you truly are and start living a life of prosperity, sensuality, and balance:

1. **Set boundaries.** Know how to set a healthy boundary. Many women set boundaries they expect other people to respect. A boundary must be within YOUR power to control.
2. **Give yourself permission.**
3. **Let go of guilt.**
4. **Let go of victim mentality.**
5. **Decide.**
6. **Decide again.**
7. **Choose you first and then change the world.**
8. **Plug into the three women every day.**
9. **Find a mentor or a coach to support you.** Stop trying to do everything yourself. Find a mentor who understands the truth of being a real woman and a community of women who are ready and willing to play all out and not settle in life.

Women are changing the world. We are meant to. We are the only ones who can. If you are reading this, you are experiencing the shift in consciousness, and you may feel it is time to take part. I believe that women will be the defining factor IF we can get out of our own way. It is time to let go of any guilt and fear. Step into your greatness. Yes, you can do this. Yes, you are enough. Yes, you WERE meant for more. Start by honoring yourself and see what happens to those around you. Step into your power as a woman. We need you; it is women like us who align to change it all. How can you contribute? Ask yourself today how you can more fully step into your power and then do it!

Use your FemmeTypes; give yourself permission to be sensual, prosperous, and balanced. You CAN have it all. You were meant to. It is up to you. It is time! It is your time!

About the Author

Tara Marino is a women's lifestyle coach and creator of the FemmeType Formula. She has a master's degree in spiritual psychology and an international business degree in French. Almost nine years ago, Tara took her first steps on her altruistic path by counseling women in need through stages of grief and transition. Her company, Elegant Femme, has a mission to empower women through beauty on a social, economic, and political platform and inspire women to live the life they were meant to live.

Tara has helped thousands of women transform their lives through the FemmeType formula. Her clients range from stay-at-home moms to executives ready to take their business to the next level of prosperity. She is passionate about unlocking a deep-seated pain within women's consciousness and supporting them in stepping out into the world in a way only they can.

Tara operates several successful businesses through which she has allowed her dreams to blossom. She has a love for fashion and design and incorporates all things feminine into her work with women. She currently resides in Los Angeles, California, and travels often with her husband and children.

Visit the Elegant Femme Society at http://FemmeTypeFormula.com, where women are stepping into their true power and effecting change on a global scale.

$\mathscr{F}$inding Your Way Through a Maze of Mixed Messages

by Kammy Haynes, Ph.D.

Like many of you, I grew up in a time when there was a lot of discussion about men's and women's roles and debate around what appropriate behaviors were for each gender. As a result, I was confused by the mixed messages. Unfortunately, that confusion didn't end when I reached adulthood; and I carried some destructive messages and ineffective coping strategies around with me for decades. I've managed to jettison most, but there are still a few thoughts hanging on for dear life. So while I continue to be a work in progress, I can share some key lessons I've learned so far in hopes of helping you speed up your growth and development. I am sharing this journey with you in hopes that you can learn from my mistakes, use some of my strategies, and free yourself from any unproductive emotions, thoughts, and actions that are holding you back.

The mixed messages that I'm focusing on come from the distinction between masculine and feminine expectations. My parents were essentially poster children for their time. My dad firmly believed that a woman's place was in the home, that children should be seen and not heard, and that he was always right. My mom didn't work outside the home until I was older, always had dinner on the table, took full responsibility for all childcare related activities, and often deferred to my dad to avoid an argument.

For as long as I can remember, my mom was supportive, encouraging, and told me I could be anything I wanted to be. The same went for my maternal grandparents. That was a stark contrast to my dad's perspective.

Finding Your Way Through a Maze of Mixed Messages

Some people are cut out to be parents and some are not. My dad was not prepared for the responsibility of raising a child, especially a girl. He had little patience for children, so even when I was very young, I was expected to act like an adult. I was not allowed to express opinions or preferences. The message was clear: he was the head of the household, so we would do as we were told. End of discussion.

I learned early on not to question his authority (or other authority figures). All he had to do was give me "that look" or raise his voice and I knew that the discussion was over before it ever started. Rather than his hand, belt, or paddle, his weapon of choice was words. He told me I was stupid, selfish, and lazy. It seemed to me that he took every opportunity to show me that I was small, helpless, and insignificant. I still remember his reaction to a report card with six As and one B. He pointed at the B and said, "What happened here?" with a disapproving tone.

He made it clear that I wasn't good enough from the very start, no matter what I did. My main crime was being a girl, and my punishment would be fighting an uphill battle for the rest of my life. I was 17 when I realized I would never get his approval, although a little part of me still hoped. Fortunately, I was surrounded by my mom, teachers, friends' parents, and family members, who thought I was a great kid and encouraged me.

However, research consistently shows that we are more likely to remember negative comments than compliments and give them more credence. That was certainly the case for me. Therefore, it's important to look at those kinds of deeply ingrained and emotionally laden messages that stick with you and how they influence your life (and the choices you make). Once you see patterns, you can begin to make sense of your decisions and understand why you made them. More importantly, you can decide whether you want to continue using those same paths as you move forward.

The contrast between masculine and feminine in my house was very distinct. The masculine model encourages competition, winning, beating the other person, triumph, and championship. The feminine model is based on collaboration, cooperation, sharing, being nice, not bragging, and putting others' needs before your own. As a child, I didn't see much middle ground, so it got more confusing. What's a girl to do? Your father expects you to be perfect and to excel at everything, and your mother tells you to do your best but cautions you about celebrating too much if you win. In psychology, this is called a double bind situation.

When we're faced with a choice, we go through a mental checklist of pros and cons to determine which choice will provide the most benefit or create the least amount of pain. As women, we often concern ourselves with whether or not our choice will disappoint, upset, disturb, or inconvenience others. I only "over-celebrated" a victory once, but I still remember how sorry I was for embarrassing my mom in front of the other moms.

While being considerate is a worthy trait, it can be destructive when we worry more about what others will think and not enough about how the decision will impact our own lives. We can make decisions to make others feel good that ultimately make us feel bad. We often wonder what the heck we were thinking and why we were so worried about what our parents, spouse, sibling, teacher, or family member would think. After all, we're the ones who have to live with our decisions day in and day out. Ultimately we reap the benefits or consequences of our choices.

After going through the checklist (unconsciously at that age), I embraced the masculine concept of competition and enjoyed winning. I was highly competitive (everything from board games to test scores to sports to number of Girl Scout badges and cookies sold to being the first off the line when the traffic light turned green). I felt compelled to outperform others (studying longer, working later, going above and beyond) in order to get some recognition. At the same time, I avoided situations where I didn't think I was capable of achieving the task or winning. (If I didn't think I had at least an 85 percent chance of success, I wouldn't try.)

If I had to describe my thinking, it would go something like this: *If I'm the best, then they can't criticize me. If I work hard, they'll recognize and approve of me. If I don't try, I can't fail. I can't fail because that would confirm others' beliefs that I am unworthy, imperfect, and not good enough.*

That's a prime example of how these sneaky negative messages can team up and wiggle into the smallest nook and cranny of your mind. They become so common and comfortable that you have no reason to doubt them. It's an endless tape loop that plays in your head over and over again.

Sometimes I felt like I couldn't really enjoy my successes because I'd hear *don't brag* or *don't hurt others' feelings* rattling around in my head. Dealing with the contradictory messages was stressful. Therefore, as a nod to the feminine side, I added some self-deprecating humor to disarm my (potential) enemies. My rationale was if I pointed out my shortcomings first, then I'd taken away their power to disapprove or find fault. That gave me some room to be "slightly imperfect" without admitting defeat. If I exceeded expectations, I'd carefully deflect any compliments so that I could receive the praise without being accused of bragging. (Even as I'm discussing the feminine side, I'm using masculine, aggressive words such as *disarm, enemies,* and *defeat* because of the need to protect myself.)

By viewing the two models as opposites or contradictory, my mind and emotions were in turmoil. I'd end up apologizing or making excuses for winning. ("You got a really hard question.") I'd discount my accomplishment in order to make the other person feel better. ("It was close!") I made myself smaller or dimmed my light. I pretended to be someone that I wasn't, which only reinforced that the real me wasn't good enough. In essence, I was continuing to treat myself the same way my father did.

Early on, I felt like I was essentially faced with a choice between being a winner and disliked or liked and mediocre. That's a lousy choice to have to make, and boys don't seem to have to make it. Boys and men who excel in their field (sports, academics, or business) are revered. I doubt anyone asked Donald Trump or Michael Jordan if they worried that their success would scare off any potential spouses or told them that their behavior was unmanly (the flip side of unladylike)!

The idea of mediocrity makes me think of the term *settling*. Based on my personal experience (along with family, friends, and clients), I believe that most women settle because they lack the confidence to ask for more, often because they've come to believe they don't deserve it. Perhaps the lack of confidence came from a dysfunctional family or a specific incident where she failed (so there is now a fear of failure and hesitation to try again). Maybe she is afraid of success and the changes that would happen if she took action. She may have a warped picture of what would happen to her life and relationships if she got a raise or promotion, took the job transfer, left her abusive partner, or started her own business. Rather than take a chance, she opts to stay in her comfort zone, doing what she's always done and getting more of the same.

That fear (of both success and failure) often pushes us to make decisions that "protect" us from either outcome. For example, when I was in graduate school, we were all expected to find summer internships where we could gain work experience related to our major. The best way to secure an internship was through a referral from your professor.

I found it difficult to approach my professors because I was fighting all of these negative and conflicting messages in my head ("I've got good grades, but I'm not good enough.") plus the added element of gender. Put simply, I was afraid to ask my male professors for an inside track on these internship opportunities without looking like I was flirting with them. Add that to my discomfort with bragging about my abilities and my fear of disappointing them if they put me in an assignment where I wasn't perfect, and the equation added up to a big fat zero—no internship on my resume.

Maybe they were just waiting for me to ask, to show some initiative. I'll never know. I settled for less than I deserved, and it probably cost me $5,000-10,000 on my starting salary. That makes "Do you know of any internship opportunities?" a $10,000 question. Hindsight stinks.

Unfortunately, I took most of these same negative and disempowering beliefs into the corporate environment. Now I had a Ph.D., so my reputation was on the line. As a human resources consultant, I could affect others' careers, too. In order to be effective, I needed to develop good relationships with the key players so that I could understand their issues and offer sound advice. Since most of my clients were men, I had to be careful not to do or say anything that could be perceived as inappropriate or that would reflect poorly on women in the workforce. My fear of failure continued despite repeated successes and consistent promotions.

I also self-selected myself out of some great job opportunities because I wasn't 100 percent qualified. Let me explain with this quick fictitious story. I rationalized that I should not apply for a job because they asked for experience with Aardvarks, Bears, Cats, and Dogs and I only had experience with Aardvarks, Cats, and Dogs. Rather than risk failure or embarrassment, I didn't apply. I could almost hear them saying, "Are you stupid? We clearly asked for experience with Bears and you have none." Later, I found out that the person they hired only had experience with Bears and Dogs and that the company was willing to train him on the rest.

Why didn't I ever consider that? I was too busy thinking small and disqualifying myself rather than considering the growth possibilities. I was focused on why it wouldn't work and what could go wrong rather than on how I could make it work. Once in a while, I still catch myself starting to do the same thing. It's a tough habit to break.

I should have known better. In my first corporate job, my boss hired me based on potential rather than the experience that I actually brought to the table. (Remember, I didn't have an internship.) He looked beyond my resume to other qualities (willingness to learn, strong communication and teamwork skills) and gave me a chance to grow into the position. He was willing to bet on my potential when I didn't have the courage to do so.

Without learning the lesson, I left Corporate America to join a small consulting company where I counted on my partners to bring in new business because I wasn't confident enough in my sales abilities. Although I took umpteen training courses to learn the right techniques, I still didn't have much success, and I was getting discouraged.

After a while, I realized that a big part of the problem was the way I was thinking about sales (pushy, aggressive, stretching the truth). Because I was uncomfortable with that masculine approach to selling, I was resisting it. No wonder I wasn't bringing in new clients!

Later, when one of my coaches reframed selling as teaching, I realized that was what I'd been doing all along but just hadn't been thinking of it that way. I was teaching my clients about what I had to offer and how those products and services would benefit them. That new perspective helped me get past my negative feelings about selling.

I've invested considerable time, money, and effort searching for explanations as to why I couldn't shake those nagging thoughts and beliefs. I've learned some key lessons that have enabled me to find a path through the mixed messages and approach situations with a new (and more positive) perspective. That's not to say that self-doubt doesn't creep in or that I'm not triggered when people put me down, but I'm not bogged down by childhood baggage.

It all started to come together when I *accepted* these six things. Although I know I've "learned" these things several times over in my lifetime, apparently I wasn't ready to accept them. When the time is right, it really is like a light bulb comes on and suddenly things are so clear.

1. **No one really expects me to be perfect.** When I remember that, I relieve a tremendous amount of pressure and increase my productivity (because I'm not sweating every detail and worrying about making a mistake). One of my favorite quotes is from Mike Ditka, former coach of the Chicago Bears: "Success isn't permanent and failure isn't fatal."

2. **Others' perceptions and beliefs about me do NOT define who I am.** They are free to express their views, but it's 100 percent up to me whether or not I accept or internalize what they say. The more I know and accept myself, the less influenced (and upset) I am by others' opinions. I have complete control over whether I ignore, dismiss, or consider their comments. It still hurts my feelings when others disapprove (but only if their opinions are important to me). Then I remember what Dr. Seuss said: "Be who you are and say what you feel because those who matter don't mind and those who mind don't matter."

3. **Every difficult experience teaches you valuable lessons about yourself.** For example, I stayed in a miserable relationship for almost

a year because I wanted to "prove" to myself that I wasn't selfish (something both the guy and my dad had accused me of). I now have plenty of evidence to the contrary.

4. **I am not helpless or insignificant.** I'm quite self-sufficient (by nature and out of necessity). It feels good to know I can handle things on my own and that I don't need someone else to make me complete. I want a partner, not a rescuer, so Prince Charming would be disappointed that I don't "need" him enough.

5. **Lighten your load.** Even with wheels, lugging heavy baggage around is exhausting. Revisiting the negative things that have happened is like opening up the wound and pouring salt in it. Acknowledge and learn from what happened, but focus your attention on the present and future. You can't change the past. People have said and done certain things. I interpreted and acted upon them in certain ways. Those are the facts. Now it's time to examine those emotions, thoughts, and actions and decide if they are serving me or not. If not, they do not make it into the suitcase for the next leg of my journey.

6. **Don't invent choices or dilemmas where they don't exist.** As a child, I felt I had to choose between masculine and feminine because I didn't see a good way to combine them. Now rather than seeing them as opposite ends of a continuum, I see them as a collection of items in a buffet, where I can select the portions of each that I want.

These specific lessons may or may not apply to your personal experience. So in case you didn't have an "aha" or "me too" moment, let me give you a strategy or outline for making the discoveries that will be of greatest value to you.

When it comes right down to it, in order to be successful, there are only a few things that you have to remember. To gain (or regain) control of your life, you need to decide on your destination and then focus on your E-T-A. Your level of commitment to these steps will define your journey and determine your Estimated Time of Arrival at your desired destination. (However, in this case E-T-A stands for emotions, thoughts, and actions.)

E – Emotions   Your emotions can either work for you or against you. Therefore, it's important that you learn to direct your emotions in a way that helps rather than hinders you. By understanding your emotions, you can prevent them from controlling you and improve your decision making. You cannot count on being able to change anyone's perceptions but your own. Don't allow others to dictate your level of happiness or success.

T – Thoughts   What you think determines what you'll try, how you'll react to success and failure, and eventually what you will be able to accomplish. Self-talk is a critical element here. Make sure you are focused on positive messages and not buying into old, worn-out thoughts put in your head by someone else—perhaps a long time ago. Turn off the tape. Stop listening to thoughts that make you feel bad about yourself or discourage you from moving forward.

A – Action   Ideas without action are useless. The same goes for acquiring knowledge and skills. If you don't apply that knowledge, you won't receive the full value. If you've ever purchased exercise equipment that turned into a clothes hanger or went to a training class and didn't follow up on any of the ideas, you know exactly what I mean. Don't let your attempts at self-help turn into a closet full of "shelf-help." Implement what you learn as quickly as you can.

My purpose in sharing these stories and life lessons is to shed some light on the destructive power of negative thought and beliefs that each of us may be carrying around. I don't want you to spend decades beating yourself up, wondering what's wrong with you, or settling for less than what you deserve and can achieve. I want you to stop selling yourself short, quitting before you try, and putting yourself down. The world sends out enough negative messages. We don't need to add our own voices to that noise.

We can't realize our potential until we clear away the internal obstacles. It's difficult to take on external challenges (new job, inconsiderate spouse, difficult children, aging parents, starting a business) when you are fighting an internal battle with negative thoughts and emotions.

As the world evolves, new approaches and strategies will be needed to deal with the changes. It's time to realize that we all need to work together, leveraging all of our strengths in order to succeed. That means taking the best of the masculine and feminine approaches and blending them.

I've come to realize that I'm most successful (and comfortable in my own skin) when I take the pieces from both the masculine and feminine approach that fit me and/or the situation. There are times when taking a more directive and assertive approach is what is needed to resolve a situation—or at least it's expedient and effective. Other times, a kinder, gentler, and more personal approach will yield better results—without risking any damage to the relationship. That proper balance depends on you, the other person (or people), and the specific circumstances. There is no one right answer, and there's some chance that you'll choose an ineffective mix. That's okay. That's how we get experience, learn from our mis-steps, and grow as human beings. Perfection is an illusion, and it's not worth chasing.

When all is said and done, I encourage you to be yourself. Listen to your inner voice—to what you know in your heart to be true—rather than to what other people say. Use your unique combination of masculine and feminine traits to ensure your voice is heard and that your ideas are recognized, considered, and implemented. Show others how to achieve extraordinary results by respecting and empowering them. Form the teams, communities, and coalitions that you need to make your desired changes, whether they are for you, your family, or your environment. Finally, take time to celebrate your successes no matter how small. That courage will liberate the many talents that you have at your disposal and allow you to accomplish more than you ever expected.

About the Author

Kammy Haynes, Ph.D., is an entrepreneur, management consultant, trainer, speaker, and author. Kammy's mission as the founder of the EMERGE Community is to give women the tools and strategies they need to expand their personal and professional potential. By increasing levels of respect, collaboration, and empowerment, we can change our lives at work and at home.

Kammy brings both a practical and humorous approach to some serious subjects based on her 20 years of experience working with Fortune 500 companies, small businesses, and entrepreneurs as well as her doctorate in industrial organizational psychology. She continues to read books and attend teleseminars, workshops, and conferences to gain more insight into herself and others. By integrating this information, she has created the "Seven-Es" approach for tapping into and leveraging your unique set of skills, abilities, and desires. This approach serves as the basis for the content in the EMERGE community and helps women unlock and unleash their full potential.

Kammy has written the soon-to-be published *Exceptional Managers Success Series™* (a blueprint for getting amazing results through others), and *Words of Wisdom: Quotes to Motivate and Inspire You and Your Staff to Achieve Extraordinary Results,* as well as numerous chapters in the McGraw-Hill and American Society for Training and Development handbooks. She specializes in skills assessment, team facilitation and problem solving, employee surveys, employee engagement, supervisory skills, and organizational change. You can download a free report on Women in Leadership roles at www.KammyHaynes.com.

Visit the EMERGE Community at http://TheEmergeCommunity.com.

$\mathcal{T}$here's No Business Like Soul Business

by Penny Wanger and Nanci Moore

My name is Penny Wanger, and this is the story of how I went from ordinary to extraordinary. Growing up, it never entered my head that one day I could be wealthy and successful. I was part of a large, middle-class family living in Detroit, and my loftiest goal was a secure job. The attribute that has always been a part of me is my love for people and my ability to see the best in them. This quality, and my feminine nurturing instinct, made me well suited for my chosen 33-year career as a dental hygienist.

I married, had a son, divorced, remarried, and had another son. I worked part time and loved motherhood and my work. I seemed happy and fulfilled on the outside. But if I had been financially able to maintain my lifestyle in those days, I would not have remained married.

My husband was a good-hearted, honest man who wanted to change; but early in our marriage his anger ruled him, and I was very unhappy. Though I railed against it and even separated, I allowed myself to be a victim. It took us years to conquer our issues. I know now that feeling trapped disempowers the spirit and magnifies everything. I spent many years chained to a secret sadness because I was unable to claim my power, accept myself as twice divorced, and stop judging myself harshly.

Today as a successful businesswoman, I find it hard to recognize myself as that person. Because I believe that financial abundance supports and increases our ability to choose, I am passionate about inspiring women to live empowered lives and exercise choice. I wonder if things would have changed if I had not finally said "yes" to my entrepreneurial calling.

Opportunity had arisen numerous times, but I had always reasoned my way out of "taking a chance for change." The biggest difference this time was that I started asking, *What next?* After so many years of using my hands, I started to experience numbness, burning, and pain. I wondered, *What if I can't work?* We still had both boys to put through college, and I was not ready to give up my independence. The Universe answered my question, placing me in front of a dynamic and inspirational speaker who presented a business opportunity that resonated with me. Even though I had never been in sales, a voice said, *You can do this!* I was scared, yet it was exciting to think about starting my own business and using my skills with people as well as my master's degree in nutrition. I had been asking, so I needed to pay attention to what came up.

I experienced fear, challenges, walls, doubts, and tears, yet I was certain that this was my path. I had asked for something different. As I moved forward, others saw the seeds of success in me before I had the inner resources to see them in myself. These people nourished and believed in me. I began to see a bigger picture of myself. Several times daily I would return to trust and commitment. Trust can dispel fear. Trust can facilitate acceptance. Trust can override our egos and make us bold. Trust allows us to fail and start over. Trust that we are inherently deserving of prosperity and owning our own lives can send us flying out of the box. Acting with trust despite the fear brought growth, accomplishment, pride, confidence, and success! I did not know at the time that my business would become the business my soul needed—growing me, molding me, and empowering me. But I became stronger and unwilling to accept unhealthy habits or unhealthy relationships in my life. I grew in love, leadership, purpose, and vision, equipping me to offer service and value beyond all my expectations.

Even though I had enjoyed my dental hygiene career, there was no personal growth or challenge in it. I was good at it, period. I remember an early training in my new business during which we were asked to write down our goals. Terrified, I prayed no one would call on me to share because I realized in that moment that I had no goals or dreams. I had been in survival mode for so long that I had never allowed myself to look forward.

Since then, I have mastered the ability to dream, vision, and manifest! My life is full of the things I love: time, freedom, travel with my family, and sharing a business that makes others healthier and wealthier and enables them to own their lives. With a sense of purpose, I am now able to assist women to experience the same deep passion, fulfillment, and financial success. The soul calling that I answered is available to all who ask.

As my children grew up and my nest emptied, my world expanded, filling my new nest to overflowing. As I became more empowered, confident, and certain of my purpose, everything in my life improved, including my relationship. When I changed and began to lead an inspired life, those around me changed—or left! In the flow of my life I began to attract what I required to continue a rich and fulfilling journey of purpose. And so it was no accident that at the very time I started my business and began visualizing business partners I met my future Soul BIZ Sister, Nanci.

My name is Nanci Moore. I was born a child of joy, welcomed into a traveling family of musicians, writers, readers, poets, artists, leaders, and adventurers. Since we grew up in a military family, my parents encouraged my brothers and me to immerse ourselves in the cultures of many countries. I was raised safe and free, cherished by my family.

It has been an incredible journey, and now I am a Woman of Vision— my heart is in my life and my soul is in my business. In addition to my outward travels, I have traveled miles and miles on inner journeys and have come to discover they all lead to the same place—my sassy, lively soul.

As a child, I struggled to learn. I didn't discover until a trip to Asia that different people learn in different ways—some learn more easily using the right side of the brain and others using the left. Having this aha moment, I fell in love with my right-brain learning style and began to attract mentors who were in the body work and massage therapy field. Learning from innovative healers in the 1970s, I soon recognized my own strengths as a healer and became a massage therapist. Compassion, love-acceptance (my word), silence, joy, trust, and pure healing intentions were the gifts I gave to each client who entered my massage studio.

In most areas of my life I felt incredibly fulfilled; however, I had settled for a modest life. I was unable to finance many activities my children longed to join, and there was no extra money for causes. But then I had a vision:

A medicine woman appeared. Her purpose was to provide health, comfort, and ceremony to the people of her community. In return, the community took care of all of her needs: they provided shelter and clothing and kindly brought her meals each day.

For me, a vision can be visual (like a movie) or auditory (like a radio or speaker); but this vision filled my whole being! I knew it was important to listen, and this is the message I retrieved:

In ancient times communities were devoted to caring for their tribal medicine woman or man. In modern times healers—like everyone else— must be attentive to their finances, buying their own food and shelter.

My listening becomes acute when a vision appears. I want to hear the message that will lead me to my next step in life. I have always followed the guidance of my visions, often using them to create ceremony and lead other women. Now I was ready to go to my next level.

New questions began to form as my vision helped me realize that as a healer I desired and deserved financial abundance. My 30-year massage career had helped me develop into a skilled therapist, but it had not set the foundation for a lifetime of income. I wanted to create a stable, long-term income source! Could I create money that would be congruent with my values, my desire to help people, and my integrity?

It was at this time that I met Penny. She introduced me to a new community built around a business based on extraordinary liquid whole-food nutrition. I saw lives changed by the community, the nutrition, and money flowing from this new business. I knew I could align with it and that this business would be a powerful addition to my practice. However, I soon discovered that the world of business was very different from the massage room, and I began to feel uncomfortable, afraid, and lost.

I wondered if I had made the right choice. The unfamiliar leadership responsibilities were exhausting and overwhelming. As a visionary and a healer, could I become the successful entrepreneur that I wanted to be? I realized that I felt disconnected from my soul. Could I reconcile my heart and business intellect? Could I lead women in business as well as in ceremony? Yes, as long as my soul is in my business.

Penny became a dear friend as well as a business partner, and we embraced my questions and began a deep inner exploration into the ways business can be carried out when led by soul. I gathered my courage, asked questions, trusted the answers, and then had another guiding vision:

I am sitting on the ground, flowers all around me. Almost dozing, I am awakened by a nudge. Standing on my right is a magnificent lion. He walks to the edge of a steep cliff. I follow. We look out at the glorious expanse. Without thought of hesitation, I step off of the cliff into mid air. The lion's massive jaws reach to hold me and I feel him ask, "Would you like for me to hold you, or would you like to fly?"

"FLY!" I say, and I begin to drop through the air. I am dropping, my heart skips, and my intention to fly is now laser focused . . . I am Flying! I feel the warm sun on my back and the cool air on my face. As I soar, the lion is now loping through the air beside me. We fly side by side and land among the flowers, resting together.

After this vision, I was transformed. I felt whole. The masculine strength and protection of my lion, interpreted as the intellect, had flown side by side with the power and freedom of the feminine heart. This confirmation raised me from feeling "lost" in the world of business to feeling extraordinarily confident. I knew that the intellect of business could create a dance of excellence and love with the heart of business. This courtship of heart and intellect is the Soul Dance of my Soul Business. I am grateful to have this internal balance of masculine and feminine, drive and intuition.

As this unique idea became integrated and my passion grew, so did my part-time business and my bank account. I became grounded and connected to myself. With my new money awareness I was becoming a money magnet, and my husband was noticing. Subtle changes were happening in our life. For the first time ever, I was contributing extra money to my family and hearing myself say "yes" to their requests, such as my son's big wedding, my daughter's travel plans, and my own romantic motorcycle trips. Soon I closed my massage studio and followed my calling to assist others to step boldly into their Soul Businesses.

The journey of my life—living in other cultures, embracing my learning style, and celebrating a healthy relationship with money—has equipped me to connect with women to design Soul Business roadmaps. Through this journey I have been given many precious life gifts, but three of them stand out: who I have become in order to be a savvy Soul Businesswoman; the new life my Soul Business created; and my relationships with magnificent businesswomen, especially my partnership with my Soul BIZ sister, Penny.

We have been in business together for over eight years. Though we individually work our home businesses, we also work as partners and foster a large team of entrepreneurs. We have developed through our businesses and each other, experiencing accomplishment, joy, challenge, wisdom, and the value and rewards of a business that has soul.

What is a Soul Business, and why would you want to have one? In a Soul Business, the soul of your business serves the purpose of your soul. Here is how this new model can serve you:

Purpose

Through our business we are able to discover and express our life purpose. We are led to our Soul Business by connecting inside. While our purpose may or may not be immediately apparent, the more we listen and trust ourselves, the clearer it becomes. We are often required to practice "commitment before clarity" as we trust our path and commit to it. Our Soul

Business uses our unique, and sometimes dormant, talents. Our entire life path and experiences have prepared us for this new way of doing business. When you "lead from the soul," a Soul Business is created out of your unique experiences.

Growth

When you have a Soul Business, it is not separate from who you are or from your life purpose. The qualities that must be developed for success are exactly the same ones we need to live to our full potential. Continuous learning and growing are required. All the skills that you learn not only make you better leaders and role models in business but also assist you to live your best life, enhancing communication, relationships, and authenticity. A Soul Business is about who you become in the process.

Balance

One of the biggest challenges for women is maintaining balance. We know how to nurture and care for others, but how do we create the space to connect to ourselves? A Soul Business insists that we nurture ourselves, take time for quietness, and look within. The actions that are required for accomplishment are initiated from this place of inner knowing. When we get too busy, we become overwhelmed and emotionally drained. It is only in the present moment that we can hear the inner voice that keeps us connected to our Soul Business. Actions arising from this personal place keep us energized and clear. The breath is our tool to keep us centered and in the moment. If we are not connected to our soul, there is no Soul Business!

Passion

One of the most rewarding benefits of a Soul Business is a life of passion. There is a shift in our belief, our fulfillment, and our joy when we are directed from a deeper place. When we fully grasped the outcome of our Soul Business—growing us and assisting us and others to own their lives—our passion was ignited. Passion is the fuel that keeps us alive and energized, and it is contagious. There are many ways to realize a passionate life of purpose. You can find it as an entrepreneur, a mother, an employee, or a volunteer. When you know your path is right for you, from the inside, you create a life of wealth in all areas. That doesn't mean there aren't challenges, but our passion and commitment keep us working through them and learning from them.

Visionary women are looking for the same connection, collaboration, and support that we experience as business partners. Our shared beliefs gave birth to the Soul BIZ Sisters Community. We are committed to our wholeness; and yet, as two halves of a business brain, we complement each other's qualities and synergistically create a powerful business alliance. We know that our business must serve the purpose of our soul.

One of the greatest benefits of our partnership is that we support each other's personal and business development and are honest about areas in which we need to grow. This relationship would not be possible without trust. When trust is high, the freedom to explore, grow, fail, and recover is created. Together we embrace both our laughter and tears.

We have set up a template for other women to follow, and we attract many magnificent and amazing women to our business team. One of the first and most critical factors in bringing the dream to reality is making a decision. Early in our own careers, neither of us saw a clear picture of ourselves as women excelling in business and leadership. However, we made a decision to become thriving business women. It was our path, and we committed to it.

We began to attract strong, influential role models—women who became our teachers. Since the five people you hang out with the most affect your personal success and income, the fact that our mentors all had fabulous incomes created another shift in our lives. We discovered that success in business is not born, and it is not an accident for the lucky few. It is learned. It is the result of being coachable, committing to a decision, and mastering a set of necessary skills.

There's No Business Like Soul Business

Once you make the decision to follow the direction of your soul, opportunities, people, and synchronistic events will begin to spontaneously show up in your life. Be careful what you ask for, because you will get it! Then you'll be required to live outside your comfort zone and stretch.

One of the empowering qualities for expressing your gifts and touching lives is finding your authentic voice. This voice expresses the genuine essence of who you are and what you believe. We discovered that being connected to our inner voice and being comfortable speaking in front of people, especially groups, are two different things. When we set our intention to make a difference in many people's lives with our business, the Universe answered! We found ourselves in front of many groups, knowing our message but often struggling to get our words out.

A Soul Business has a purpose and a message, so the ability to communicate them clearly, confidently, and authentically is vital. The first step is to examine your core beliefs about your message. When your deep belief is congruent with your words, your message will contain your conviction. Next, what is the value or service you bring to others? Connect with that. When we are aligned with our message and the value of what we offer, we let go of our ego and communicate powerfully. We are not focused on looking or sounding perfect but on our life-changing message.

Right now we are all waking up to a global shift in business. The old model of adrenalin-driven business no longer fits for women; in fact, it exhausts them. Dog-eat-dog and heart-centered models just cannot coexist in the same arena. "Business as usual" has been based on an atmosphere of competition, the idea that we can't all succeed together. Only one person can be at the top, and you have to fight your way to get there. Today, women are choosing to do business within a cooperative model. Instead of climbing a corporate ladder by stepping on the backs of fellow workers, we choose to ascend a wide staircase, arriving at the summit together.

Women aren't comfortable in restrictive, powerless work environments where personal creativity and expression are not encouraged. Are you experiencing dis-ease in your career? Are you excited to get out of bed in the morning? Do you go to sleep peacefully, with the realization you have contributed to a better world today? Are you passionate? You may not even realize why you are feeling disconnected from your essence. You may be comfortable, but just not inspired, not being your magnificent, authentic self. You may be asking, *Why am I not happy here?*

In our experience, once we begin to ask the important questions, the answers come from many directions. This is an exciting and extraordinary time to ask soul questions, listen for the answers, and develop a Soul Business. Support and new thought are showing up everywhere. Entrepreneurial women now are at the forefront of a new world of business. This isn't your father's business, Sister!

The number of conscious, heart-connected women is increasing every day—women who are visionary, who embrace change and choice, who claim their abundance. Today's inspired woman knows she can have it all and takes purposeful action. Women are curious and open to new ways of creating. And they are sharing their wisdom and experience, leading and guiding other women who desire a new way of living business. In an atmosphere of understanding and learning, women are coming together from diverse cultures and creating the prosperity to make shift possible. It is only through creating personal wealth ourselves that we can contribute to community and global wealth, helping to heal the world and feed its children. New levels of trust are created with our global sisters as we see ourselves as the energy that will facilitate change in the world.

A Soul Business opens us and makes us bigger in the world. It creates abundance and freedom through purpose and collaboration. It puts us intimately in touch with energy, which is boundless and connects us to ourselves and all living things. Out of our Soul Business a vision came to Nanci, and we both embrace it. It is a vision of a new country without geographic boundaries, where citizens from around the world are united by understanding and acceptance and an intention for peace and prosperity.

We believe that as BraveHeart Women living our purposes in our lives and through our Soul Businesses we are fostering this powerful future. As we connect, communicate, and collaborate with women all over the globe, we are planting the seeds of necessary change and shifting the consciousness of the world. Business is evolving; it is a medium through which we are creating our freedom. Choose to be a part of this transformation.

One thing we know for sure, "There's no business like Soul Business!"

About the Authors

Penny Wanger lives in Durango, Colorado. She is the mother of two grown sons and currently shares her home with her willingly evolving husband and two chocolate labs. After 33 years as a dental hygienist, Penny found her passion and purpose as an entrepreneur in the network marketing industry. She leads an inspired life of service-based leadership, learning, travel, and adventure and is a sought-after trainer and international speaker.

When she was an eight year old in pigtails and blue jeans, **Nanci Moore** launched her first entrepreneurial enterprise selling comic books. The excitement of giving a great value and receiving monetary reward influenced a lifetime of creative independent businesses. Experience in the court system, medical system, ski industry, and 30 years as a massage therapist have given her compassionate insight into how women and men step into personal, communal, and global excellence. Spunky, warm wisdom guides her coaching style. Nanci and her husband live in the Colorado Rocky Mountains. They have two grown children and two grandchildren.

Penny and Nanci began an amazing journey as friends and business partners in 2002. Their evolution in creating a successful business with consciousness, heart, and purpose birthed the BraveHeart Women Soul BIZ Sisters Community. They embrace this new global paradigm shift in business and share a commitment to empower human potential through transformation. They mentor people in their business and their community.

To find out more, visit http://SoulBIZSisters.com or contact them at penny@gobrainstorm.net or nanci@gobrainstorm.net.

$\mathscr{A}$ Passion to Empower

by Tari Bussard

I was born in a small town of 18,000 people about 2 hours southwest of Chicago. I was the second oldest of the four "Ruiz Girls." Being a middle child, I grew up with the perception that I was never important enough and that I didn't matter. My older sister was very beautiful and talented in many ways. She was also pretty spoiled, according to some people. My two younger sisters were just as beautiful, getting lots of attention. But I always felt overlooked.

Growing up with my sisters and our neighborhood girlfriends was a lot of fun. We made up a variety of imaginative games and "produced" mini beauty pageants, which I never entered because I never felt pretty or talented enough. I was always one of the judges. We also played thousands of games of jump rope, hopscotch, and my favorite game, jacks. We were lucky enough to live by the local swimming pool and always had summer passes. When we were old enough, we walked to the pool every day and usually had a little money to buy pop and popcorn or the occasional hotdog. Once in a while we were lucky enough to go swimming at a pond by the dairy just outside of town. Life was very simple then. We didn't have much, and we didn't need much.

When we were in grade school, my mother went back to school to become an RN so she'd have something to do when we all grew up and left the house. I really admired her for this and was very proud of her. Dad was around, but Mom was the one who really took care of all us girls. I know that wasn't always easy. Sometimes she went outside and just sat quietly on the retaining wall in the front yard. I am sure she was crying. Mom never said anything; she just simply and quietly walked out and then quietly came back. She kept to herself and never complained about anything.

At the age of 52 my mother became sick. She died of pancreatic cancer a year later. I always wondered if she got sick because she kept all her emotions inside and never shared her pain. At one point during her illness, I was outside her door crying, trying to hold it back so she wouldn't hear me. I couldn't believe I was watching my mother die. I couldn't believe I couldn't talk to her about it. I wanted it to be okay, but I had no control over this outcome. Internally I was freaking out. I screamed at God: "Is this the way you want to play this game? Come on! You can do better than this! You can heal her! You have the power! I can't save her! Is this really what you want? Why are you taking the good ones when there are so many bad ones who should go first? What is up with this?"

Mom heard me and ordered, "STOP IT!" I don't think she could bear to watch us suffer over her dying, so she simply didn't allow it.

My sisters and I went home to see her at Christmas, knowing there wasn't much time left. She was frail and sickly. But she still had that beautiful smile on her face and that special glow that only mothers seem to have. She was still trying to be the glue that held the family together even though she knew that it was slowly melting away. We had a beautiful Christmas. Two days after I returned to California, I got a call and had to go back to Illinois. I arrived on Wednesday, but my sister from Oklahoma couldn't get in until Friday. Even though my mom was pretty much in a morphine coma, she waited until she could be hugged by each one of her children. What a powerful experience death is—ugliness and beauty all in one!

There were times in my childhood when I felt really hurt by my family because they weren't being open and honest about certain things. This bothered me deep down in the core of my being. On many occasions, I would see a sibling manipulate a story or tell an untruth to get her own way. I saw the pain this caused my parents, and I couldn't stand it.

During our childhood, my sisters and I discovered that we had two half brothers and a half sister. We were able to meet our brothers but didn't get to know them until we were all much older. My parents had told us about my half sister, and we even had her high-school graduation picture in our kitchen. We knew certain things about her. For instance, we knew she had been in a lawn-mowing accident on her parents' farm at the age of ten. She had lost her arm and almost lost her life. But we never really got a straight answer about where she lived—until she found us!

One day she was in a laundromat in town at the same time our neighbor happened to be there. Our neighbor noticed her arm first and then her resemblance to us. Explaining that she'd seen her picture in our kitchen, the neighbor told her that she must be our sister. Things started becoming clear to her all of a sudden. She never resembled her other siblings, and she always had felt that she didn't fit in. She decided that she had to meet us, and the very next day she came to see us.

She looked like us and talked like us, yet she was different. I can't describe how awkward, peculiar, and powerful that experience was for all of us. I will never forget the look on my father's face. I had never seen him cry before. I remember thinking, *She is one of us!*

She moved in with us, but it wasn't long before rivalries between my older sister and her surfaced. My older sister didn't want to give up her position as the oldest—and now I really had become the middle child.

My half sister was not as fortunate as we were. She had been told lies about who she really was and where she came from. She suffered in many ways because of it. No one had told her that she had another father or siblings, and the man she thought was her father had been abusive to her for many years. In addition, she had been raised to hate Mexican people, and suddenly she found out that she was Mexican herself. She had to process all of this. Can you imagine walking into a laundromat to wash your clothes one day and having the whole course of your future change?

Over the years, I witnessed how brutal some people can be to someone who has a handicap. I would have never believed it if I hadn't seen how they treated my sister. At times, I was ashamed of the human race.

A few years later, I was about to graduate from high school and was having the time of my life. I still wasn't sure what direction I wanted to take in life, but I was open to change and opportunities. My plans to attend a classy cosmetology school in Iowa with a friend didn't really excite me anymore. I had aspirations to become a talented, stylish beautician with my own very hip, high-end salon in Chicago. As it turned out, fate had something else in mind for both of us. She moved to Florida.

A couple of weeks after school was out, I had planned to hook up with my best friend, Velinda, to go swimming at the pond by the diary and then head out to our softball game later in the day. On this hot, stuffy summer day there was something in the air, something thick and gloomy. It wasn't the humidity. I didn't know if it was a presence or my intuition trying to tell me something. I couldn't quite put my finger on it. It was a funky feeling deep inside of me.

There were no cell phones back then, so if you missed a call there wasn't much you could do about it. I thought Velinda was coming to my house; but once the meeting time had passed, I assumed I was wrong and headed out with another friend to see if she was at the pond. She wasn't! I remember hearing "Another One Bites the Dust" and "Take the Long Way Home" playing over the loud speakers while we searched for our friend during the next hour and a half. Once again, there was a strange feeling pressing on me. I wanted to leave because something in the air just wasn't right.

We headed back to the house to see if Velinda had been there and left a note. We'd missed her again, and at this point I didn't know how to catch up with her. I was frustrated, and that gnawing, uneasy feeling within me was expanding. I was no longer in the mood to play in the softball game. This was completely out of character for me. I have always been a very responsible person. But that feeling was too strong for me to ignore. Although I really felt guilty, I decided not to go to the game.

My other friend and I headed for the south of town, hoping to find Velinda at her boyfriend's house, which was kind of the central party place.

I knew she would be headed there after the game.

After we'd been playing cards for a few hours, Velinda showed up. She wasn't happy with me because of the mix up, and we argued. Finally, she announced that she was going to the pub just outside the state park, where many of the towns meet on the river. It was a great place for socializing, and Velinda felt really comfortable there.

I thought about joining her, but by now this feeling was burning and churning and I was still upset about the argument. I had to waitress the next morning anyway, so I decided to go home and get to bed early.

The next morning I was working the window at the restaurant when the phone rang. I picked up and said, "Welcome to Silver Frost. How can I help you?" It was my friend LuLu asking if I was okay. "Yes, I'm okay. Why wouldn't I be?"

LuLu said, "You had a game last night. Weren't you with Velinda? Haven't you heard what happened to her?"

"What are you talking about?" I asked. "I didn't go out to the pub. I went home early. What happened, LuLu?"

"Oh my gosh, Tari. You haven't heard yet! Velinda died in a car crash coming home from the pub last night."

I was speechless, but inside I was screaming, *NOOOOOOOOOOO!!!!!*

Backing myself into the corner, I was about to lose it when I saw my dad coming through the front of the restaurant to get me. I soon discovered that things were even worse, because Velinda wasn't alone in the car. Three other friends on the team had been with her after the game. Everyone except me! They were all badly hurt and were in the hospital.

Let me tell you, I was a mess! You see, I was the one who yelled at Velinda and made her slow down when she drove too fast. I was the one who took her keys from her and drove her car when she couldn't. I was the one who told her she was going to kill herself or somebody else one day! I was the one who wasn't there for her! I was the one who didn't rescue her! I was the one who never got to tell her I was sorry for not meeting up with her that day. I was the one who never got to tell her I loved her. I was the one who could have saved her! Why wasn't I there for her?

I was in a daze for weeks, trying to process the whole thing. At that time in my life, I knew God but didn't have a personal and close relationship. I think I knew God was keeping me from connecting with Velinda that day, but I didn't understand why I'd been spared. Over the next few years, I started to realize that God had a higher purpose for me. I just wasn't sure what it was.

My parents had a wealthy friend in California who had a huge aerospace company. Since my beauty-school days were over, they thought it would be best to send me there to start a new life. I spent the next 20 years of my life working for this man whom I adored. He was extremely powerful—a very handsome, controlling, and eccentric Irish entrepreneur. I was amazed by the number of people he bullied. I don't know if it was because they were afraid of him or afraid of losing their jobs, but not many men went up against him. I loved his family and the company. I learned to do what it takes, pay the dues, shut my mouth, and do what I was told.

Like most wealthy men with power, he was led by his ego. Dishonesty and affairs can weasel their way into any relationship, but tie that in with family and you have a big mess on your hands. I went through so much pain trying to figure out why some people allow their families to be destroyed. I loved this man with all my heart and felt torn between protecting him and speaking my truth.

I was able to see him from a different perspective than most people did. He had visited us often since I'd been a child. So while many people at work treated him like a god, I treated him like an uncle. When he was giving from his heart, I saw his huge generosity. I was amazed at the things he could do for people. I truly learned how to give from him, and giving of myself became part of my journey. When I became a wife and a mother, this generous man paid me a full salary for five years so that I could stay home and take care of my children. I am forever indebted.

During my years with this company, I really enjoyed working with men because I felt valued and appreciated. I also preferred to mingle with men rather than with women because I didn't like the way women sometimes treated each other. Too often they were catty, gossipy, and mean spirited. I observed the pain that they consciously or unconsciously caused each other and often wondered if this could be changed.

Ask, seek, knock, and the door will open!

For the next 14 years, I was very blessed to be a stay-at-home mom taking care of my two boys. When they were about four and six, I started to have this strange feeling again. This time I recognized it. Something was going on inside me, and it was familiar. This time it was touching me deep down in my soul. It made me uncomfortable enough to acknowledge it. I had a beautiful home on ten acres of land, a wonderful husband, and two fantastic kids, so why wasn't I happy? Wasn't this what every woman wants? Something in my heart told me to keep searching.

I also had joined a church and was trying my best to follow its fundamental beliefs. I became a model Christian, doing everything that religion told me to do. So how come I still wasn't happy? One problem was that this church kept telling me that all the other world views were wrong and that only their beliefs were right. That didn't resonate with me. Didn't God love everybody? Was it right for us to judge these other beliefs? Once again, something in my heart told me to keep searching. And I did! The feeling was still there, becoming stronger, more powerful.

During this time I kept asking for guidance and assistance for my future. Ask, seek, and knock, and the door will open! Teachers and guides started appearing. I have an amazing neighbor, Julie, who is a Reiki master. She stopped by on one of those days when I was very down and depressed. She said she felt that energy and came by to see if I was okay. I told her that I was in a funk! There was this feeling that I had again. She gave me a couple of books to read. One was about angels, and the other one was about chakras. Once I opened the books, I became obsessed with reading, expanding my mind and my perceptions. I loved working on myself as well as helping other women work on themselves. It was all very empowering!

Several times in my life I have had people lay their hands on me and say that I am going to do something very powerful in my life. One man who reads colors also told me that I am going to do something very powerful in my life, but he added that I am a healer. And so I continued to seek!

For nine years I pursued home-based businesses on health products, discovering empowerment and self-mastery. While I wasn't passionate about sales, I WAS passionate about promoting products that I believed in.

Then came 9/11, and the feeling was back stronger than ever. This time I went down into my barn, got down on my knees, wretched, released, and surrendered every ounce of anxiety, anger, fear, and pain I had inside of me.

Finally I realized that this feeling is God leading and guiding me. God protected me that hot summer day of the car crash. I understood that without this Higher Power I was nothing and could do nothing. So I talked with Him and said I was willing to be His servant and that I loved to help people. If He would open the doors for me, I would be willing to walk through them. Ask, seek, knock, and the door will open!

What I have learned in my life is to ask God for guidance. I continue to seek Him and am willing to be opened minded about the things He is trying to show me. Some lessons are short and sweet; others can take many years. I believe and trust that the doors will open for me. I intuitively feel His power guiding me, and then I take the action that is required.

I resonate with like-minded women who have a vision and a voice for change. I love and accept every friend and loved one for where they are today in their own personal growth. I am here to assist them with growth and expansion. I love to empower women by nourishing and cultivating them.

At one time in my life, I resisted change. Now I welcome it! I choose to come from a place of acceptance, forgiveness, and unconditional love. I choose to have an amazing and positive attitude no matter what cards life deals me. Life is what you make of it. I choose to enjoy the journey!

I want women to be the change that we expect in the world. Someone has to lead, and I think it's time that women step up to the plate. I believe that it's mothers' love and the accompanying protective power that will rise up to save the human race and our planet. Right now many of us are coming into our power and becoming stronger. Now is the time for us to come together. Those of us who are awakened and conscious know what we have to do. We all have to envision, believe, and trust the process.

Nations of the world now have the power to destroy and eliminate each other. Is this what we have evolved to do? We are going to have to change, or we will all die! It's time for us as women to ask for guidance, believe and trust in that guidance, and then act!

Are you with us?

About the Author

Tari Bussard is a passionate, driven woman dedicated to empowering women on a global level. She worked with an aerospace industry company for 20 years as a procurement specialist and then "retired" early to devote more time to her husband and two young sons. She considers herself very blessed to have been a stay-at-home mom over the next 14 years. While she raised her children, she found spirituality. As she created a home-based business during these years, her passions grew; and she realized she wanted to empower women globally.

Once she found her passions, her own life expanded and she became completely unstoppable. Now Tari chooses to share and collaborate with like-minded women who would like to lead and be the change in the world. She is also an advocate of bringing passion and personal growth into our education system.

Tari is the founder of the Empowerment 101 Community and can be contacted at http://Empowerment101Community.com, where she loves to nourish and cultivate women and to help them raise their inner power!

The Simmering Pot

by Nancy Markham

Growing More

This is the story of a pot that simmered for quite some time. I always say God's timing is perfect; but even I have to chuckle when in my mind's eye I picture God smiling and saying, "I bet you never could have imagined this!" You know what? He's right!

Many of the years I've lived would probably be considered rather typical, especially for a woman of my generation. Born in 1942 and a product of the Midwest, my early childhood had a Tom Sawyer quality about it. What a blessing. It helped to nourish my love of books, animals, nature in all its beauty, and joy in simplicity.

I wasn't one of the kids who know from the get go what their life purpose is. So after graduating from high school and because I felt I needed to do something, I settled on nursing school. My friends were going, and so off I went. A Halloween dance given by the school introduced me to my husband-to-be. When he graduated from college a year later, he decided to take care of his military obligation. He had grown up in California and so asked for the West Coast as his area of choice. They sent him to Guam. A couple of months after he arrived on "the rock," he wrote me a letter asking me to join him. I went. We were married there. I was barely 19.

The years that followed happily brought us four sons. My life was a whirlwind of activity, both with my family and helping out now and again in my husband's business. I was knee-deep in diapers throughout the "free love

231

'60s," which is so ironic it makes me laugh. I experienced the normal ups and downs, twists and turns comprising the tapestry of a life. The moments that I would "come up for air" and fleetingly consider additional facets of possibility, life would intervene and once again submerge my thoughts and feelings to linger there awhile longer. I've since come to realize that I was allowing it to do so. I didn't know what I wanted and didn't have a real understanding of how to gain that clarity. Thus, it was easier not to rock the boat. Be that as it may, it wasn't until I was in my 50s that the simmering began to bubble a bit more.

In order to keep busy, I tried on a couple of things to see how they fit. Initially, I took a part-time job. After that, it was trading commodities. I got into that because of a booklet that came in the mail. It was an opportunity to make good money, I could work from home and dictate the time I worked, and it was a challenge. There is an art as well as a science to being a good trader. I am exceedingly grateful for the experience, the people I met, and the lessons learned. Stepping through my fear was one. Back then, I really didn't recognize it as such, but it was one of the breadcrumbs that would lead me along my path. The search for the fork in the road had begun.

During the later part of my trading days, I started getting this deep, recurring feeling, this knowing, that I was getting ready for something. I had no idea what it was, and it was driving me crazy. I guess I thought I was preparing for a party because I attempted to get ready by going shopping. In a funny way, I was. But I am here to tell you, no amount of retail therapy worked on this one. Heaven knows I tried!

I ran through the gamut of thoughts and emotions. After all, when you get to be my age you should have this stuff down—right? So I thought. These were trying times, not only for me but also for my husband. I was going into uncharted waters, changing course. I was on a constant search for answers; but it was the balancing of the internal that I was unknowingly seeking, not the external I was stubbornly pursuing. It was the understanding and remembering that the one precedes the other that I was looking for.

Would you believe that the turning point came in an e-mail? It was the type of marketing message I would normally have deleted, but I chose to read this one. And when I finished reading, I immediately called and placed an order. There was no hesitation or waiting, just a strong knowing that this was what I needed to do. Pay attention to what pops out at you and to what your intuition is trying to tell you! Messages come in so many different ways. When you are having trouble making a decision, take a moment to step back, breathe, get quiet, focus on your heart, and listen.

The order I received was a home-study course in qigong, an ancient Chinese healing system involving meditation, controlled-breathing techniques, postures, and movement exercises designed to improve physical and mental well-being and prevent disease. I have always been interested in the healing arts, and the whole concept felt like exactly the right thing for me. The key is that it *felt* right. I certainly knew that I needed to restore my energy balance, and I'm sure that's what drew the strong response to the e-mail. At first my thinking, my concentration, was on the physical benefits. Who doesn't want more tranquility, vitality, and better health? I later truly came to understand that it is a state of being.

When the course arrived, I was in the midst of other things; so after a quick look-see, I put it on the shelf. I was just starting to delve into it a couple of months later when a letter arrived announcing a seminar in our area. At first I thought that perhaps it was premature for me to attend; but because I was having a knee problem at the time, I decided to go.

The next seminar I attended was a combination of different speakers where I not only was able to pursue my learning quest in the area of qigong but also developed an interest in feng shui. So it went. I was starting to discover that it all interweaves.

That led me to other seminars, retreats, and classes in qigong, feng shui, transformational studies, and so on. Once I became aware of the breadcrumbs, I couldn't seem to stop picking them up. My spirit was craving those morsels of preparation.

Don't ignore creative outlets when traveling your spiritual path. I discovered a love of painting that I didn't realize existed. It came in the form of a flyer from a local college. In my case, it seems God has been really big on sending messages through the printed word! I guess He's using whatever will best grab my attention and thinking that surely she will catch this one. Lately, He has become more diverse. It's probably more accurate to say that, thankfully, I'm not missing as many messages.

The flyer caught my attention because a couple of friends had been telling me I should try doing something creative. You might say I had just brushed it off! I had always loved art, but it had never occurred to me to create art myself. I always thought I couldn't draw. I don't remember why. So, because I thought I couldn't, I didn't even try. Be ever so careful about the thoughts and words you use. They can sabotage you. That's something I'm still working on.

All I can say is that it must have been my spirit that moved me to take the class. How wonderful it was to be able to express and incorporate my love of nature and color in one fell swoop. It got me out of that analytical left-brain side of me. It turned out to be another one of the breadcrumbs and was instrumental in helping to open my heart more, freeing and creating space for new to arrive.

Did I know when I stepped onto this path exactly where it was leading? No. Was it easy? Not always. Long-standing habits, clutter, limiting beliefs, doubt, and fear all made an appearance at one time or another, putting forth their best efforts to erect roadblocks. Isn't it interesting how hard we fight at times to stymie change? We seem to be able to think up an endless supply of excuses in order to maintain the status quo and avoid letting go. It's a continual work in progress.

At times I was physically tired. One time I almost missed a flight because I dozed off while waiting to board the plane for a seminar. I awoke suddenly to hear them calling my name. I had had maybe three or four hours sleep in the prior three days because I had stressed my sciatic nerve and it was certainly letting me know about it, but a part of me knew that it was important that I be at that seminar. After making the decision to go, synchronicity took over. I have found that if you are in the flow of what is in truth for you, all that you require will show up. Ask, ask, and ask.

At times I would question, *Where am I going with all this?* Turning back was out of the question, and I wouldn't have wanted to even if I could have. It took decision, action, and commitment on my part. It still does.

Search out the support and education you require. There is so much gratitude and love in my heart for all the masters who extended their giving hearts to me. They shared the gifts of healing, knowledge, and wisdom lovingly, saying in essence, *Don't worry. I've got you.*

I don't ever remember a time that I didn't believe in a Higher Power. For me, that was never the issue. I had to once again understand how to put all the pieces of the puzzle together, making it whole. Life will still happen, but living in love and joy is a choice. It's indeed an "inside job."

I'm living proof that it is truly never too late. Realization of your spirit is the journey. Whether you are aware of it or not, the longing to come home dwells within you. What you choose to create and allow will take you there. Sometimes you will repeat your experience over and over again until you learn what it is you need to know. That can be challenging. Each of us must come to it in our own way, unrushed and unhurried. Nothing stays the same, and growing requires us to be uncomfortable for a period of time. It requires that we do things we haven't tried before and for us to be open to whole new experiences. At some point, however, we must stand in our own power.

Keep putting one foot in front of the other doing the work, letting your intuition lead you. Step through the fear with a trusting heart. There is nothing to wait for. Every day you step out into the unknown. The safety is on the other side! Bring your voice to the world and do it through your heart. It's the person that impresses, not the words. Remember, you start dying when you stop learning and growing.

The rippling, intermingling, flowing waters of our Fountain of Youth create remembering of how we can honor our spirit, keep the energy flowing, and prevent stagnation. The following nine ripples I selected for the garden of our heart are a blending of the Laws of Nature, spirituality, and personal growth:

1. **Contagious Joy** is the uplifting, freeing vibration of love and peace that lives in our heart. It is not dependant upon circumstance. Joy and happiness walk hand in hand; but remember, if happiness is your permanent goal, it will remain elusive. Each day you wake up decide to focus on the joy in your life. What we desire, we create. Living in joy may be one of the best things we can do for our physical and mental health. Love is the strength of the soul.

2. **Eternal Gratitude** is an infinite amount, or state, of thankfulness. To quote Meister Eckhart, "If the only prayer you said in your whole life was 'thank you,' that would suffice." Gratitude is the feeling that occurs after receiving. Do not confuse it with indebtedness or obligation. Like joy, it is a strong factor in determining your well-being. By choosing to focus on what is right in our life, we shift into love and out of wallowing in the negative.

3. **A Trusting Heart** is a heart that is devoted, has direction, and makes decisions. It's a heart that has learned to relax and not "sweat the small stuff" because it's all "small stuff." Its opposite is a heart that is stressed and lives in fear. If we are ultimately going to succeed, we have to be based in the eternal to provide consistent motivating action. When we're coming from a place of truth and love, contentment and hope replace the worry. They fuel inspired action.

4. **Forgiving Spirit** describes the full, complete, unreserved act of forgiving ourselves and others. In forgiving, we release the past and create new beginnings. Forgiveness is not earned, and it's nonjudgmental. In giving forgiveness we unblock the flow of energy to us and from us. Forgiveness erases and gets rid of the anger that we are feeding. Although forgiveness can be one of life's toughest challenges, it is essential that we forgive; otherwise, the anger will bury us under its weight.

5. **Abundant Giving** is a flow of energy. You give freely and openly receive to keep it flowing. Quite simply, you give what it is you are wanting. Giving happily and without expectation is required. If we expect something in return when we give, we create a negative vibration that

severs the connection with spirit. By the same token, if we don't allow ourselves to receive, we again block the flow of energy. Stagnation is the result in both cases. There are so many ways besides the material that we can give. It can be a kind act, a smile, a compliment. The list is endless. There is always something we can do for the good of others if we desire to do so.

6. **Fearless Resiliency** is the ability to press forward so that our action does not become paralyzed. It's being able to bounce forward from change. Fear begets fear. Assess what is occurring right now in the present unemotionally. Then persist without exceptions. That is the mark of a great pathfinder. Determine what you have control of and what you don't. The Serenity Prayer by St. Francis of Assisi is a good reminder if you start veering off course. Being resilient means weathering the storms so we may once again set sail.

7. **Harmonious Balance** is flowing stability. When all the parts of your life are balanced with each other and the world around you, then you are in harmonious balance. It doesn't mean you eliminate all problems and conflicts. How you choose to distribute energy so that it fits your personal comfort zone creates that feeling of flowing stability. All of us have experienced times when we've had a whole lot of balls in the air. An important first step in creating balance and harmony is to know your goals and intentions and then proportion your energy accordingly.

8. **Expressive Creativity** is beautifully explained in a great quote by Alan Alda: "The creative is the place where no one else has ever been. You have to leave the city of your comfort and go into the wilderness of your intuition. What you'll discover will be wonderful. What you'll discover is yourself." The process can be used to provide healing. The scope of creativity includes much more than such things as painting or writing. It includes any time you venture onto a side path of the unknown and nurture your imagination in a land with no boundaries.

9. **Ageless Attitude** is a viewpoint of timelessness. It's the remembering of our spirit as a child would. Regardless of the numbers that we write

in the age box and all that goes with it, we transcend time when we choose to embrace this gift of life and live it with gusto.

Each of us creates our own life, but we are all on the same journey—just in different classes of experience. We are all a piece of the whole, but so often we lose touch with our spirit as we grow through our years on this Earth. When we start believing that our ego—our personality—is who we are, that's when "trouble in River City" begins. It leads us into situations and solutions that no longer serve us.

There is a great deal of fear and negativity surrounding us in the world today. Therefore, it's more important than ever before that we "show up." Our world depends on it. We are love and so very loved, but we do have to choose to live our lives in love and joy. It's a mindset. It takes practice. It takes letting go of that bag of "stuff" we all carry around that keeps us stuck. Having support is a critical key. Do the things that will help you to adjust. Start small and work up if the leap seems too large. Examine what you feel. Do your choices make for a feeling of expansion or one of retraction? Do they lift you up or shoot you down? Your intuition is your Higher Self. Let it guide you. Trust it! Trusting your vibes will open up a whole new world.

I'm reminded of the story of the two wolves, which is symbolic of the battle inside all of us. Do we want joy in our life or anger? generosity or greed? truth or lies? The answer to which one wins, of course, is the one that you feed.

Dreams count in number, along with the people who dream them. They are infinite in shape and size, and all have that profound rippling effect. By choosing love and joy, your effect will be felt and your life will be blessed without measure.

Walk with the dreamers, the believers, the courageous, the cheerful, the planners, the doers, the successful people with their heads in the clouds and their feet on the ground. Let their spirit ignite a fire within you, to leave this world better than when you found it.   -Wilfred Peterson

About the Author

Nancy Markham is a wife, mom, and grandma who values the sacred beauty in all things. It's her desire to share the intense love and joy she feels for life and the precious gift we have been given. Her art and writing are an expression of that love. In providing a supportive gathering place where the experience, creativity, knowledge, and wisdom of our life's journey can spill out, there is the opportunity and possibility to create even more ripples of inspiration. She believes that no matter what your age number is, exploration, learning, and collaboration form a vessel where action can grow and flourish.

Nancy believes we can make a difference in the world. Every moment is a moment of reinvention, and when we choose to allow the "Nine Ripples" of the "Fountain of Youth" to flow in and around us, we can create a "life masterpiece." By trusting our hearts, we will be rippling out and receiving the beauty of love.

Nancy's vision of GrowMore Community is a place of support and learning where women can collaborate, create, inspire, and be an encouraging, proactive presence in a world that can use what we have to offer. Join her in the GrowMore Community, where she explores "Sixty is the new Sixty," by visiting http://GrowMoreCommunity.com.

$\mathcal{T}$he Birth of a Poet

by Rebecca Hofeldt

Humble Beginning

This is an almost unbelievable yet true life story,
One in which I do find my joy and a bit of glory,
A real awakening at any age,
Certainly on a whole new stage.

As I had lay there in my hotel bed
Lines with rhymes, racing around my head,
Hard to believe or really understand
Pen and paper were now in hand.

It was really quite late at night
But here was a poem I had to write.
It all came about most unexpectedly
And so it seemed quite suddenly.

It snuck up on me so quietly, cleverly disguised,
Completely hidden from my own eyes,
At first a shock, a scare, and then a really sweet surprise.
Was I kidding myself, could it really be?
A poet lay hidden inside of me.

Destiny

I was discovering my purpose in life at last
Yet it was happening all so very fast.
I told myself NO, NO, it can't be true
That is something you would have knew.
Things like this just don't happen, only to someone else,
But who could and would believe it to be to one's own self?
Stranger things have happened, I guess
I'll just continue on this journey, my new conquest.

Now there are poems of cobwebs and dancing stars
At times I feel I must have gone crazy and my mind has landed on Mars.
Who Am I to write such things?
This is only done by other great human beings.

What has happened to me
Was actually, eventually my Destiny.
No longer do I live as I did in my past.
Now believing in myself, bravely and boldly I begin
Embracing, expressing, and sharing the poet within.

The Next Chapter of Life

What masterpiece lays dormant inside of you,
Awaiting, awakening?
You may not understand, but there is always a reason
This is now your season.

A life can begin at any time
Reborn, refreshed, renewed.
Standing in the doorway, as a ray of sunshine,
The next chapter of life you will now determine,
Drinking it in like the coffee freshly brewed.

Your God-given talents you cannot waste.
It is yours to live, empower, and then to embrace.

My dream, my wish is that you see
How much you are just like me
And yet individually each of us a bit unique.
Live your life now, not later as an antique.

The Calling of Your Inner Voice

Give your voice the power to speak.
Don't merely hold it, tongue in cheek.
Today it is your choice
To answer the calling of your inner voice.

Then your own song you will be singing
To your life you will start bringing
A reason, a meaning, to that feeling you observed
Knowing that you are here to be, to do, and to serve.

Following your purpose, your passions, your creativity
This is something you set free.
You can bring a smile to someone's face.
Through your works, the world can be a better place.

Words can give life new expression,
A new flavor and zest, a taste of spice,
Like looking in the mirror at your reflection
Seeing there is more than one chance to roll the dice.
Life is a wonderful, magical game,
Adventurously played, no longer each day the same.

A New Song

In this world there is so much to see, to accomplish, and to be,
In this world there is so much natural beauty,
So much laughter, so much love

When we look at the skies and what is above,
Surrounded by miracles, sights, and sounds,
Guided by intuition, followed through by intention.

Our paths will cross at some point in time
Tied together our hearts, yours to mine.
Joined soul to soul, hand in hand
No barriers shall exist in our lands.

A new song, from our hearts, through our voice, we will sing
And with that boldly and bravely we will bring
Harmony, balance, peace, joy, and above all grace
To a special place, where we will all embrace,
Where love will have no boundaries, no one face,
Everything is limitless in time, in space.
Together we can live in this place.

The Book of Humanity

Consciously aware of who we are,
Guided by one shining star,
Compassion and mercy are at our core.
Our children shall know what they are here for.

As the old world relinquishes to this renewed power
May we stand unified as one, each and every hour
For honor and dignity
And above all our integrity
Shall hold us to the truths of this universe.
Then each person will clearly and honestly see
What was written in each verse
Of the book of humanity.

This book is written by each one of us every day
For our footprints are here to stay.
The future belongs to the next generation.
Let us leave it a place of exploration,
A world where they are allowed to follow their inspiration.

About the Author

Rebecca "Becky" Hofeldt was born and raised in Southwest Colorado and moved to Wyoming in 1980, where she met and married her soul mate. They have been married for over 26 years and have an amazing son. They live on a small ranch where they raise, ride, and show cutting horses. Becky was an employee of a gas pipeline company for 23 years. Then in 2000 she decided to take a different path in life and stay home for a while. She devoted the next few years to relaxation and self-exploration.

During this time she found herself evolving into an entrepreneur and finding new interests in life. This is when her true "awakening" occurred. In late 2006 Becky discovered her long-hidden talent of writing poetry. Discovering this gift has been the beginning of a major transformation in her life.

Becky now enjoys writing all types of poetry: inspirational, spiritual, from poems of love to clouds, horses, sea shores, and so much more. While most of her poetry comes to her while she meditates, it may also come while she's driving down the road, riding, or enjoying nature. It can happen any time or any place.

Becky believes there is a poet within everyone—it only requires discovery. To share her gift and assist others in expressing their own poetry, she has started The Poet Within Community. To find out more, visit http://ThePoetWithinCommunity.com or e-mail her at jbj@wildblue.net .

Discovering Ten Personal Peace Portals

by Rijuta Tooker

Listening to My Soul

As I stepped through the doorway of my little cottage into the moonlit night, the intoxicating fragrance of night jasmine filled me with its sweetness. I walked down the narrow path and rounded a corner of the house that we used for yoga classes. A few more steps and I was on the soft, cool sand. Gentle waves splashed over my toes as I walked up and down the beachfront.

I really loved being here on Paradise Island at the Yoga Retreat. The Bahamian sun, sand, and sea, tropical fruits, yoga, and swimming every day made my work seem like play. It all began as an answer to my prayers.

But tonight I had something on my mind and an emptiness in my heart. After my divorce, I had come here from Connecticut with the hopes of finding myself. I had been teaching elementary school children as an enrichment teacher. I also danced with the Hartford Ballet Company and choreographed for our local Little Theatre group. There was a house, money, and social life; but a feeling of emptiness had been growing within me that was hard to explain to my friends. Was this all there was to life?

Much of my childhood had been wonderful, yet there were periods of emotional chaos, turbulence, noise, dysfunction, and neglect. Being the eldest of four, I felt the responsibility of being the peacemaker and assumed that role for years. My longing for a life of peace and calm and an understanding of the deeper meaning of life was to shape my entire adulthood.

Now, here in this idyllic setting, I was beginning to have the same kinds of feelings I had before my divorce—something was missing.

In Connecticut I was taking hatha yoga classes and found the postures to be very soothing. We meditated; and although I had difficulties keeping my mind still, there were moments of deep peace.

My husband had no interest in these things. There was little effort on his part to understand or to even have a conversation. We were growing further and further apart. We finally divorced. It was time for me to move on.

After I had become certified as a yoga instructor, one of my yoga friends came to see me. He said that an Indian man from New York had given a talk and meditation the night before. He invited me to another that evening.

Little do we know the significance certain events will have in our lives when they first occur. I went to the meeting-meditation and heard the person who was to become my spiritual master: Sri Chinmoy. All that he said resonated with me, answering questions I had been recently asking myself. Although I felt connected to what he said, I did not become his student right away. I did not realize what it meant to have a spiritual teacher, nor was I consciously looking for one. My soul was trying to tell me that I had found the "missing something," but the message was not clear to me.

There is a saying: "When the student is ready, the teacher will appear." The teacher had appeared, but was I ready? No one had asked me out loud, "Do you want this Indian man as your spiritual teacher?" So the experience came and went. However, I would soon meet one of his students.

Invited to accept a job at the Paradise Island Yoga Retreat, I was thrilled with the prospect of something new and exciting. Bravely, I handed in my resignation to the Board of Education.

The forces of destiny had not given up easily. I had been at the Yoga Retreat for a couple of weeks when a woman and her husband came down from New York. We became good friends, and I soon learned that they were students of the same spiritual master I had met in Connecticut.

I asked many questions about their philosophy, meditations, and activities. My interest was piqued, but I still didn't realize this might be a way of life for me. My new friend offered me a teaching job if ever I decided to leave the island. At the time, I was not interested, just curious.

I continued to walk in the Bahamian moonlight. I'd been on the island for more than two months, and now I was having the same feelings of emptiness and unrest again. How could this be? All of my life I had been dreaming of a calm, quiet, no-turmoil, peaceful life. Here on Paradise Island, I originally thought I would have everything I could possibly want. I was happier. I felt more at peace. Yet now I felt I was not where I was supposed to be. Resolving nothing, I headed back to my little cottage.

I soon realized that I had to leave. Calling my friend in New York, I gratefully accepted her invitation to go there and teach for her. The door to New York had just opened, so perhaps this was the next step. I was allowing the forces to draw me toward my destiny.

Settled in New York and teaching yoga for my friend, I began to join her at the meetings and meditations of her spiritual teacher. This path of yoga and meditation began to fulfill my earlier yearnings. A life focused on peace and loving oneness was exactly what I needed. I "officially" requested to become a student and was gratefully accepted.

Due to an inner feeling I could not deny, I finally saw the connection between my seeking and what was being placed before me. I was blessed that I did not listen to the fears and doubts of those around me in Connecticut. Gratefully, the whispering voice of my soul proclaimed victory when I took action and made the necessary changes to move my life forward.

My meditation life began to blossom, and I reaped the rewards of having a living spiritual master of the highest caliber. Consciously living a life of meditation and spirituality under the guidance of a spiritual master was a new experience. Someone who has already walked along the path of meditation can illumine many of life's mysteries. The missing element during my marriage and while working in the Bahamas could only be found in New York. I was meant to be on this particular spiritual path with this particular spiritual master. I now began to find true fulfillment.

Beginning to understand higher truths, I incorporated what I could into my life. My teacher was helping to awaken my aspiring heart through his inspiration and example. I could feel his spiritual presence of peace and love and received inner knowingness from the connection with him. The daily teachings and practices were life changing, life enhancing, and life fulfilling for me—lessons I have come to live by. They have brought me peace, clarity, inner poise, joy, and a sense of loving oneness.

Discovering I Am a Peace Seeker

While in college, I recall one of the students asking me, "What is the one thing you would want most of all if you could have it?" I quickly and spontaneously answered, "World Peace!" surprising myself. So it was no surprise that I found myself working at the United Nations. Inspired by the visionaries who had shaped this international community of almost 200 countries, I relished working with many people of different cultures and beliefs. The absolute necessity of working together as a team added to my growing experience of realizing that all people are indeed one, regardless of the differences we perceive with our five senses.

An activity that had a profound influence on my personal peace-seeking efforts was a twice-weekly peace meditation for staff and delegates held at the U.N. by my spiritual teacher. These quiet times of stillness and meditation inspired me to keep a part of every day for peace and silence.

While at the U.N., I worked with many wives of ambassadors and delegates. We met once a month for lunch at one of the homes of the wives and always ended our meetings with a 7-minute peace meditation. During our meetings women were encouraged to continually strive to take their lives to the next higher level—to greater peace and oneness.

Each morning in my office at the U.N., 10 to 12 directors—men of varying religions and spiritual beliefs who actually worked for world peace every day of their lives—met for a 7-minute peace meditation. A totally unique group, these men were dedicated to attend each morning for silence and inspiration, taking turns bringing in quotes on peace to be read aloud.

Each year while traveling widely on holiday, I taught peace meditation techniques to many, thus fulfilling my desire to contribute to the inner and outer peace of this world. My outer experiences as well as my inner meditation have helped me learn many life lessons and have opened many portals that helped me to establish my own personal peace.

Ten Personal Peace Portals

In this rapidly changing world, it is necessary that each woman move forward with speed and excellence to find, commit to, and live by her own set of heart-centered principles. Women are looking for peace. They are looking for change—personal, professional, and, especially, change within our institutions, many of which are crumbling before our very eyes.

Women everywhere can become an aspiring force for change in the shift of consciousness on Earth. We must change our perspective to a new way of thinking, feeling, and becoming. By internalizing simple principles and practices, each woman can learn to align herself with her highest values to transform her life into a new and more perfect reality. For a peaceful global change to come about, one must start with one's noble self.

For those who wish to contribute to creative changes that will impact humanity locally and globally, I offer ten Personal Peace Portals that I have been blessed to learn and live by during my life journey.

1. Be happy.

To be happy requires only an inner attitude, not outer circumstances. Be happy in the moment with what you have and with what you are. View your personal world with happy eyes. Make no complaints; offer only gratitude.

Do whatever it takes to be happy. Deny everyday stressors the opportunity of taking away your joy and peace. Doubts, worries, anger, and resentment cannot stay long in your heart of happiness. Remember to use your inner light to illumine and transform all negativities—immediately.

Think happy thoughts. Look for happy feelings. If need be, move your thoughts and feelings up a level closer to happiness. Act in ways that bring happiness. To have a happy heart, serve others selflessly. One of the easiest and quickest ways to be happy is to put a smile on your face and repeat to yourself, "I am happy! I am happy!"

2. Live from your heart and soul.

To live from your heart and soul of oneness is most important in order to bring about inner peace for yourself and, ultimately, outer peace to the global community. Living in your mind is a life of separativeness. Living in your heart is connectivity, collaboration, creativity. Your mind is a wonderful tool, but your heart is where you live.

You are not the body or the mind; you are not your personality or your emotions. You are the heart and soul. Live from your heart and soul and be free to live your truth. When you seek to access and hold sacred the very highest in you, you will be living from your heart and soul.

We know ourselves through our limited body: I am hot; I am cold. This is mental, limited knowledge that leads us to spend most of our time in struggle, competition, fear, and worry. When we live from our heart and soul, we spend our time in ease and flow, in oneness-love and peaceful collaboration. This is expansive, limitless wisdom knowledge.

In order to "know thyself," you must discover your true essence, your inner capacities that allow you to go beyond limitation. You may wish to establish the discipline of inner search through prayer and meditation in order to discover the many inner secrets of living from your heart and soul.

3. Dance with life.

To dance with life, simply move your life. Dance with your body, ideas, emotions, words, and actions. Create your own dance of life. Dance it daily, as if no one were watching to criticize or limit you.

The best movement is the kind you enjoy. When there is no movement, there is stagnation. With movement, there is newness, growth, creativity, aliveness. Life is about constant change. Movement facilitates change.

Movement of the body brings good health and a special freedom that allows you to go forward with ease. Movement of the mind brings greater knowledge, more clarity, broader perspectives. Movement of your emotions in an upward direction takes you toward a higher resonating experience.

Dance your life with love. Love yourself first; then you can love others. Dance your life with gratitude for all that you are; you will become more of what you desire to be. When you can flow with and enjoy your own dance with life, you have excelled in the most important dance class.

4. Discover your inner silence.

Inner silence is more than an absence of all speech, sound, and noise. It is a stillness, a quietude that we can find by going deep within our hearts. Silence is fullness, oneness, our highest reality. We can find it most easily by focusing on our love and light with inner poise and tranquility.

To experience inner silence, one must have a sacred space. It is in your heart. Wherever you go, you will have a "silence temple" within you.

We all need time each day for inner silence. This can be as informal as a solo walk in the park or as formal as prayer or meditation. A daily disciplined intention to enjoy regular silent time helps. Silence can assist in making your world more beautiful, more peaceful. In inner silence you can find your highest truth, hear your inner voice, and know the real in you.

Once you have discovered and connected freely with your inner silence, go ahead and create your outer sacred silence space. Make it beautiful!

5. Celebrate!

Who are the happiest persons? The happiest persons are those who find cause to celebrate life's victories, large and small.

Celebrate everything! Celebrate getting up five minutes earlier in the morning. Celebrate receiving a college degree. Celebrate all birthdays, anniversaries, national holidays. Celebrate for yourself. Celebrate with your family, friends, colleagues, and the groups you belong to.

We are here on Earth to experience as much joy as possible, so celebrate with joy. Find at least one thing daily that you can honestly celebrate.

6. Go in peace.

Wherever you go, go in peace. Whatever you say, say in peace. Whatever you do, do in peace. Your peaceful intentions will foster peaceful intentions in others. You can never feel peace in your doubting and frustrated mind; however, you can always go to your peace-loving heart of satisfaction. Personal peace is your inner wealth. Honor this above all else.

Only when we establish peace within can we experience peace without. This world desperately needs your inner peace, your commitment and aspiration to change the chaos and turmoil surrounding your everyday life.

Harmony and peace are one. Be in harmony with your surroundings and with all those around you. If you cannot sing the same note, find a note that harmonizes. Live in harmony with nature. Honor and treat your Earth with dignity and respect, just as you would wish to be treated.

Commit to establishing your own inner peace for your sake, for the sake of the world. We can co-create a world of greater peace, love, light, and joy through our oneness collaboration if we always go in peace. *God has many children, but His fondest child is peace.* -Sri Chinmoy

7. Find your true voice.

Your true voice can only be found through your heart and soul, your inner silence. You can hear your own voice. Let it speak through your conscience. Words are sculptors of your future. Be wise when you speak. If it does not add to the conversation, do not say it. Every word counts.

Special words have built up a resonance or vibration from being used in a certain way with certain feeling over the years. Check the words you use repeatedly throughout the day. Do they inspire? detract? encourage? support? The inspiring words that you use can be coming from your heart and soul. These inspiring words give hints about your true voice.

Can you hear your own unique VOICE? What are your thoughts, feelings, aspirations, and commitments? Keep your internal freedom by staying true to your inner voice. This is who you really are. Don't let outer circumstances dictate what your true voice can say. Be in total alignment with your highest values to help you find your true voice.

8. Use your power of love.

Love conquers all. The power of a mother's unconditional love for her child enables her to move heavy objects in order to protect her child.

The power of love to heal is well known. Healing energy is now being used by practitioners who facilitate the healing energy of the client to bring about near miraculous healings. The power of love to inspire others is historical. Many leaders have led remarkably with their love power.

You also have the power of love. Use it as often as possible. Wrap all encountered negativity in love and send it on. At every moment you have a choice: you can fly upward with love or you can fall downward with separativeness. You can help to heal every time you surrender to your highest aspirations and use your power of love.

9. Aspire to go higher.

Aspiration is your inner cry to go beyond that which you are currently experiencing. You aspire for progress and have a goal that moves a little higher than where you find yourself. When you aspire, you constantly desire to reach a place of higher consciousness; you become a person who increases her excellence in all that she thinks, feels, says, and does. Aspiration is like the fuel one needs to keep going on, to continue climbing higher, always in an expansive direction.

First start with inspiration. Something or someone inspires you outwardly. Then add your inner aspiration. The inner and the outer must go together. Be inspired. Aspire. Commit. Manifest.

10. Never give up.

When you find something that will take your life to the next level or that will add to your happiness, make a commitment to go in that direction. Continue on until you reach your goal, one step at a time. Keep trying. She who gives up, loses. She who continues on can still be a winner.

If there is no apparent solution, experiment until you find one or create a new one that suits you. There is a solution for everything.

Live with hope. One with hope in her heart will never give up. Conquer fear and doubt. Leave aside all of life's obstructions. Even if you lose your way a great many times, the answer can be just around the next corner.

The current shift of consciousness is bringing an end to much of what we knew and held dear, yet at the same time there is a yawning gap to fulfill the desperate need of a new reality. Who will create the massive changes needed for our new world? You and I and the oneness hearts of our sisters and brothers. We are in the budding stages of a new creation here on Earth, moving toward a time when more and more individuals can live their own personal truth. Around us we see the colossal collapse of our institutions. Let us avoid entirely the old paradigms of thinking and being.

My hope is for each woman to move into her own inner sacred heart space. Here she can access and utilize her heart and soul power in order to create from purity, oneness, and the highest truth. When we align ourselves with things that do not serve our highest good, our experience defaults to the stream of forces that surround us at any given time. When we align ourselves with the highest within us, we create with ease and flow.

My vision is that forward-looking women will co-create the life they desire through collaboration with other women globally. With aspiration, they can create a new and beautiful reality for the highest good of all. To enjoy a higher and more peaceful life, we must avoid fear, doubt, worry, resentment, and other negativities. Let us attract and create oneness, trust, beauty, peace, joy, love, and light by becoming that which we seek.

All women must come to know and express their inner power of creativity and love. Each woman must blossom into her rightful power as a co-creator of a oneness world family. She must feel that she not only has a personal right but also a duty to feel and speak her own truth. In this way she can become a most beautiful instrument of peace, joy, love, and light.

About the Author

Rijuta Tooker is a creative health and lifestyle coach who lives in the New York City area. She aspires daily to access that special inner love-light energy of creativity, passion, joy, and soul power so she can better serve others that they may do the same.

Rijuta specializes in teaching concentration and meditation techniques, assisting many to illumine and transform their lives so they can enjoy a more enriched and sacred lifestyle. She has guided thousands to discover rich, inner resources that come from tapping into their inner heart and soul power and then learn to express their inner truth outwardly.

Rijuta has a master's degree in education, has been a student of spiritual master Sri Chinmoy for over 30 years, and shares a life experience of over 25 years teaching and coaching in many countries around the world.

Rijuta founded the Creative Concentration Community in order to offer techniques and tools to assist the individual to move through blocks and resistance to a more purposeful and fulfilling life. Women learn to create with magical ease and flow as they manifest their unique greatness. They learn to direct their creative energies in a more peaceful, joyful, and loving way. Through collaboration and oneness, women are co-creating a new paradigm to manifest a beautifully sustainable future for all.

You can e-mail her at rijuta@earthlink.net. For more about her community, visit http://CreativeConcentrationCommunity.com.

$\mathcal{E}$xploring the Frontier Within

by Lynette Chartier

The journey began in the fall of 1982, when I gave birth to a beautiful baby girl named Chantalle. Unfortunately, we only had her with us for a very short time since she was born with a heart defect, transposition of the great arteries. In spite of treatment and surgery, she was unable to pull through.

Chantalle was a rose that never had the opportunity to bloom. It took me many years to grasp the full meaning of the law of nature and to integrate that experience. Children are like seeds in a flower garden. When we plant the seeds, they do not all grow. Sadly and at times very difficult to understand, not all children are meant to live a long, healthy life. They come into our life for a reason. The joy they bring is very real and intense, and we are to cherish them. Yet due to no one's fault, they leave too quickly.

Shortly after Chantalle's passing, I decided that I would never stay home full time to raise children because the idea of losing another child was unbearable. I knew that I needed a structure to my days. Therefore, ten days following Chantalle's death, I signed a teaching contract that would allow me to develop my craft in a grade-one classroom.

What I didn't realize as a young woman was that the strategy of pushing down emotions in order to keep moving forward would not prove effective long term. Eventually we need to work through our emotional material because it is by working through our emotions that we can birth our spiritual lessons. Emotions that are continuously repressed cause energetic blocks. For the most part, we tend to be unaware of these blocks and of their negative impact on our daily lives.

The years that followed Chantalle's passing moved quickly and were focused mainly on building a career, having and raising two sons, and devoting three years to teaching in the Yukon. Going North was a way of spending more time in nature, experiencing new adventures, and gaining broader perspectives on life. In 1993 my family and I moved back to our home town of Winnipeg, Manitoba, in order to be closer to friends and family and get back into the educational system we had previously known.

Throughout those busy years and often stress-filled times, I was experiencing some health challenges. Part of me knew that they were due to my driven nature, my deep desire to please others, my habit of taking on worries and responsibilities that were not mine to own, and my fear of failure. Yet I was unable to let go.

The stress headaches and intestinal-track issues were frequently debilitating. I remember a two-week stretch where I consumed a bottle of 100 extra strength Tylenol®. When that was not effective, the doctor prescribed something stronger. The headaches would leave, but I was left exhausted and unable to focus. It was only years later, when I decided that I would research headaches and their causes, that I came to recognize the physiological cycle that I had put myself into. By changing my diet, exercising, and finding ways to de-stress, I managed to turn my health around. Now headaches are a thing of the past for me.

As a young mom and busy teacher, I wasn't making the time to listen to the quiet voice within that was trying desperately to be heard. I ignored all nudges and intuition, and I chalked up the internal discord within my body as being so-called "normal." After all, others around me were experiencing the same type of story, only the circumstances were different.

In 1999 I was presented with a business opportunity, and I decided that perhaps a home business would be an eventual solution to my challenges. I could build my business part time and leave my teaching career when the time was right. You see, teaching had become all-consuming—there were so many needs to be met and possibilities to explore, yet there were never enough hours in a day. Although I loved working with children, somehow between the educational politics, a system that was slow in changing, the late nights prepping and marking, the unrealistic demands from society, and the general public's perception of educators, I had forgotten why I had become a teacher in the first place. Today I know that many of the non-serving beliefs and perceptions I had back then were due to my own unrealistic expectations of myself. The Universe is simply a mirror!

Not knowing how to say "No" nor how to set up appropriate boundaries and make time for my own well-being, I was one stressed-out chic on the inside; yet on the outside I appeared to have it pretty much together. The morning I awoke thinking that suicide was a way out of a life gone amuck, I actually scared myself to the point of knowing something desperately needed to be changed. The thought of working from home and being my own boss appealed to me.

The time I spent in two network marketing companies broadened my horizons by bringing me new insights, travel opportunities, and a chance to acquire a new skill set and make new connections. Even though I did not turn the opportunity into a great financial success, it was a most valuable education.

Although my husband and I got along fine, the daily pace did not leave us much time to look closely at ourselves and our own issues. Brushing things under the carpet believing they would get resolved with time added further discord to my internal state. Once again, ignoring certain clues and not being able to really connect with the voice within pulled me further away from my true self.

Let's fast forward to June 23, 2004. With one week left before my summer holidays, I had spent the afternoon in a staff meeting. When I got home, my eldest son informed me that Grandma had been taken to the hospital and I was to call my sister. My mother had just experienced a massive stroke at the age of 69, and it brought her to her untimely death within 24 hours. I was not particularly close to my mother at the time, yet I had always felt drawn to her, trying to understand who she was.

It was only after her death, while writing her eulogy and then later while sorting through her things, that I tapped deeply into a subconscious knowing that I had had all along. My mother was clearly a misunderstood woman. And then the aha moment came. The fact was that she could not be understood because she herself did not really know who she was and why she was. As a result, she was one more statistic, one more person who had died with her music still in her, forever to remain unplayed.

Every time I walk into a cemetery and see tombstones, it is the thought of all that music not played that brings me sadness: Which book has not been written? Which business did not get started? Which "I love you!" was not spoken? Which solution was not invented?

I made a decision during that summer of 2004 that I was not going to die with my music in me. I was going to sing my song, maximize my potential, and walk my true path for several generations: hers, mine, Chantalle's, and perhaps even for my future grandchildren. I decided to put an end to certain aspects of my French Catholic upbringing and cultural way of being that had been holding me back. These included letting go of fear and guilt one layer at a time and putting an end to playing small so that others could be comfortable.

Several months later, picking up a newspaper that my husband had left on the kitchen table, I came across an ad promoting a weekend conference on finances. I had a feeling that I needed to be there, not so much for the content I would hear but because of someone I was destined to meet.

On that fateful weekend in March 2005, I met a psychologist/coach who became my mentor. Although I had already spent several years diving into personal development and attending workshops, I was about to embark on something different, something I had at some level really been looking for. I was excited, grateful, uncomfortable, and even a little afraid when he said, "We are about to crack the veneer." What had I gotten myself into?

Some people choose to go on for years living with situations and circumstances that are not for their highest good just to avoid "15 minutes" of pain. The question for me became, "Lynette, are you willing to go through the awkwardness, the discomfort, the necessary conversations in order to get to the other side of the bridge?" My answer was "Yes."

For the following 15 months, I devoted the beginning of each day to reading, studying, and digging deep within. The coaching calls, the conversations, and the personal changes that ensued were not always easy. Yet they stretched me beyond anywhere I had ever been stretched before. They allowed me to gain a much deeper understanding of myself, of others, and therefore of the world. I started to recognize the power and courage I had within. It actually frightened me at first.

In the summer of 2006, I stepped away from my job security to work full time from home, believing that I would leap and the net would appear. That proved to be only somewhat true. I had forgotten about divine timing! I had other lessons to learn before reaching my goals of joy, success, and abundance; and the Universe would deliver these lessons in divine order. Through working my business, doing contract work, traveling, avoiding a bankruptcy, attending conferences, and taking more classes, the little voice within was speaking up louder and louder. I could choose to ignore it, but I could no longer deny its presence.

Coming to a fork in the road in the spring of 2009, I needed to choose a path. I knew that whatever path we choose in life, there will be moments of sadness, different layers of issues to confront, and fears to override if we want to walk our true path. Although my immediate choice was not taking me to my final career destination, it was a path that I believed would allow me to continue to get closer to my life's purpose, to grow, and to allow deeper personal unmasking.

In April I decided that I would go back to the Department of Education and take on a management position. I felt that doing this would assist me to be fully grounded, to regroup, to make course corrections, and to set off anew on the next leg of my journey.

One of the key lessons I had internalized by then was that you can never give away what you do not own. If you do not truly accept and love yourself, you cannot deeply love and accept another human being. If you cannot forgive yourself, you will always at some level be critical of another.

At this point I had enough self-acceptance, self-esteem, and self-confidence to understand that going back to something I had known and left was not a failure. It was a gift to myself. Such an opportunity would allow me to take care of my basic needs and make the next major shift.

Having recently completed more internal work, I saw that I needed to officially end my marriage after nearly 29 years. In truth, it had already been over for years. Ironically, once I realized that at a subconscious level stepping away from the marriage had represented for me the "ultimate failure," I could finally voice my feelings and start the procedures.

If you have ever sewn, you have certainly stitched some seams that needed to be undone and resewn. There are two ways of doing so: either you yank the thread out and risk marring the fabric in the process; or you choose to slowly and carefully pull the thread out, lay the fabric anew, and sew a new seam, all the while leaving the fabric intact. Roland and I chose the latter as a way to end the marriage. We chose to see to each other's and to our grown children's well-being. At the time of this writing, the house has been sold; and we have three weeks left before we each move into our own condos. We were able to list everything we owned on a sheet of paper, do a walk-through of the house, and within an hour agree to who was taking which pieces of furniture and other items. Imagine—no lawyers and no negotiations, no big bills, simply a willingness and intention to see that we are both well in the process.

There have been moments of annoyance, resentment, and confusion over the past year, yet we have avoided many storms due to our commitment to take responsibility for our life experience, our determination to continue on the path of self growth, and our willingness to turn within and tap into our true essence.

It was frequently well-meaning friends and acquaintances who caused some grief by saying such things as "That's not a separation!" Obviously, ours was not the path of the masses. Yet we trusted our own internal voices enough to know we had to do it our way.

I am confident that we will always maintain this deep respect, that we will have an appreciation for each other and a treasured friendship. After all, Alain and Rémi brought an incredible amount of joy into our lives as they were growing up, and they continue to do so now that they are grown and have moved out on their own. Roland and I have been at our best while raising and spending time with them.

Currently I am looking forward to the new chapter that is about to unfold and to the inspiring and purpose-driven projects that are on the horizon. I am deeply grateful for the life lessons that I have learned.

Speaking of life lessons and challenges, over the last eight years my willingness to be open and honest with myself and to persistently walk the path of personal development has allowed me to transcend some key challenges, such as giving my power away; being frequently ungrounded by spreading myself too thin; lacking discernment; harbouring many fears such as the fear of failure; and being unable to find my voice, know my true purpose, and tap into my own wisdom because I kept looking outward. Were the moments of discomfort, fear, sadness, anxiety, and sheer frustration, along with all the tears shed throughout the entire process, worth it? Yes!

Allow me to share with you some of the wisdom I picked up along the spiritual path. By the way, these are gold nuggets that I have personally experienced and benefitted from, not merely read and understood. There is a huge difference between doing the work of shaping the soul and being around the work. Being around the work can feel cool; doing the work is messy. However, it is truly in the mess that you experience the clarity and see further than you have ever seen before.

1. In order to change our personal circumstances we must first know who we are. We must return to a place of wholeness. Being whole requires that we learn to turn within, where our true answers lie. By turning within, we develop the ability to integrate the ego, soul, and essence of our being and to tap into our divine gifts and our purpose.

The answers that are true and unique to each of us are found by looking within and not by looking without. Only when we truly know ourselves can we really know another, see the world from a 35,000-foot view, and then positively impact the world around us.

By learning to get quiet within and create space between my thoughts, I could finally hear my own "soululor phone" (a term used by Jeff Brown in his book *Soulshaping: A Journey of Self-Creation).* This enabled me to connect with my inner voice. I can now intuit more accurately and tap into my own wisdom. The space created between thoughts allowed my subconscious knowing to bubble up.

2. It does not matter where you start on the path of personal growth—whether you choose to start in the emotional, physical, spiritual or mental realm—because everything touches everything. With time, what you do in one area of your life will impact the others.

Although you can start anywhere, you will probably want to make feeling better physically a priority fairly early in the process. When you are not at ease physically, it is much harder to keep the mind focused on the positive.

3. Taking small steps gets you where you want to go faster. When taking baby steps, you actually build up your self-confidence and have the time to do some course corrections. You can avoid becoming overwhelmed and stepping into the realm of drama and chaos.

Learning to move like a turtle was quite effective for me. I recommend sticking your neck and head out for a while. Be bold and brave. Then pull yourself back in, where you can integrate the learning and gestate if need be. As long as you keep stepping out, it doesn't matter how many breaks you take along the way. Simply do what feels right. "Three steps forward and two steps back" is still progress!

4. Discover where your personal energy leaks are coming from and put a plug in them. Energy leaks come in various shapes and sizes and from many places. You can lose energy by allowing negative words and images to influence your mind. An overdose of the nightly news and mass media doom and gloom will ultimately sow the seeds of fear.

Relationships that drain you emotionally and focus on keeping you stuck and playing small are definite energy leaks. It has been said that if you look at the five people with whom you spend the most time, it will give you a good indication of where you are headed, what money you will earn, and which types of relationships you will keep attracting.

Simple things like foods that do not nourish you but leave you feeling lethargic and dis-eased are energy leaks that can be easily and quickly plugged. By becoming aware of what you put into your mouth, you can make simple yet profound shifts that last a lifetime. Fresh fruits, vegetables, pure water with trace minerals, and sea salts go a long way in increasing one's sense of well-being. Breathing deeply and exercising the body are both great healers.

Women frequently create energy leaks by spreading themselves too thin and trying to do too much at once. For years, I was a huge fan of multi-tasking. Since it frequently took up extra time and led me to being unfocused, I have changed my perspective somewhat. Some things simply need a block of undivided and uninterrupted time.

Observing other women around me, I became very aware of our gender's frequent inability to set appropriate boundaries. Learning to say "No" can be hard. Yet for everything you say "Yes" to, you are saying "No" to something else that could be more valuable long term.

Regularly turning within and combining experiences for personal growth such as being coached, attending conferences, participating in workshops, and seeking various healing modalities will lead you to unmask yourself. Being willing to unmask leads you to your truth and to being your authentic self. For those of us who have spent years disconnected from our true selves, it can be quite uncomfortable when we finally allow ourselves to get close. It can be lonely on the spiritual path as we let go of people, situations, and circumstances consciously or as they drop away naturally.

There are times we must walk part of the path by ourselves until we find what Jeff Brown calls our "soulpod" (the person or group of people with whom our soul finds the most resonance at any given moment).

The internal, or spiritual, journey is a continuous one. However, there does come a point where the inner strength you have developed, the courage you have cultivated, and the wisdom you are able to tap into will grow exponentially rather than in a linear fashion. All of this will leave you feeling centered and confident that what you are searching for is searching for you and that it is just around the corner. You will connect with your life's purpose and feel a deep sense of satisfaction.

My personal toolbox now contains the following: a clear understanding of myself and others, compassion, courage, well-developed discernment, the ability to be grounded, and my accumulated wisdom. Using these tools enables me to fulfill my life's purpose—helping people understand and make sense of their world. For now, I pursue the projects and services that I am most passionate about during my hours away from the office until I am in a position to transition to them full time.

If you can remember only one thing from reading these pages, I hope it will be this: Do not die with your music in you! You have gifts, talents, and potential waiting to be uncovered. You are here on Earth at this point in time for a reason that only you can fulfill. If you forget to sing your song, it will remain forever unsung.

Know that to be able to sing your own song you must truly know who you are. This enables you to align with your gifts and life purpose. And you can only know who you are if you consciously choose to turn within and to unmask. Exploring the frontier within is the journey that will liberate you. It is not a journey for the faint of heart. However, it is a journey that will give you a strong foundation and an ability to tap into your gifts and your power. It is a journey that will lead to joy, contentment, satisfaction, success (internal and external), and abundance.

Only you can get quiet enough in order to hear your "soulular phone" when it rings. The choice is yours. What will you choose?

About the Author

Lynette Chartier is an educational entrepreneur, a mother of two awesome young men, and a woman expressing her voice and following her purpose of helping others understand their world.

She is passionate about exploring the dimensions of the inner world and walking her soul path in order to live a more authentic life. By sharing her accumulated experiences, knowledge, and wisdom, Lynette assists other women to incorporate simple success rituals into their daily activities and to develop habits and strategies they require to manifest more joy, internal success, and abundance in their life.

"You can never give away what you yourself do not possess—whether that is on a physical, mental, spiritual, or emotional basis." With this core belief, Lynette is currently working in collaboration with the BodyMind Institute of Calgary, Alberta, Canada, where her latest project is to create condensed, cutting-edge curriculum for the purpose of teaching women around the world the attitudes, knowledge, and skills that will facilitate their work with children. Lynette dreams of a world with happy, confident children who know themselves and can express their gifts and talents, a world where kids grow up with a higher level of consciousness, ready and able to contribute to the emerging new world.

Lynette is the founder of the Ritual Diva Community, where she assists women in discovering, recognizing, integrating, and mastering simple success rituals, thus allowing them to align their abilities with their purpose and passion. This, in turn, enhances their capacity to create a life of joy, fulfillment, abundance, and inner peace. To visit her community, go to http://RitualDivasCommunity.com.

$\mathscr{A}$ Business Legacy

by Arlene Schmidek and Cathy Dool

Like many people, we have a desire to jump out of bed in the morning, do what we love, contribute, and make an impact on the world. There is a need within each one of us to find our purpose—the reason for our life's journey—and share it. As sisters, we took different routes individually but ultimately came together in business.

Cathy, as the oldest of five children, was responsible for managing home life while our mom and dad worked. She carried this into her marriage, the loss of two children, a divorce, and then starting over in another city with a job marketing a college. She felt frustrated and stuck.

Arlene was the youngest. She experimented with many career options before becoming a high-school teacher. Watching many of her students struggle and graduate without a sparkle in their eyes, she felt like she and the system had failed them.

Then opportunity knocked on our door—an opportunity that would allow us to leave our jobs and have a business together. We aligned ourselves with an international educational company, and it was through their programs that we learned tools for success. Immersing ourselves quickly, we started marketing and facilitating their programs all over North America. In retrospect, our previous JOBS involved some form of development, consulting, or advising; so it was almost inevitable that we would strike out on our own, becoming facilitators, trainers, coaches, and strategists.

Being in business was a natural transition for us as our parents had always been business owners. We had never been involved in the family business—a heavy truck-and-trailer dealership—until our father became ill with cancer. Our parents asked us to help out so they could focus on Dad's health. At that time, there were only seven people involved in the dealership, including both of our parents and two siblings. Unfortunately, Dad never got better, and his passing was a huge loss to our family.

After Dad died, we thought our involvement in the business would be fairly straightforward, since it had been sustainable for 25 years. But that was not true. Sales were decreasing while expenses were increasing. There was a net loss, and competitors were lurking.

Since our attention was now on the family business, the two of us limited the clients we were working with and made the family business our main focus. Major changes were required. As is the case in many businesses, there was no succession plan. There were no effective systems, such as a sales and customer database, detailed financial reporting, marketing strategies, or human resource management. We implemented vision with values, systems, profitable products and service, and a team while respecting the 25 years of "mom and pop" tradition.

The business grew to a large organization, and we rode that wave up to where we had $25 million in sales and a very nice 6-figure profit, which we shared with our team. Moving into a new 22,400-square-foot facility, we presented customers with a one-stop shop that offered truck and trailer sales, retail parts, service, rentals, consignments, and a business office. We were successful in turning the family business around, so we allowed our team to handle the day-to-day activities and turned our focus back to our own business.

We were content with the success of the family business. Little did we know we were about to learn a very valuable lesson—**keep your eye on business!** (You would have thought we'd learned this lesson when Dad died.) The family had stopped paying attention to the details because we were making money. We became like other businesses and got "fat" in the expense and debt lines; our inventory was too high, and we did not understand the true focus of a business. Before we realized this lesson, the economy shifted and business changed dramatically.

Our revenues dropped as every one of our markets had been affected, causing us to have huge losses. We could not react quickly enough to the changing situation. Even though we immediately cut all the expenses we could, the family still needed to invest additional money and decrease our compensation so we could continue day-to-day operations and pay our employees and vendors. We did everything in our power to turn things around. This time we had to admit it was our mistake that got us into this position, not our parents'.

What we have learned is that the journey is what's most important, not the destination. It really has been about the experiences and hard lessons that shaped our lives. Not only have we "walked our talk," but it has impacted our purpose. We are grateful that we can share this knowledge, helping others to create a sustainable business and share their voice.

There is global shift occurring that is causing more women to take the risk of going into business for themselves. The attraction of a business is the whole freedom aspect of doing what you truly want and making a difference. *Do what you love, and the money will follow.* Many people have amazing stories or gifts to share, and they decide that others need to hear or will benefit from them. But can they turn this into a business? Will building a business around something you are passionate about equal success? Will turning a hobby into a business ensure profitability? The question we ask our clients is *Can you make a living doing it?* A business should give you financial profitability or else the risk and the stress aren't worth it. You would be better off working for someone else.

When deciding to share your voice through a business, there is only one criterion: Is there a need in the market? Does your product or service fulfill that need? Will someone pay to fulfill that need? No customers equal no business. We all have great ideas, but until "many" will pay for the idea to solve a need, there is no reason for a business. The idea or passion can still be shared, but keep it as a hobby until you are able to solve a need.

Basic Business Keys

Many business owners want their business to be successful, but they get stuck on how to change things and may not have strategies to take it to the next level. Because of our experiences, others ask us what they should focus on. Here are our top four keys that we focus on daily.

Mindset

You need to manage and direct your mindset. This includes your thoughts, intentions, habits, attitudes, beliefs, and expectations. Your mindset determines your responses and interpretation of situations. It is the quality of your mindset that determines your success.

"You move towards what you think about." Concentrate on what you want and where you want to go versus where you are or have been. Most people dwell on their mistakes or worry about the future. Worrying is negative goal setting. Learn and continue to move forward.

You must believe in your skills and abilities. A belief is something that you accept to be true; and thus you act and behave in accordance with it. Your beliefs can either stop you from or support you in growing to the next level. What do you believe to be true about your business, skills, abilities, and leadership? Here are some typical beliefs that may be hindering your growth: *I can't do this. There is no money. I don't have the education. I don't know the right people. Nobody is buying. I can't charge that. I don't understand my financials. I am not good at selling. Business is a man's world. I can't have both a business and a family.*

Whatever you believe, it tends to come true, so it is imperative for you to be aware of your beliefs and keep them positive. We focus daily on what we want, on our skills, on our experiences, on not comparing ourselves with others but rather "being the best me I can be in business and in life."

One way to become the best you is through your habits. Ninety-six percent of our actions are habitual. Your habits create your results. The key is to do the right things every day. The other part is identifying what are the right things, what are the highest income and highest impact-producing activities that you as the business owner should be focused on every single day. Focus on three daily actions that will affect your sales, cash, and bottom line. This can be calling three new leads, reviewing your financial drivers, following up on customers, or streamlining processes.

In today's high-tech world, it is easy to get off track. With the increase of e-mails and social media like Facebook and Twitter, you can lose yourself for hours. Unless you can justify these activities and know they are making an impact on your business, keep them to a minimum or make them the last thing you do each day.

We all have the same 24 hours in a day. It's how we invest our energy that makes a difference. As Nido Qubein, businessman and author, says, "It is about energy management, not time management." Ask yourself how you are investing your energy. Build the habit of leveraging your time and energy through technology, team, systems, and outsourcing.

In order to improve your business, you need to improve yourself. You can invest in yourself in several ways:

- through books, programs, seminars, coaching, and mentoring. Make sure you are applying the information or else it is a waste of energy and money.
- by masterminding and collaborating with groups, especially other business owners in the same industry and other industries. This gives you an opportunity to learn and share best practices.
- by scheduling time for yourself. You can easily get overwhelmed with information. It is when you take the time to be quiet and allow your genius to percolate that creative ideas, strategies, and solutions arise. Listen and be guided by your intuition.
- by reflecting back on life's lessons—it's that trial and error that you don't learn from books or others. It is your own experiences that will give you insights into the future.

Another part of mindset is to have values that guide you daily. Your decisions should be based on your values. Knowing your own values will help you determine your course. Here are some of our values:

- **Be authentic.** Stay true to yourself, your voice, your expertise—be you. Many opportunities may present themselves to sway you from your goal. Just because others are doing it—the hottest and latest craze—does not mean you should follow.
- **Be accountable.** Be 100 percent accountable for decisions, actions, and results.
- **Cultivate balance and harmony.** Your business is one part of your life. Make sure the choices you make benefit all areas, including your health, your relationships, and your leisure time.
- **Leave a legacy.** Is your life, your work, or your contribution making a difference? Dr. J. W. Grant MacEwan, Cathy's mentor, said, "Leave the vineyard better than you found it." It was very important for us to continue our parents' legacy, but it is also important for us to be aware of the legacy we are leaving too.

The quality of your mindset affects the quality of your decisions. A good business owner reacts to challenges and turns them into opportunities.

Marketing

You can market positively or negatively, but you cannot "not" market. Marketing is the expression of who you are. It encompasses all the activities you do to raise awareness and perception of your value and what you have to offer through your products and services. It is about producing what you can sell rather than just selling what you can produce. The foundation of good marketing is to know your market and determine if there is a need for your product or service. The best strategy is to identify what a customer wants or needs and then supply it at the price the customer is willing to pay.

Marketing should be one of your main focuses as a business owner because you know your products and services better than anyone. You need to determine the activities and the flow of them that lead to building leads, converting leads to sales, and retaining customer relationships. You can always delegate or outsource the "how" of the activities, but you should always be involved.

There are many off-line (traditional) and on-line (electronic) activities for customer engagement. From this partial list, pick a few activities—maybe three or four—and do them well before implementing additional ones.

Off-Line Activities

- Overall Brand—name, logo, slogan
- Business Cards/Stationery
- Brochures/Print Mailings
- Fax Cover Sheets
- On-Hold Messages
- Voice-Mail Messages
- Postcards
- Special Events
- Signage
- Radio and Television
- Networking
- Sponsorship
- Trade Shows
- Promotional Items
- Referrals—Word of Mouth
- Articles or Books
- Billboards
- Speeches and Presentations
- Customer-Appreciation Event

On-Line Activities

- Domain Names
- Websites
- E-mail signature
- Social Media—Facebook, Twitter, LinkedIn
- Video Marketing
- Webinars
- Internet Advertising
- e-newsletters
- e-articles
- e-commerce
- Sales Pages
- Search Engine Optimization

Some businesses do not "officially" market at all and are successful despite themselves. Others are not sure which activities are making the biggest impact. Unfortunately, it is easy to make mistakes with marketing. Here are a few marketing guidelines:

Be clear on who your target market is. We all want to believe our product or service fulfills a need for the masses, but it is very difficult to create and implement any marketing activities without an "ideal" client in mind. The more you know about your target market and what sets it apart as a group, the more effective your marketing. It is easier focusing on a target audience versus running an ad to the masses.

The purpose of off-line and on-line activities is top-of-mind awareness: TOMA. As a business owner, you want to be at the top of your customers' or prospects' minds when they are thinking about purchasing a product or service you offer. Just placing an ad in a newspaper or newsletter one time will not make as much impact as placing that same ad seven times. Your marketing efforts should be created for long-term results. Ask yourself what it would take for your customers to see you as the primary source to fulfill their needs. The more talk about your product or service, the more awareness exists. The more awareness exists, the higher the probability of being in that top-of-mind position.

Choose your marketing strategically, and be determined to follow through on that activity until you can confidently say it is a success or a failure. You can't give up on your monthly newsletter after the second month. You need to test and measure. Are you getting inquiries and customers? Is there a return on your investment of time and money? Marketing drives your sales. If your sales are low, then look at your marketing activities and make sure they appeal to your ideal client.

Financials

Do you know the financial state of your business? Most businesses operate from a reactive approach, and 90-95 percent of business owners don't have any idea of what their sales or their expenses are or even what their net worth is. This is one of the most common mistakes of business.

Business owners give various reasons why their businesses do not have or produce monthly financial statements, such as: *I know how much money is in the bank. I only get them at year end. I don't understand what the numbers mean. I don't know what to do with them but file them.*

The numbers are the result of business activities. The only way you can really see how well your business is doing is through your numbers. Once you have your numbers, preferably weekly or monthly, you can determine the effectiveness of your products, services, marketing, and decision making. You need these three statements: Income (Profit and Loss) Statement; Balance Sheet (Assets, Liabilities, and Net Worth) and Cash Flow (money coming in and out) Statement. You can get them from your accountant or bookkeeper or invest in a business accounting software that is easy to use if you are doing this task yourself.

The **Income Statement** is a "movie" that depicts what happened over a month, quarter, or year. It is based on a formula: your revenue (what your products and services are making in sales), minus the expenses (related product or services costs and overhead expenses in a business). This equals your Profit or Loss. Usually 20 percent of your products or services contribute to 80 percent of your sales. When you understand this, you will be able to eliminate the ones that are not making you money and may even be costing you money. You should review your overhead expenses such as marketing, freight, gas and mileage, utilities, meals, entertainment, telephones, taxes, wages, benefits, and other perks on a line-by-line basis at least once a quarter or every six months. The Income Statement lets you know if you have made a Profit or Loss. Don't confuse Profit with cash in the bank. For tax purposes we get in the mindset of keeping this number low. Be careful with this strategy.

The **Balance Sheet** is a snapshot of your financial position at a certain time. It includes Assets such as cash, inventory, equipment, and accounts receivable (A/R) and Liabilities such as accounts payable (A/P), bank loans, car loans, and lines of credit. It also shows the owner's equity and whether it is getting better or worse. For most businesses, cash/liquidity is an issue, and the Balance Sheet is an integral part of evaluating your position.

The **Cash Flow Statement** is a summary of the actual or anticipated incomings and outgoings of cash over a time period. It answers the questions: *Where did the cash come from or where will it come from? Where* *did it go or where will it go?* Use this statement to plan and forecast your cash balance on a monthly, quarterly, or yearly basis.

The Income Statement (Profit and Loss), Balance Sheet, and Cash Flow Statement make up the critical set of financial information required to manage a business. By understanding the activities that drive your numbers, you can play the "what if" scenario to see how your decisions impact these statements and your business.

Your financial focus in your business should be to:

- invest in yourself to understand your numbers.
- increase sales. Charge what your products and services are worth, including your time.
- minimize expenses. Look at ways to lower your product or service costs.
- increase and manage cash flow—the lifeline of a business. No cash equals no business. Cash comes from sales, collecting your account receivables, minimizing the inventory you stock, and paying your bills just in time.
- invest in assets. The assets you purchase should contribute to sales. The tendency is to purchase "want" items that have nothing to with creating more sales.
- decrease debt. You should have a safety net in place in case the economy or your market shifts. Decrease the amount of debt you carry on credit cards, bank loans, and credit lines.
- increase Net Worth. Net Worth is a way of calculating how much a business has and also is considered the "liquidation" value. If you sold all of your Assets (things you own) and repaid your Liabilities (things you owe), Net Worth is the amount you would have left over. Many business owners think that their business is an asset; but until you calculate this, you don't know.

Feedback

Most business owners are in the daily operations of the business. Rarely do they take the time to get accurate feedback. You must have effective processes and systems to track and measure the activities.

Customer feedback can give you insights to improvements. Complaints usually come from loyal customers rather than disloyal ones. Loyal customers usually will tell you what is wrong, hoping that it will improve the situation so they don't have to go elsewhere.

Other feedback can come from but is not limited to financial, marketing and sales, team efficiency and productivity, technology, inventory, and investments. If you are not getting feedback, start asking questions. The point of feedback is to focus your energy and attention on what is working and to stop doing what isn't working.

As you grow your business, you will experience opportunities, challenges, highs, and lows. But focusing daily on these four basic business keys of Mindset, Marketing, Financials and Feedback will set you on the right course to be a savvy and successful business owner.

About the Authors

Arlene Schmidek and **Cathy Dool** are business partners, best friends, and sisters who have been coaching and teaching for over 20 years. They work with women business owners across North America to maximize their business and have a great life. They know what it takes in the real world to take a small "mom and pop"company, nourish it, and provide it with the room to grow into a dynamic, multi-million-dollar corporation.

Arlene is a dynamic, powerful speaker and teacher who brings her business, wellness, and lifestyle experience to her audiences. She wants to see individuals living wonderful lives that are fulfilled and authentic. Cathy's high-energy, down-to-business style combines hands-on experience with education. She speaks to audiences who want to take their businesses to higher levels, and she practices what she preaches.

For more information, visit www.profitandlifestyle.com.

$\mathcal{T}$he Many Layers of Surrender

by Lisa Buckalew

As an awakened woman, I have observed that my life has consisted of cycles of growth where I have had periods of deep, soul-searching intensity—periods where I question everything—followed by periods of healing and then subsequent blossoming or receiving of the "gifts" of life. There isn't just one repeating cycle; rather, there are many overlapping cycles within my life. Some last moments and some last much longer. The healing and blossoming haven't always been all that evident either. Sometimes there is a long space between the intensity and the healing or the healing and the blossoming. In some cases I have not completely healed or blossomed at all; yet my experience shows me that when I nurture and take care of my Self, when I commit to and lovingly develop my relationship with my Self, I experience the many cycles of growth in a much faster and much more peaceful way. My inner personal growth feels like it's not only being measured as slow, steady, and consistent but also contains quite a few leaps and bounds, or what I call aha moments, scattered within.

Like most women I know, I have spent a great part of my life living within a reality created by my inherent need to nurture combined with the side effects of being a good student. This reality embodies the essence of molding my Self to "fit in" with what I was told I was supposed to be as a woman, a mother, a daughter, a sister, a friend. This fitting in with what I thought I was supposed to be was exhausting work. I did my best to maintain my home, nurture my family, and contribute to the household income by working outside of the home.

For the most part, I had been a stay-at-home mom for 15 years. I transitioned from the occasional part-time job to full time, getting out of bed each morning believing I was making a difference. Although our financial situation was improved, our home life was strained. Our lives became an almost frantic struggle to keep up. The few short hours after school where the boys were unsupervised began to create problems between them and in the neighborhood. Life wasn't about living but was more about getting by.

There was new tension in the house that I was not sure how to cope with. I struggled with the tasks of balancing home, family, and my desire to pursue some sort of career. I wished to create something artistic, something visual that carried feeling or a collection of feelings. I considered several possibilities, believing that somewhere out there would be a market that would appreciate whatever avenue of creative work I chose to do. I made time to experiment with these possibilities, creating on my computer. I doodled while on the phone at work and dreamed about having more time to explore my creative inspirations.

I've always had a natural talent for artistic things; however, the artistic "me" had been put neatly in boxes and bags and was packed away in closets and attics for a very long time. It seemed as though art and nurturing my creativity was more a luxury than a necessity. Although I locked my artistic self in the closet, my creativity would not remain hidden and leaked out into many areas of my life. I learned to decorate cakes, cut hair, embroider, and make all kinds of crafty things.

Life took an abrupt and sudden turn and in many ways came to a screeching halt in the spring of 2000 when my oldest son, Jeff Jr., was in an auto accident in which he was thrown from the vehicle and sustained severe head trauma. He was flown from the Trauma Center here in New Jersey to the Children's Hospital of Philadelphia, where he spent the next five weeks in a coma and on a roller coaster ride of one "system failure" after another.

It had been 12 years, but we had been there before. When Jeff was five years old, he spent seven months in the same hospital recovering from corrective heart surgery. During those seven months, there were at least a dozen occasions when the hospital staff expected him to die. He was an inspiration to all involved in his care, and the fact that he had made it out of the hospital made him a walking miracle.

Although Jeff's heart was functional enough for him to live a productive life, its surgically enhanced functionality was a workaround for a congenital defect. His heart still required certain conditions to function normally and sustain a quality life. The head trauma required an entirely different set of conditions. Treatment became a balancing act of treating the head and the heart—almost like a seesaw. The head of his bed would be elevated to assist his heart, yet the feet also required elevation to assist his head and brain to heal. In spite of all efforts to save him, he passed away five weeks later, on Easter Sunday, April 23, 2000.

I had expected and thus taken for granted that my children would outlive me. But now my child had died—the very channel through which many miracles had already flowed. I plummeted into the depths of grief, despair, and anger. What was all that for? Why give and then take away? I did not understand why God would decide to take my son. I wondered why God was punishing me. I couldn't make any sense of it. I couldn't believe it.

With the funeral behind us, well-meaning friends and family encouraged me to return to work, telling me it was what was best for me and what I needed to do. I know this advice was given with love and caring, yet I could not accept anyone else's version of what was best for me or anyone telling me what I NEEDED to do. I decided to quit my full-time job. I felt that my sons needed me to be home as much as I needed to be home with them.

It was a decision made with good intentions, yet it was made from desperation. I soon lost the connection to the good intentions as the pain and confusion of losing a child pressed down harder and harder on me. I fell hard into what felt like a deep, dark, black pit. Everyone was lining up at the door wanting something from me, yet all I could manage to say was "Get in line!" I wondered how I could ever smile again. Would I, could I ever again feel true happiness inside? If I were to laugh or feel happy, would I dishonor the memory of my son? Was my life now to be one of eternal grief?

On the morning of Jeff's passing, a few hours before we made the decision to remove all life support, I experienced what I can only describe as a vision. It appeared like a picture painted on an invisible movie screen above the head of Jeff's bed. He was standing with his arms out and was smiling and laughing and saying, "It's all good!" The moment was filled with an energy that was pure love and pure peace. I could see in my son's face and feel in the pure joy that exuded from him the energy of divine wisdom. It was as though from where he was looking the world was perfect and it all made sense. It was as though he was experiencing an enormous aha moment as he hovered between life and death and stood on the edge of the other side. The vision faded just as quickly as it came, and I wondered if I was losing my mind; yet this same vision has been an incredible comfort to me in some of my darkest times.

As I sank into depression, I did not see how I could ever rise above the deep grief and sadness and live a normal life again. I had been forever changed. I sank deeper. I questioned everything, searching for understanding. I asked over and over, *What's this life for?* I wanted to die. I wanted to go to that divine place from my vision. I wanted to be in that place of peace, joy, and love and once again be able to hear what my son had so often told me, "It's all good, Mom! Enjoy the ride!"

I did not want to take my own life, yet I realized there are other ways to die. I could just give up and surrender to death a little bit every day. Slowly and gradually I could fade away. It wouldn't be a big shock like Jeff's death. I began to think about the things I would leave behind. How would my boys and my husband cope?

Depression is a monster with many faces. It makes its home in the deepest, darkest parts of our psyche and feeds on pain. It tricks the mind with shiny baubles that at first glance appear to be the answer to relieving the pain; yet when the truth is finally revealed, as it always is, the baubles show their face as just another part of the monster.

At some point I began to realize through my own questions about Jeff's death that there would be questions about mine. I began to create artwork to express some of my deepest feelings, seeing this as a way to leave symbolic clues behind. I started working on images that would convey a feeling that words alone could not describe.

I began allowing the grief and sadness within the day-to-day journey of the aftermath of the death of my child. I spent hours at the computer, posing human figures in 3D space. It was a very emotional process for me. Moving the figures and striving for the "sweet spot," or the place where body language told the story, was an emotional roller coaster. There were many times when I found myself so focused on posing the finer details of a facial expression or finger placement that I felt like I was physically overflowing with the emotion I was trying to capture and freeze on the computer. Depending on the image I was creating or the story I wished to tell, my emotions ran through the spectrum from love to hate to sorrow to guilt to pain to fear to hopelessness. The tears came and I let them flow.

Each image I created carried some sort of message within it. I thought that I could deliver messages with my art that I could not seem to deliver with my voice. I lost myself in the computer world and in creating art. I immersed myself in the process, learning one skill at a time and then asking, *What's next?*

Something happens when you give up—when you surrender. There ceases to be an attachment to a goal. If the goal was to die, which was my form of surrender, then anything better than death is not too difficult to accomplish. Yet, in hindsight, I see that surrendering brought me many gifts I had not anticipated. With surrender there was nothing to lose. Nothing to lose meant that no risk was too great. Surrender on the deepest level was the absence of fear.

Three summers ago as I sat on the deck of a beautiful house on the beach in North Carolina, I said, much to my brother's surprise, "I love my life!" And I truly did. My husband and I were doing well enough financially to pursue our lifelong dream of owning a farm. We found a beautiful piece of property and were in the process of purchasing it. Life felt good and I felt happy. Shortly thereafter, I began to wake up.

Waking up for me has been a slow process, and it's still happening a little bit each day. Waking up meant that I began to recognize that I was a product of my environment and my conditioning as a woman, wife, mother, daughter, sister. I began to see that there were certain beliefs I had adopted as my own. These were not all necessarily healthy or self-serving beliefs but were composed mostly of what others thought I should do or be or be doing.

I began to see that I had been a good student, eagerly absorbing and striving to embody the essence of what I was being taught. As I began to awaken to the realization that there was so much more to learn, I started to wonder, *If I was programmed or conditioned to "be" this way in the world, can I also reprogram or recondition myself?* Then I began to seek ways to do just that—to let go of what did not serve me and allow something new to come in.

I became interested in hypnosis and ordered a home-study course in which I discovered the difference between the conscious and the subconscious mind. I became more conscious of my own internal programming, "the tapes" that automatically play within me all the time. I became aware of the power of meditation and creating the quiet space for new, life-affirming, positive messages to be integrated into my subconscious mind. Hypnosis assisted me to connect with my Self in a variety of new ways.

Soon I wanted to go deeper into my Self, to unlock doors that I didn't even know I possessed, let alone know that I had placed locks on. I began a daily practice of guided meditation that led me through the energy centers in my body—chakra centers—and began to experience how these energy centers relate to my everyday well-being.

I became curious about the Law of Attraction and the power of thought. I found that the more I asked, *What if . . . ?* or *What's next?* the more information seemed to flow to me—in the next book I happened to pick up, in e-mails, through web links, or through sharing with friends. One of these e-mail links led me to the BraveHeart Women Global Community, which led me to the Prosperity Hormone Training Calls and then to Rise, the annual BraveHeart Women conference.

The weekend I spent attending Rise in Los Angeles was incredible and liberating. The sharing of journeys and stories inspired me, since there were so many things I could relate to my Self and my own journey. I began to see my Self differently as a woman and to understand that I alone hold the keys to my happiness.

Making a commitment to invest in my Self and my personal growth, I signed up to attend a very powerful and transformative Release weekend with Dr. Sugar. Through the process of releasing my old beliefs and embracing new ones that are more aligned with my personal development, I also discovered the secret of allowing life's lessons to be transformed into life's gifts. One of these gifts is the understanding of the power of surrender.

Ten years ago I chose to die. Three years ago I began to awaken and chose me. Six months ago I chose to LIVE.

What does it mean to consciously choose life? Does it carry the same energy as surrendering to death? Does choosing life also mean there is nothing to lose? Does choosing life mean that there is nothing to fear? Does surrendering to life provide the same freedom that surrendering to death did?

I feel that the first step in choosing life is to heal, yet I wondered if I could heal my own wounds. Isn't that like the cat guarding the canary or the fox guarding the henhouse? If I allow that I am merely Mind and Body, perhaps that would be true; however, there is another factor present that is often ignored because it is "unseen." I am also connected to Spirit.

As a product of nature and a child of God, I have an invisible yet deeply soulful connection to the divine energy that created me. The connection is much like the one that I feel with my own children—an invisible energy bond where we are connected in spirit.

When I allow the true and good nature of my spirit to reside in harmony and balance with my mind and body, I then become the healer, able to heal my Self.

The Many Layers of Surrender

What tools are required to heal my Self? to continue to grow? How do I assist my Self to grow beyond the limitations of my experience in life and to create new experiences that are limitless? How do I let go of what other people think I "should" be doing and allow my Self to simply be me?

Some of the inspiration and guidance that has assisted me to awaken to the answers have come to me as aha moments experienced through the power of celebrity that has been shared through the BraveHeart Women Global Community.

I recognize that the word *celebrity* is a "sore spot" for some people, and I feel that is in part due to how we as a society have used a broad brush that paints the definition of the word *celebrity* simply as "someone in the public eye." To me, the word *celebrity* describes someone who is lit from within. Celebrities are people who are doing what they were born to do, who are living their purpose, who inspire through their life's work, whatever that may be. Celebrities are people who, when the spotlight is trained on them, choose to be conscious and to stay true to that divine inner light of inspiration. They choose to celebrate their gift by sharing it, to make a difference by using the power of celebrity to inspire, share, and heal. Celebrities are people who celebrate their own gifts by nurturing them and then share them with others.

I am deeply grateful for the light of celebrity that is shining within the BraveHeart Women Global Community. These shining lights assist me to know my Self and celebrate that which I feel called to do. To me, this light appears as a lighthouse lit from within, turning around its source in a circle, completing successions of 360 degree rotations that illuminate in all directions, seemingly at once.

This light, having a choice to pause a bit in one spot in its rotation, to linger at one degree on the wheel just a moment longer, illuminating this area just a bit more, sending more warm and loving light in a single, chosen direction, illuminates a path that resonates with me. In the darkness of night, this light gives direction and promise of safe harbor, renews hope that the light of day will follow, and provides a focal point to head toward a beacon in the night where I can rest.

I may never be a celebrity in the public eye; yet the choice to celebrate my purpose or calling makes me a celebrity in my own eyes and in the eyes of God. This celebration assists me to pause for a moment in recognition of my Divine Self and to direct my own light in a similar direction or degree on the wheel. I am thankful for the beacons of warm, loving, and guiding light that assist me to find my way on my journey and illuminate my relationship with my Self and others, assisting me to heal and strengthen the energy of my own light so that I may grow.

In surrendering to and celebrating life, I start where I am. I take full responsibility for my Self and my life. I let go of "should" and instead allow "could." I identify and release that which does not serve me. I love my Self unconditionally. I clean out my toolbox and refill it with tools that are more aligned to my purpose. I learn from those who are already doing what I wish to create in my life. I understand that no one has my answers and I do not have anyone else's; yet the stories, practices, and aha moments that are shared among women can assist us each to discover our own path and unlock the answers that are within each of us. I do not set out to be "just like" someone else. I strive to be me with the same energy that others who inspire me are who they are. I understand that there are many ways to do the same thing or achieve the same result. No way is the "right way;" rather, all ways are right ways. I detach from the goal and practice being in the moment. I commit to me. I am my highest priority. When I allow and nurture unity of my own Mind, Body, and Spirit, I can grow, blossom, and thrive.

A side benefit of investing in my Self and committing to doing the inner work required for my continued growth is the incredible gift of sisters. BraveHeart Women are bound first as women. Each of us is unique; yet our differences, personal perspectives, stories, journeys, and our own power of celebrity embody something much larger that could not exist without each of us doing our part and participating.

Through my BraveHeart sisters I am learning to connect with my Self on a deeper level in all areas of my life. By observing and allowing the uniqueness of others and being open to their messages, I am beginning to see and to celebrate some of the qualities I admire about my sisters as they appear in my Self. Through my sisters I am discovering how to be bold in my zest for life, yet to do so with the energy of being in service. This being in service honors me, my purpose, and my relationships.

Through my sisters I am dusting off the many facets of the diamond that I am, and I am discovering how to let my inner light shine. I understand that I am not defined by my story or by what happened to me and that when I release my story, I receive gifts of wisdom that were hidden within it.

Through my sisters I am awakening to different energies and vibrations and am developing soul connections with my Self and others. I am learning how to let go of the protective shell I have been hiding within for so long and allowing my true inner light to shine.

My choice to embrace, surrender to, and celebrate life calls me to heal and embrace the woman that I am and to continue to grow and blossom into my own feminine wisdom. This is a personal daily practice that is also a small portion of a much larger blossoming of the essence of feminine wisdom. This collective of wisdom assists us all to grow together in balance of Mind, Body, and Spirit and to experience a unity where we not only grow, we thrive.

Growing and blossoming is not always easy; yet when I nurture balance in Mind, Body, and Spirit, I allow and assist my Self to love my life. With love and gratitude for my life and living it as though I were a flower in a vase on the dining-room table, my own sometimes painful transformation from seed to bud to flower, happening again and again, seems to occur within my life with an ease that leaves me smiling and remembering the wise words that echo in my heart, paint pictures in my mind, and whisper to my soul: "It's all good, Mom! Enjoy the ride!"

It's ALL good! Enjoy the ride!

About the Author

Lisa Buckalew is a digital artist who enjoys a rural life with her husband and family in a historic small town in central New Jersey's farm country. Having grown up on a farm, she has a deep appreciation for the country life and chooses to spend as much time in and around nature as possible. She laughs as she says, "There's a certain gift in being chased out of a barn by an angry goose. It keeps you humble."

When asked about her favorite things to do, she talks about long days outside experiencing nature, followed by long evenings spent around the campfire with family and friends. Her family and friends have been a huge inspiration in her awakening. "They help me to keep the dream alive," she says. "They believe in me at times when I feel like giving up."

The dream she speaks of—one that she shares with her husband and their children—is becoming more of a reality each day. "We all share a need to be outside in the experience of nature. We were fortunate to be able to purchase a large piece of forested property and are planning our farm, which is neither forestry nor farming in the traditional sense but is called Forest Farming, or agroforestry. I find the practices, principles, and requirements of healing a forest very similar to those required in the healing and blossoming of my Self. Both seek to stabilize and restore the original natural diversity and balance through which nature not only grows, it thrives."

Something else that helped Lisa in her awakening was her art. She began to express her emotions via digital art during the time when she had given up on life and discovered that "one of the many paths to healing lies within art itself."

To see some of the 3D plants that she has created, visit www. lisasbotanicals.net.

$\mathcal{M}$y Journey to Becoming More

by Bonnie Hooper

Hello, my name is Bonnie Hooper. I'm married, the mother of two sons, and have been working for the same company for the past 30 years. In 5 more years I'll be eligible to retire. (I tell everyone I started when I was 10!)

I have always believed that things happen for a reason. Sometimes the reason is immediately clear, but at other times it may be quite murky. This belief is what has gotten me through some very tough and sad times. My whole life has been filled with periods of sadness, tragic loss of loved ones, issues of abandonment, betrayal, infidelity, abuse, low self-esteem, hopelessness, guilt, depression, and pain—both emotional and physical.

From 1998 to 2008 I suffered off and on with lower back pain. However, I continued to work hard and play hard. I have always played ball during the summer and curled during the winter. I started golfing in 1993 and playing soccer year round in 2000. In 2008 my back pain worsened and became constant. Both of my legs would go numb and then I started having constant pain shooting down both legs. I had two choices: have back surgery or end up in a wheelchair for the rest of my life. I chose the former.

While I was waiting to see a surgeon, I continued to work and play. The pain was the worst at night, when I was trying to sleep. More often than not, I wasn't able to turn or get up on my own. My husband would have to get out of bed to lift or turn me. To make matters worse, I was experiencing horrible night sweats and mood swings. It was like suffering with PMS multiplied by a million. I would argue about silly things. Although I knew I was being irrational, I couldn't seem to stop myself. Feeling totally out of control, I thought I was going crazy. Eventually, for the sake of my own sanity and the sanity of my family, I went to my doctor. She knew instantly what was going on with me and assured me that I wasn't going crazy. The problem was that I was pre-menopausal, so she put me on medication. In less than a week I felt that my moods were almost "normal" again, but the back and leg pain was getting worse.

On October 30, 2009, I finally had back surgery, decompression from my L3 to S1. When I woke up after surgery, I couldn't lift my right foot. My surgeon told me that he was confident that this condition, which is called "drop foot," would not be permanent. I walked with a walker for the next three months, trying to make the best of numerous restrictions: no lifting anything over five pounds, no cooking, and no driving. This was okay for the first six weeks while I was healing from the surgery; however, after that I started to feel like a burden on my family and friends. I have always been independent, so relying on others to drive me anywhere I wanted or needed to go felt horrible. To top it all off, I wasn't allowed to go back to work until April 2010.

Slipping into a depression, I put on weight at an incredible speed, gaining 40 pounds in 3 months. Not only did I feel like a useless burden but I also walked funny and none of my clothes fit me anymore. In the midst of my depression, I received a call from my General Manager, who had been my leader and mentor for the past 30 years, announcing he was retiring. Gripped in panic, I wondered, *What's going to happen now? Who is going to replace him? Will anyone else ever believe in me the way he did?*

Falling deeper into my depression, I talked to my doctor; she put me on a higher dose of the anti-depressant I was already taking and referred me for counseling. All doped up with anti-depressants and seeing two different counselors, I didn't feel that anything was helping; but I continued anyway because I didn't know what else to do.

Slowly I began to isolate myself from everyone, yet I pretended I was all right when I talked to family and friends on the phone. This was very exhausting and mentally draining. I hated myself and how I looked and felt. My friends wanted to visit with me or pick me up and take me out with them, but I would make all kinds of excuses to avoid letting anyone see me. I was in such a dark place that it scared me. I felt hopeless and remember thinking, *Why am I here? What have I done with my life? I'm going to be 50 this year, and I don't even know who I am. I'm such a failure as a mother and a wife.*

In February 2010 a close friend of mine invited me to a BraveHeart Women Meet and Greet. My first instinct was to say I couldn't go, but for some reason I told her I would. When the day of the Meet and Greet arrived, I tried to think of an excuse not to go. But again, for some reason that I can't explain, a voice inside me said, *No, you need to go.*

My son drove me to the event. I remember keeping my jacket on the whole time, as if it was my invisibility cloak, and sitting at the back of the room. Having already used up most of my energy just getting there, I wanted nothing to do with anyone.

Then a woman named Darlene came onstage and started telling us a little bit about herself. I heard her say that she grew up in Esterhazy, Saskatchewan. Immediately I felt connected with her, since I grew up in Lintlaw, Saskatchewan, which is nearby. When she talked about being in a "dark place in her life," I knew exactly what she was talking about. As I listened to her story and how she got to this moment in time, I thought, *I wish I could be like her.*

After she finished her own story, Darlene introduced Dr. Sugar Singleton. When Dr. Sugar spoke, I heard her describe my life: "You get up in the morning, go to work, come home, make dinner, watch some TV, go to bed, get up in the morning, go to work, come home, make dinner, throw some laundry in the washer and dryer, watch some TV, go to bed, get up in the morning . . . ." You get the idea. Dr. Sugar went on to discuss how we can release the blocks that are getting in the way of having true fulfillment and prosperity. She even mentioned a Release workshop that she facilitates once a month in Scottsdale, Arizona.

I knew in my gut that I needed to attend this workshop, so at the break I filled out the registration form. That night I told my husband that I was going and asked if he was okay with it—as if he really had a say! All he said was, "If this helps you, I'm all for it."

However, my sons wanted to know where I was going, what Release was, and why I was going. I told them as much as I knew, which really wasn't much about "what it was." As for "why," I said, "I'm almost 50, and I have no idea what my purpose or passion is."

My oldest responded, "Sounds like you are just going through a mid-life crisis." Then he started grilling me, wondering if it might be a cult that I was getting into. That made me laugh out loud. Did he think I would come home with my head shaved and serve up purple Kool-Aid® to my family?

I replied, "If I get nothing else out of this, I get to fly to Phoenix, be picked up in a Hummer limo and chauffeured to a mansion in Scottsdale, where I'll be fed for four days."

He admitted, "Well, when you put it that way, I guess it's a really good deal."

As it turned out, attending Release was one of the most amazing experiences of my life. When I arrived at Casa de BraveHeart, I was in a dark, dark place. I couldn't see anything. When I tried to stretch my arms out, I couldn't because the walls were closing in all around me. After Release, I suddenly saw only light all around me, and I felt that I could stretch out my arms and fly anywhere I wanted. I felt no limitations. It was as if I had been in a cocoon, and now I had transformed into a butterfly and could fly anywhere! For the first time in my life I actually felt comfortable in my own skin. I have never felt so at peace.

Dr. Sugar was so right when she said to us on the first day of Release, "You are right where you are supposed to be." I am so grateful to have experienced a safe and non-judgmental arena to release all the painful baggage that was blocking me from my true potential. With one decision I changed my life!

As I mentioned earlier, I have always believed that all things happen for a reason. What I didn't tell you is that for the past 19 years I have always participated in a ladies curling bonspiel on the same weekend of the BraveHeart Meet and Greet. If it hadn't been for my "drop foot," I would have been out of town that weekend and would not have attended the Meet and Greet. I love my foot—and now I love my life!

I'm still not sure what my purpose is, but what I do know is that up until now I have only been living life. From now on, I want to really EXPERIENCE life! Since attending Release, I have had numerous amazing opportunities presented to me, one of which was being invited to speak at another BraveHeart Meet and Greet. Before attending Release I would have rather gone for a root canal than get in front of anyone to speak, but when I spoke that day in front of over 50 women I never felt so empowered!

Attending Release has changed my life. My husband, children, friends, co-workers, and doctor immediately noticed a positive change in me. I also was presented with a wonderful new business opportunity that has enabled me to start making money immediately. Every day is a new day, and I can choose how I want it to be. My choices create my reality. And I have chosen to become more!

I have learned that it is so important to take time for myself, to reflect and to be grateful for all the good I have been blessed with in my life. I get up about an hour before I need to get ready for work. This is one of my favorite times of the day because no one else is around and the house is quiet. This is my time to meditate, to visualize, to pray, to thank my creator for all that I am grateful for.

In the summer I stand out on the deck and do some deep breathing. When I look at my surroundings now, I am so aware of the beauty all around me. Was it always there? I believe it was, but I am just now seeing it, really seeing and experiencing it, for the very first time—the trees, the shrubs, the flowers, the birds, and all the sounds of life around me that I had previously blocked out.

All the living things that had what I thought to be imperfections I now see as total perfection. For me this means that if imperfection is beauty, then we are all beautiful and perfect. Wow! I don't know about you, but that is a big one to wrap my head around. If that's true, then why am I still so motivated to become more? Well, I believe that even though a tree is beautiful just the way it is, imperfections and all, it still keeps growing. And I believe this holds true for all living things, including me.

Even though I am beautiful and perfect the way I am, I still have not found the purpose for which I was born. Every day I strive to find my purpose. I know it's locked down inside my soul just waiting for me to show up with the key to let it out. I too want to continue to grow—just like every living thing.

Even though I have released much of the baggage from my past that was no longer serving me, even though I have a better understanding of when I feel resistance and what to do about it, I could still very easily fall back on what I always did in the past, which was nothing. Or I can face my resistance head on and work through it by acknowledging it, identifying it, and then letting it go. Recently, I have been choosing to do the latter. Even though this can be quite challenging, when I am finally able to let go, it is also the most empowering feeling that I have ever experienced.

What else have I learned so far? I know that it was my desperation that forced me to listen to my gut, my intuition. When the invitation to the BraveHeart Meet and Greet was presented to me, it was my intuition that pushed me to go, even though I really didn't want to be there. It was my intuition that urged me to sign up for Release. When I finally started listening to my intuition and taking action, I suddenly started to feel that there was hope for me when previously I had felt none. Even when my sons grilled me and questioned my decision to go to Release, I had no doubt that I was supposed to go. To me it was a sign I was finally on the right path; and because I believed this, I knew I had to be open when I got to Release. Because I was open and I listened to and trusted my intuition, it took me into a whole new direction that I could have easily ignored and then I would have missed out on so many great opportunities.

My whole life I have always looked externally for approval, acceptance, love, happiness, and, ultimately, peace. I have tried to be what other people wanted me to be or what I thought I was supposed to be like; I have tried to do things a certain way to be accepted as "normal"—to the point that I didn't even know who I was. Maybe I didn't know who I was because I never liked myself and didn't think anyone else would like me either. It is my prayer that not all women have to be in such despair as I was in order to start listening to their intuition, trusting it, and then taking action. My personal belief is that my intuition is God guiding me down the right path that will lead me to the purpose I was born to fulfill.

My aha moment came when I realized that I had to start looking inside myself for all those things and to listen to and trust my intuition. Since I have started allowing myself to be open, so many great opportunities have been presented to me; and, more importantly, I have been letting my intuition guide me. I don't even know how to explain everything that I have felt and experienced since I have started down this new and exciting path. I have made some lifelong friends, met and continue to meet so many beautiful and amazing women.

I just know that I am right where I am supposed to be, and it feels right. When I was presented with a business opportunity that involved marketing, my initial reaction was *I can't do this*. But listening to my gut, I knew I could; and I have been very successful. When I was asked to write my story for this book, I was so honored yet so afraid at the same time; but once again I listened to my intuition and pushed past my fears of imperfection and failure. I know this is what I am supposed to do.

The more I talk to my women friends, I mean really talk to them and share with them where I was before and how afraid I was, I realize that I'm not alone. I also understand that we are all on our own journey, yet we all are searching for the same things: internal and external peace, to be accepted and loved for who we are, to find our purpose and to live it. It has been on my life journey that I have learned love, compassion, and forgiveness. I have already learned so much; yet the more I learn, the more I realize that I still have so much more to learn.

I have learned to be open even though I am feeling fearful. When I let my fear rule my actions and ignore my intuition, my soul seems to try to reach out to me through my body. For example, I continued to feel dis-ease even after my surgery and received help for my pre-menopausal mood swings. When I am open and listen to my intuition, it leads me to exactly where I am supposed to be. I have learned that being open is leading me down the right path, and for the first time in my life I am feeling a sense of empowerment because I realize that I can choose a life of ease instead of a life of dis-ease. Since going back to work after my surgery, I have also learned that even though I have loved my job for the past 30 years, it is not my passion. Although I am good at my job, it is not what defines me.

As I become more, I am so aware of the positive impact I am having on my family and the people in my life. With all the uncertainty in our quickly shifting world, I can feel and see women searching, wanting to make a difference and wanting something better. I believe that globally all women dream about what they wish their life was like. They want to live their purpose. They want to make a difference. And if they are like me, not sure of what their purpose is, they want to know how to find out.

Can you just imagine what this world would be like if all women realized that when we are living our purpose our energy is strong? Can you visualize women all over the world with this energy? Can you see the impact this would have and the difference we would make across the globe? Believe it. See it. It starts one woman at a time. It starts with women like you and me. All of us together can and will make a huge difference.

About the Author

Bonnie Hooper is a wife, mother, businesswoman, and seeker who lives in Calgary, Alberta, Canada. Recently she started a community called the "School of Becoming." She is the first student, and so far she is being coached by four amazing BraveHeart Women experts.

This is what Bonnie says about her decision to start her community: "Recently I heard a saying that I believe is so true: 'When the student is ready, the teacher will appear.' The more women I talk to, the more I realize that I am not the only one who doesn't know what her real purpose or passion is, and I am not the only one who wants to find out and thus become more. It is my intention to document my transformation process not only for my benefit but also for all women who want to become more."

To find out more about Bonnie's community and to check her progress as she transforms and becomes more, visit her at http://SchoolOfBecoming.com.

Author Information

Chapter 1: Mariel Hemingway   http://marielhemingway.com

Chapter 2: Rolonda Watts   http://rolonda.com

Chapter 3: Gloria Loring   http://glorialoring.com

Chapter 4: Kim Kiyosaki   http://richwoman.com

Chapter 5: MaryEllen Tribby   http://workingmomsonly.com

Chapter 6: Dr. Sugar Singleton   http://TheCellularWoman.com

Chapter 7: Cynthia Krejcsi   http://CareerTransitionCommunity.com

Chapter 8: Sheila Kelley   http://sfactor.com

Chapter 9: Shelley Redford Young   http://pHmiracleliving.com

Chapter 10: Anne Johnson   http://BoldandClassyWomen.com

Chapter 11: Kathy Kolbe   http://kolbe.com

Chapter 12: Radha Conrad   http://SisterhoodOfClarity.com

Chapter 13: Audie Perove   http://OurChildrenCommunity.com

Chapter 14: Janie Pighin   http://WarriorCaregivers.com

Chapter 15: Dr. Kim Silvers   http://GlowToxCommunity.com

Chapter 16: Dr. Pamela Zimmer   http://FreeYourSoulCommunity.com

Chapter 17: Dr. Angela Sorensen   http://SheOptimal.com

Chapter 18: Tara Marino   http://FemmeTypeFormula.com

Chapter 19: Kammy Haynes   http://TheEmergeCommunity.com

Chapter 20: Penny Wanger and Nanci Moore   http://SoulBIZSisters.com

Chapter 21: Tari Bussard   http://Empowerment101Community.com

Chapter 22: Nancy Markham   http://GrowMoreCommunity.com

Chapter 23: Rebecca Hofeldt   http://ThePoetWithinCommunity.com

Chapter 24: Rijuta Tooker   http://CreativeConcentrationCommunity.com

Chapter 25: Lynette Chartier   http://RitualDivasCommunity.com

Chapter 26: Arlene Schmidek and Cathy Dool   http://profitandlifestyle.com

Chapter 27: Lisa Buckalew   http://lisasbotanicals.net

Chapter 28: Bonnie Hooper   http://SchoolOfBecoming.com